VOLUME TWO

THE MEMOIRS
OF PHILIPPE
DE COMMYNES

Book Six: French Expansion in Burgundy and Louis XI's Last Years, 1477–1483 / Book Seven: The French Invasion of Italy, 1494–1495 / Book Eight: The French Retreat from Italy and Charles VIII's Last Years, 1495–1498

EDITED BY SAMUEL KINSER

TRANSLATED BY ISABELLE CAZEAUX

University of South Carolina Press / Columbia, South Carolina

Acknowledgments

I am most grateful to the staff of the University of South Carolina Press for the care and responsiveness which they have shown in preparing this new translation of the *Memoirs* for publication. In particular I should like to express my indebtedness to the late Dorothy Clyburn, former editor of that press. Without her sweet forbearance and ready understanding the first volume of this work would be much fuller of scholarly crotchets than it is. Cynthia Merman's possession of extraordinary funds of *Findigkeit* has probably never been put to a severer test than in the gathering of the illustrations for these two volumes. Finally, I wish to thank the members and staff of the Institute for Research in the Humanities at the University of Wisconsin for the many ways in which they have made the preparation of this work not only less onerous but, sometimes, even enjoyable.

Contents

Illustrations

ENDPAPERS: *Part of Gentile Bellini's oil painting of the Corpus Christi procession of 1496 in the Piazza San Marco, Venice (Galleria Accademia, Venice: photograph by Alinari). Either Commynes or Bellini has made a mistake in describing—the one in words, the other in oil—this fete day, the most solemn of the approximately two hundred religious festivals celebrated each year in fifteenth-century Venice. Commynes says on p. 500 that on Corpus Christi day a wooden walk was constructed which extended across the piazza from the ducal palace, a corner of which may be seen in the upper right portion of Bellini's painting between San Marco Cathedral and the base of the campanile or bell tower. In the center of the painting a relic of the holy cross, paraded only on Corpus Christi day, is being carried in a gold reliquary. Ecclesiastical dignitaries surround the reliquary and are followed in the procession by state officers, musicians, and other notables. The onlookers scattered about the center of the piazza lighten the heavy outline drawn by the buildings and the procession while intensifying, by means of their rich costumes and elegant stances, the sense of panoply, wealth, and power which Venetians sought, both politically and culturally, in their public life. Although they are in disagreement about details, both Commynes and Bellini saw and portrayed with great eloquence the combination of glitter and deliberative solemnity peculiar to Venice in the Renaissance.*

Illustrations

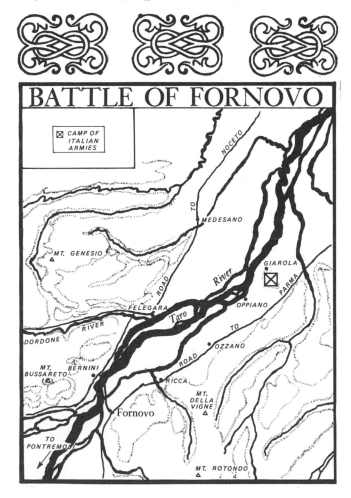

BATTLE OF FORNOVO

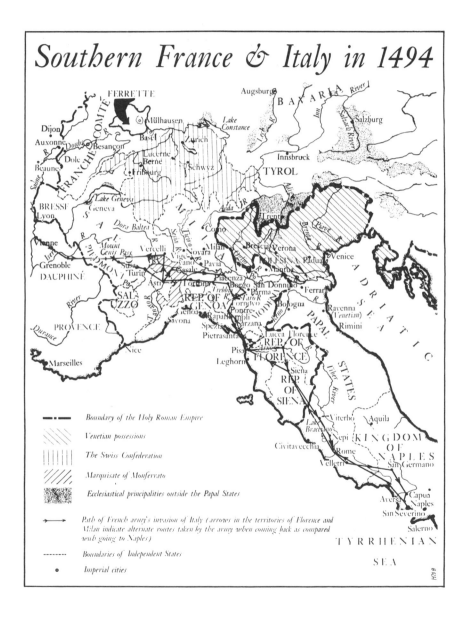

Southern France & Italy in 1494

FERRETTE

Augsburg

BAVARIA

Dijon
Auxonne
Beaune
Dole
Besançon
Mülhausen
Basel
Zurich
Lake Constance
FRANCHE COMTÉ

Lucerne
Berne
Fribourg
Schwyz
Innsbruck

TYROL
Salzburg

BRESSE
Lyon
Geneva
Lake Geneva

Vienne
Grenoble
DAUPHINÉ

Mount Cenis Pass
Susa
Turin
Asti
Casale
Vercelli
Novara
Vigevano
Pavia
PIEDMONT
Como
Milan
Brescia
Verona
BRESCIA
Padua
Mantua
Venice

Trent
Piave

SAL-UZZO

PROVENCE

Nice

Marseilles

REP. OF GENOA
Genoa
Rapallo
Savona
Spezia
Pontremoli
Sarzana
Pietrasanta

Tortona
Piacenza
Borgo San Donnino
Parma
Reggio
Modena
Bologna
Ferrara

Ravenna (Venetian)
Rimini

ADRIATIC

Lucca
Pisa
Leghorn
Florence
REP. OF FLORENCE
Siena
REP. OF SIENA

PAPAL STATES

Civitavecchia
Viterbo
Lake Bracciano
Nepi
Rome
Velletri

Aquila
KINGDOM OF NAPLES
San Germano

Aversa
Capua
Naples
San Severino
Salerno

TYRRHENIAN
SEA

——— Boundary of the Holy Roman Empire

///// Venetian possessions

|||||| The Swiss Confederation

///// Marquisate of Monferrato

▓▓▓ Ecclesiastical principalities outside the Papal States

→ Path of French army's invasion of Italy (arrows in the territories of Florence and
   Milan indicate alternate routes taken by the army when coming back as compared
   with going to Naples)

- - - - Boundaries of Independent States

• Imperial cities

Chronological Table

for Volume Two

1477–1479   *Louis XI, by exploiting the quarrels among the varied local authorities in the far-flung holdings of the duchess of Burgundy and by the skillful use of bribes, secures the duchy of Burgundy and most of the free county of Burgundy (Franche-Comté), Picardy, the county of Boulogne and much of Artois and Hainaut. (See chapters 1–3 and 5–8 of Book 6)*

1478   *Commynes is sent by Louis XI to Florence to offer condolences and aid to the Medici family on the occasion of the Pazzi conspiracy. (See chapter 4 of Book 6)*

1479–1483   *Louis XI suffers a series of attacks, possibly epileptic, resulting in a loss of speech and increased dependence on Commynes and other favorites, as well as leading to the king's frenzied attempts to protect himself from the loss of his power and from death. (See chapters 6–7 and 9–12 of Book 6)*

1477–1494   *The usurpation of Gian Galeazzo Sforza's power as duke of Milan by his uncle, Lodovico Sforza, a revolt of Neapolitan barons against King Ferrante and their coalition with heirs of the Angevin dynasty in France, and the replacement of Lorenzo de' Medici by his inept son Piero in Florence, lead to an increasingly unstable political situation in Italy. Charles VIII is freed to interfere in Italian affairs by the weakening of Burgundian power (a settlement is made between France and Burgundy in the treaty of Senlis of 1493, which Commynes helps negotiate) and by the settlement of France's disputed frontier with Spain (French claims to Roussillon and Cerdagne are abandoned in the treaty of Barcelona of 1493). The king's and his ministers' intrigues with Italian exiles and princes lead to a decision to invade the kingdom of Naples. (See chapters 1–5 of Book 7)*

1494–1495   *The invasion of Italy is too successful, not only overthrowing Aragonese rule in Naples but provoking changes in various*

Tuscan regimes, a movement to depose Pope Alexander VI, and suspicion of Louis of Orleans' designs on Milan by France's chief ally, Duke Lodovico of Milan. The "Holy League" to rid Italy of the French armies is formed at Venice during Commynes' embassy to that state. (See chapters 6–20 of Book 7)

1495   *The French army wins an ambiguous victory over the army of the Holy League at the battle of Fornovo. Badly outnumbered, the French hasten their retreat toward France, followed by the Italian army of the Holy League. Commynes urges negotiation with the enemy but is given little support. (See chapters 1–14 of Book 8)*

1495–1496   *French forces under the command of the duke of Orleans (the future Louis XII) are besieged by the army of the Holy League in Novara. Commynes is the chief instigator of the treaty of Vercelli which allows the duke of Orleans and his men to leave Novara and ends hostilities between France and the duchy of Milan, but not between France and the other members of the Holy League. Duke Lodovico of Milan does not live up to the terms of the treaty. His machinations, together with the hesitant, incoherent policy of Charles VIII and his advisers, end in the French loss of the kingdom of Naples. (See chapters 15–22 of Book 8)*

1496–1498   *Ferdinand and Isabella of Spain reap the chief profit from the failure of French policy in Italy and from the disunity of the Italians. Commynes understands this result only in part. He concludes the second part of the* Memoirs, *as he did the first part, with the argument that God has shown how petty the power of kings is by dealing death to the Spanish and French royal houses at a moment when they seemed to enjoy immense prosperity and political success. (See chapters 23–27 of Book 8)*

The Memoirs

Louis XI's features here, as compared with those in his portrait on page 147, are thin and drawn, making one inclined to date this portrait later than the other one. The eyes, while presenting the same flat gaze, stare slightly upward and sideways rather than forward and somewhat downward. They are sunken in wrinkles, and when combined with the sharpened nose, the hollows below the left cheekbone and at the left temple, and the creases in the skin drawn in two ellipses down from the left nostril and up from the chin, they seem to reflect the debilitating fear which Commynes says beset Louis in his last years. The eyes here contemplate something outward rather than something inward as in the first portrait, while the face, thrust forward on the thick, engarlanded neck as in the other portrait, bespeaks apprehension rather than calculating calm. The absence of a hat and the retention of the headcloth which is shown beneath the hat in the other portrait make Louis seem humble in spite of his rich robe and knightly necklace. The resemblance of the headcloth's drapery about the forehead to that of a monk's cowl may be not unintentional: Louis' breakdown, when it came, expressed itself in religious superstition as well as in political fear, as Commynes shows in this book.

 # BOOK SIX

N.B. *For the principles of translation and editing used in this transla-tion of the* Memoirs, *see pages 83 and 90 in Volume One. Both in trans-lating Commynes' place-names and in making the maps we have followed wherever possible the spellings and locations given in William R. Shep-herd's* Historical Atlas *(New York, 1924). As for proper names, we have used for the most part the versions offered by Joseph Calmette, latest editor of Commynes' French text. If, in spite of our efforts, the reader notices inconsistencies and errors here and there, we invite him to consider the question of authenticity. We have striven, by the means of illustrations, type-face, and ornamental interlace used in these volumes, to recreate Commynes' world visually as well as discursively. But Com-mynes and his friends were hardly concerned about how they spelled their names or any other words either, and so our critics will, we hope, regard those slips which they may discover as evidence of an uncon-scious desire to preserve in still another way the savor of the original.*

The reader will also note that illustrations occur in this volume midway in Books 6, 7, and 8, as well as at the beginnings of these books, in contrast to Volume One. These extra pauses were inserted not only to amuse and instruct the student of the Memoirs, *but also to indicate some other possible subdivisions of the text. As mentioned on page 90, book and chapter divisions are not Commynes' own, apparently. Each of the illustrations is placed at a point where Commynes' narrative begins moving in a different direction from that which it has taken before.*

It is pleasant to note several important new publications concerning Commynes and his Memoirs *which have appeared since the completion of work on volume one of this translation in 1968: Karl Bittmann has published the second volume of his analysis of the* Memoirs *(Gottingen, 1970: see page 84 for full bibliographical reference); Jean Dufournet has published a biography of Commynes incorporating many new archival findings (La vie de Philippe de Commynes, Paris, 1969); and Michael Jones has published a translation of the first six books of the* Memoirs *in the "Penguin Classics" series (Harmondsworth, England and Baltimore, Maryland, 1972).*

French Expansion into Burgundy
and Louis XI's Last Years, 1477-1483

1

It is indeed time that I should return to my main theme and continue with the subject of these memoirs which I began at your request, my lord archbishop of Vienne.[133]

As soon as the duke of Gelderland arrived before Tournai, he had everything burned as far as the suburbs. Inside the town were three or four hundred men-at-arms, who made a sally and attacked the rear of their army on their encampment; and immediately the people began to flee. The duke of Gelderland, who was very valiant, turned aside with the intention of freeing the path so that his men could retire. He was badly beaten and was hurled to the ground and killed, as were a goo·' number of these people [June 27, 1477]. Very few of the king's men were present at this enterprise. The Flemish army retired after this loss; only part of their troops were defeated.

My lady of Burgundy, according to the reports, was overjoyed about this occurrence, as were those who loved her, for it is held as certain that the people of Ghent had decided to force her to marry him [the duke of Gelderland]. And this could never have been accomplished with her consent for several reasons, as you [know from what you] have heard about him earlier.[134]

Those who will see these memoirs in the future and who will have a better understanding of the affairs of this kingdom and its neighbors than I have, may wonder why, from the death of Duke Charles of Burgundy until this point, which is almost a year, I have made no mention of the English nor how they could bear to have the king of France take over the towns which were so close to them, such as Arras, Boulogne,

133. See p. 91 for information about the archbishop of Vienne, the man to whom Commynes addressed his *Memoirs*.

134. See pp. 348-53 for the development of enmity between Mary, duchess of Burgundy (1477-1482), and the people of the city of Ghent, as it was related to her projected marriage with the duke of Gelderland. Commynes may also be referring to his account of the duke's cruel treatment of his father, recounted on p. 249 ff., and referred to once again by Commynes only three paragraphs before this passage, at the end of Book 5 (see p. 368).

Hesdin, Ardres, and several castles (and they [the French army] were quartered before Saint-Omer for several days). The reason was that our king surpassed the then-reigning King Edward of England in sense and virtue,[135] although King Edward was a very valiant prince and had won eight or nine battles in England, in which he had always fought on foot; and this was something greatly to his credit. But these dissensions were of short duration and they did not require King Edward to use his sense. For as soon as one battle was over, he was master until the next time; besides, whenever there is discord in England, in ten days or less one side or the other is on top. But our affairs over here are not the same: for it was necessary that, when carrying on a war, our king should pay attention to various parts of his kingdom and to his neighbors. He was particularly attentive, among all his other affairs, to satisfy the king of England or to keep on good terms with him with embassies and presents and fine words, so that he would not mix in our affairs.

For this lord well knew that the English, whether they be noblemen, commoners or clergy, are always ready to wage war against this kingdom, both under color of the disputes which they believe they have with us, and also because of their hope of winning; for God has allowed their predecessors to win various great battles in this kingdom and to possess territories here a long time, both in Normandy and in Guyenne, which they had possessed three hundred and fifty years at the time when King Charles VII conquered it on the first try.[136] At this time they brought into England great booty and riches which they had seized from numerous poor people and lords of France, who had been their prisoners, as well as from towns and other places which they had taken in our kingdom; and they still hope to go on doing this always. But this kind of fortune was hardly possible for them to have in the days of our master the king, for he would never have risked the loss of the kingdom to the point of putting the whole nobility of the kingdom on foot to fight them, as was done at Agincourt; and [even] if he had come to that point, he would [still] have proceeded more wisely, as you were able to see from the way he managed his affairs when King Edward came [to France].[137]

135. See my forthcoming book, *Criticizing Artifacts: A Method for the Cultural Sciences*, chapter 1, for the problem of interpreting Commynes' use of "vertu" in differing contexts in the *Memoirs*.

136. *Sic*. Eleanor of Aquitaine, sole heir of the last duke of Aquitaine, William IX, married Henry II of England in May, 1152, thus bringing that duchy, which included Guyenne, to the English crown. Guyenne was recaptured by Charles VII's forces in 1452–53, thus allowing three hundred years at most for English domination of the area.

137. See p. 271 ff. for what Commynes says about how Louis "managed his affairs when King Edward came [to France]" in 1475.

The king our master well realized that the king of England and his associates were rather inclined to maintain peace and to receive some of his gifts. Therefore he willingly paid a pension of fifty thousand *écus*, which he sent to the king of England in London (and which the English called a tribute). He also granted some sixteen thousand *écus* to the king's closest associates, namely, the chancellor; the master of the rolls who is now chancellor; the grand chamberlain Lord Hastings, a person of good sense and virtue and of great authority; Sir Thomas Montgomery; Lord Howard, who has since been associated with that bad King Richard and was made duke of Norfolk; the grand equerry, Master Cheyne; Master Saint Leger; the marquis who was the son of the queen of England by a previous marriage; and he gave very great gifts to all who came to him. Even if they came with harsh messages, he sent them back with such fine words and such beautiful presents that they were pleased with him. And however much they may have realized that the king our master did this to gain time and to pursue his advantage in the war which he had started, they closed their eyes to it because of the great profits which they got out of it.

To all these people the king had given presents in addition to their pensions. And I am sure that in less than two years' time he gave my lord Howard, in addition to his pension, at least twenty-four thousand *écus* in money and dishes; and to the chamberlain, my lord Hastings, he gave one thousand marks' worth of dishes at one stroke. The receipts from all these persons can be found in the royal countinghouse in Paris,[138] except for those of Lord Hastings, grand chamberlain of England (and there is only one of them; that is why it is an important office).

The grand chamberlain was rather reluctant to accept a pension, and I was the cause of it; for I gained his friendship for Duke Charles of Burgundy while I was in his service, and the duke gave him a pension of one thousand *écus* a year; and I told the king, whose pleasure it was similarly that I should try and gain him as his friend and servant. For in times past he had always been his great enemy, when the duke of Burgundy was still alive, and even later, when he supported the lady of Burgundy; and if he had had his way, at one time England would have helped her against the king. Thus I began to negotiate this friendship by means of letters, and the king gave him a pension of two thousand *écus*, which was double the sum which the duke of Burgundy had given him. And the king our master sent to him Pierre Clairet, one of his major-domos, with strict orders that he should obtain a receipt for it, so that in the future it might be seen and known that the grand chamberlain, the

138. I.e., the *chambre des comptes*, central accounting bureau for the kingdom.

chancellor, the admiral and the grand equerry of England, as well as several others, had been pensioners of the king of France.

Pierre Clairet was a very wise man, and he had a very private conversation with the grand chamberlain in his chamber in London with no one else present. After he had made the required speeches and had presented to him on behalf of the king those two thousand *écus* in gold (for the king never gave any other kind of money to great foreign lords), and after the chamberlain had accepted this money, Pierre Clairet begged him to sign a receipt for him as his clearance. Lord Hastings made some difficulty about it. So this Clairet asked him straight out to give him only a letter of three lines, addressed to the king, acknowledging that he had received the money, so that he would be covered when he returned to his master, and so that the king, who was rather suspicious, might not think that he had stolen it. The chamberlain, seeing that Clairet's request was no more than reasonable, said: "Master, what you say is perfectly reasonable; but this gift comes from the king your master's good pleasure and not from any request of mine. If you want me to take it, you may put it here in my sleeve, and you will get no other letter or acknowledgment of it. For I do not want to have it said of me that the grand chamberlain of England has been a pensioner of the king of France, and I do not want my receipts to be found in his countinghouse."

Clairet insisted no further, left the money with him, and returned to make his report to the king, who was very angry that he had not brought back a receipt. But he praised and esteemed the chamberlain more than all the other servants of the king of England because of this; and since that time the chamberlain was always paid without giving a receipt.[139]

Thus our king got on with these Englishmen. However, the king of England was often urged and pressed to assist the young princess [Mary of Burgundy]. Therefore the king of England sent ambassadors to the king [of France] to remonstrate with him on the subject and entreated

139. Mandrot, II, 4, n. 1 (see p. 82 for full citation of this edition of the *Memoirs*), cites a manuscript letter by Hastings dated June 27, 1475, in which Hastings does acknowledge receiving a "very great and beautiful present" from Louis. Mandrot believes (II, 5, n. 1) that the episode involving Clairet took place in 1476. The negotiation of Commynes with Hastings may have taken place at Calais in 1470, where Commynes was negotiating with Lord Wenlock on behalf of Charles the Bold (see p. 212), or in England in 1471, as Kervyn de Lettenhove surmises, I, 66, and II, 6 (see p. 84 for full citation of this collection of documents about Commynes). In any case, Charles the Bold wrote a letter on May 4, 1471, confirming that Hastings' annual pension would be one thousand *écus*, and in 1474 and 1475 Hastings did give receipts for one thousand and twelve hundred *écus* respectively to Charles (Mandrot, II, 4, n. 1). See also Calmette, *Louis XI et l'Angleterre* (Paris, 1930), p. 216 and *passim*, for a detailed investigation of Hastings' "singular independence in regard to the French" who were bribing him.

him to make peace or at least a truce. For among the Englishmen who were members of King Edward's council (and especially of their parliament, which is like [our meetings of the] three estates), were several wise and far-sighted persons; and they were not beneficiaries of pensions like the rest. These men (as well as the common people) desired very much that the king of England should willingly and wittingly give help to the young lady; they said that they were being deceived on the other side of the water, and that it was clear that the proposed marriage [between Elizabeth of England and Charles of France] would never take place, for at the treaty of Picquigny the two kings had mutually sworn and promised that within a year the daughter of the king of England, who had already been given the title of dauphiness, would be sent for, but the time had long since passed by.[140]

He paid no heed to any remonstrances which his subjects made; and there were several reasons for this. He was a stout man who was strongly addicted to pleasure, and he would not have known how to suffer the strain of war on this side of the water; he foresaw great adversities and therefore he did not want to get involved in it. Besides, the longing for the fifty thousand *écus* which were paid to him every year at his castle of London softened his heart. Also, when his ambassadors came [to France], they were so lavishly entertained and were given such handsome presents that they left contented, and they were never given a definite response, in order always to gain time; but they were told that in a few days the king would send their master good ambassadors who would clarify all the doubtful points so well that he would surely be satisfied.

Now when the ambassadors had left, three weeks or a month later, sometimes more, sometimes less, which was not a short term in such cases, the king sent people to England; and he always dispatched persons who had not been there on the preceding journey, so that if the former ambassadors had made some offer which had not been followed up, the present envoys would not know what to reply about it. And also those who were sent took great pains to give the king of England such assurances about France that he still had patience and did not make a move. For he and the queen his wife were so desirous of this marriage that, for this and the other reasons which I mentioned, he was willing to dissimulate what part of his council considered to be very prejudicial to his kingdom; and he was afraid that the marriage might be broken off,

140. Mandrot, II, 6, n. 2, points out that the text of the treaty made at Picquigny in 1475 states only that Charles will be married to Elizabeth when the two parties reach a suitable age and that Elizabeth will be brought to France under the care of and with expenses paid by Edward IV. Charles was five years old in 1475 and Elizabeth was ten.

because many in England had already made a mockery of it, especially those who desired trouble and dispute.

To clear up this matter a little bit, the king our master had never intended to conclude this marriage, for the ages of the two were disproportionate. The young lady who is now queen of England was much older than my lord the dauphin who is now our king. Thus by means of these dissimulations, one or two months being gained through the coming and going, the season during which his enemy could do harm to him was broken up. For if it had not been for the hope of this marriage, the king of England would doubtlessly not have long tolerated the taking of places so close to him without making an effort to defend them. And if he had declared himself for the lady of Burgundy from the very beginning, our king, who was afraid of leaving anything in doubt or to chance, would not have weakened the house of Burgundy to such an extent as he did.

I say these things principally to show how the affairs of this world are managed, so that one may either aid oneself or protect oneself, for perhaps this may be of service to those who have great matters in hand and who may see these memoirs. For no matter how great their sense may be, a bit of advice is sometimes useful. It is true that if my lady of Burgundy had consented to marry my lord Rivers, the queen of England's brother, the king would have helped her by sending a good number of men; but it would have been a poor match, for he was a small count and she the greatest heiress of her time.

Many negotiations were being transacted between our king and the king of England. Among other offers the king of France proposed that if he wanted to join forces with him and come over in person to some place in the lady's territories and take his share of them, he would let the king of England have the province of Flanders and hold it without homage, as well as the territory of Brabant. The king offered further to conquer at his own expense the four largest towns in Brabant and turn them over to the king of England. Moreover he proposed to pay him the cost of ten thousand Englishmen for four months, so that he could more easily sustain the expenses of his army. He would lend him a large train of artillery with men and carts to convey it and to use it. The king of England would conquer the territory of Flanders while he would make trouble for them elsewhere.

The king of England replied that the towns of Flanders were large and strong, and that the country would be hard to keep, once taken; and it would be the same in Brabant. Besides, he said, the English were not favorable to this because they trade so much [with Flanders]. But since the king was so kind as to allow him a share in his conquests, he might give him some of the places which he had already gained in Picardy, such as Boulogne and others; and if he did this, he would declare himself on his side and send soldiers to his assistance, to be paid [by the French]. This was a very shrewd answer.

2

Thus as I said before, these bargaining parties between the kings of France and England came and went, always in order to gain time, and the lady of Burgundy was becoming weaker. For out of the few soldiers who had remained with her after her father's death, many passed over to the king's side, especially after my lord of Cordes had done so, taking several others along with him [March, 1477]. Some abandoned her by necessity, because their domains were situated near or in the towns which had already sworn allegiance to the king, and others left her in hope of obtaining benefits from the king. For no other prince was so generous to his servants as our master in this respect. Furthermore, troubles increased day by day in these strong towns, and especially in Ghent, which was behind everything, as you have heard.

Everyone around the lady of Burgundy spoke of various marriage prospects for her, affirming that she must take a husband in order to defend the territories which she still possessed, or that she should marry my lord the dauphin so that everything might remain hers. Several persons were very much in favor of this marriage, and she herself was especially eager for it before those letters were disclosed which the lord of Humbercourt and the chancellor had delivered.[141] Some objected to the tender age of my lord the dauphin, who was only nine or so at the time.[142] They said that his marriage had already been promised in England and they proposed the son of the duke of Cleves. Others preferred the son of the emperor [Frederick III], Maximilian, who is at present king of the Romans.

The lady had conceived a great hatred against the king on account of these letters, for she considered this to have been the occasion of the death of the two good men mentioned above and of her shame when her letters were publicly delivered to her in the presence of so many people, as you have heard; this was what gave the people of Ghent the audacity to banish so many of her servants, to separate her from her stepmother and the lord of Ravenstein, and to instill such fear into her ladies-in-

141. See p. 326 for Commynes' account of the "letters." It will be observed that in this earlier passage Commynes shifts back and forth between singular and plural in speaking of the letter or letters in question here.

142. The future Charles VIII was only seven years old in 1477, while Mary was twenty.

waiting that they did not dare to open a letter without showing it to their mistress nor [did they dare] to speak to her in low tones.

From then on she began to keep the bishop of Liége away from her presence; he was from the house of Bourbon and wanted to arrange a marriage between her and my lord the dauphin, which would have been most advantageous and honorable for the lady, if it had not been for the extreme youth of my lord the dauphin. However, the bishop's influence did not carry so far. And so he retired to Liége and everyone stopped talking about it. It would have been very difficult to manage this affair to the satisfaction of all sides, and I believe that whoever would have been involved in it would have gained no great honor from it; and so no more was said about it.

After this a council was held to discuss the matter; the first lady-in-waiting of the lady of Burgundy was present, my lady of Hallwin, and according to what I was told she remarked that what they needed was a man and not a child; her mistress was capable of bearing children, and that was what her territory needed. And this opinion prevailed. Some blamed the lady for speaking so frankly, and others praised her for it, saying that she was speaking only of marriage and of the urgent needs of the province. Thus they spoke of nothing except of how to find this man. And I truly believe that if the king had wanted to marry her to the present lord of Angoulême [Charles, later father of King Francis I,] she would have consented to do it, so much did she desire to remain allied to the house of France.

God, however, decided to bring about another marriage, and we probably still do not know why He willed it so. Judging from what happened, we can see that this marriage resulted in much greater wars on this side and on that than would have been the case if she had married my lord of Angoulême; and because of this marriage the territories of Flanders and Brabant and others suffered great persecutions.

The duke of Cleves was in Ghent with the lady, and he was trying hard to make friends there in order to arrange a marriage between his son and the lady; but she was not inclined to accept this proposition because she did not like the character of the son of Cleves, and neither did anyone else from her entourage.

And so they began negotiating about a marriage between her and the emperor's son, at present king of the Romans; there had been words about it between the emperor and Duke Charles, and these two had agreed about it. In fact the young lady at her father's command had written him a letter and had sent him a diamond ring [November, 1476]. The letter stated that in accordance with the good pleasure of her lord and father she promised the duke of Austria, son of the emperor, to conclude the proposed marriage in the manner and according to the good pleasure of her said lord and father.

The emperor sent several ambassadors to the lady, who was in Ghent; but as soon as they arrived in Brussels [April, 1477], they received letters instructing them to remain there for a while and promising that envoys would be sent to them. This was done by the duke of Cleves, who was not happy to have them come and was trying to have them return home dissatisfied. But these ambassadors already had sources of contact with the house [of Burgundy], and particularly with the dowager duchess of Burgundy, who had been removed, as you have heard, and separated from the young lady; and so they disregarded these orders, for she had advised them, as I was told, to proceed ahead in spite of these letters. She also told them how they should act upon their arrival in Ghent and assured them that the lady and many persons of her retinue were favorably disposed toward them.

The emperor's ambassadors heeded this advice and proceeded directly to Ghent, although they had been instructed not to, and as a result the duke of Cleves was much displeased. However, he did not yet know what would be the choice of the ladies. It was decided in their council that the ambassadors would be granted an audience, and that after they had delivered their message the lady would tell them that they were very welcome, that she would have a council meeting to discuss their requests, and that she would have an answer sent to them; more than that she would not say. And thus the lady concluded the matter.

The above-mentioned ambassadors presented their letters upon request and stated their case, which was to remind her that the above-mentioned marriage had been concluded with her knowledge and consent between the emperor and her father the duke of Burgundy, as was evident from letters written in her own hand, which they produced, and the diamond, which they said had been given to him and sent as a pledge of marriage. And the ambassadors on behalf of their master strongly entreated the lady to carry out the marriage according to the will and the promise of her lord and father and her own, and to declare before everyone present whether or not she had written the letter and whether she intended to honor her promise.

On hearing these words and without asking for any advice, the lady replied that she had written the letters and had sent the diamond according to her father's will and command, and that she acknowledged the contents [of the letters]. The ambassadors thanked her profusely and returned joyfully to their lodgings.

The duke of Cleves was greatly displeased with her answer, which was contrary to what had been decided in council, and complained strongly to the lady that she had spoken unwisely. She replied that she could not have done otherwise, since the marriage had been promised, so that she could not act to the contrary.

When he heard her words and realized that many persons from her entourage agreed with her, he resolved a few days later to retire to his territory and to desist from his suit. And thus the marriage was concluded [August 19, 1477], for Duke Maximilian came to Cologne, where some of the lady's servants went to meet him; and I believe indeed that they found him with very few funds, and they brought him money, for his father was a perfectly stingy man—more so than any prince or other person who lived in our time.

The emperor's son was conducted to Ghent, accompanied by seven or eight hundred horsemen, and the marriage was celebrated; from the outset it brought no great advantage to the lady's subjects, because instead of bringing them money, it resulted in their having to supply him with it. His army was not large enough to contend with such a power as the king's. Moreover, the furnishings of his men did not please the subjects of the house of Burgundy, for they had been raised under rich princes who gave them good situations and maintained a household with honor and pomp, with respect both to furniture and also to table service and apparel for themselves and their servants.

The Germans are very different, for they are rude people and they live rudely. I have no doubt that it was as a result of great and wise deliberation and in addition by the grace of God that the law or ordinance was made in France, according to which daughters would not inherit the kingdom, so as to avoid its falling into the hands of a foreign prince or other foreigners, for the French would scarcely have been able to bear it.

As a matter of fact, neither do other nations, and in the long run there is no territory, especially among the large ones, which does not remain in the possession of its natives. You can see this in France, where the English held important territories for four hundred years, but are now left with only Calais and two small castles which are very expensive for them to maintain. The rest they lost much more easily than they conquered it, for they lost more in one day than they had gained in a year. Other examples are the kingdom of Naples, the island of Sicily, and other provinces which the French possessed for many years; and now the only sign or memory of them there is the tombs of their predecessors.

Even if it were possible to endure the presence of a foreign prince, accompanied by a small, well-behaved retinue, and he himself being wise, it would be more difficult to accept him with a large train. And if he brings with him or sends for his subjects, on some occasion of a war which he has, once they come it will be hardly possible that envy, discord and division should not arise, because of the diversity of their manners and character, as well as for the violences that they often do; for they do not love the country like those who are born there, especially if they want to have the offices and benefices and positions of high authority in the country. Therefore a prince must be very wise when he goes to a foreign country, if he is to adjust all these differences. And if a prince is not blessed with this quality, which above all others stems exclusively from the grace of God, no matter how many other fine traits he may have, he will hardly be able to come out on top. And if he lives to a normal age, he will have great troubles and annoyances, as will all those who live under him, especially when he reaches old age and his officials and servants have no more hope of his amendment.

After the above-mentioned marriage took place, the affairs of the duke and duchess of Austria hardly improved, for they were both very young. Duke Maximilian had no understanding of anything, on account of his youth and his being in a foreign country. Besides, he had been rather badly educated, or at least he had no knowledge of great affairs. And he did not have enough of an army to accomplish anything significant. For this reason the country has been in great trouble up to now, and it still seems to be. It is most disadvantageous to a country to have to seek a ruler from a foreign nation, as I have said; and God has granted a great favor to France by allowing it to establish the ordinance which I mentioned earlier, which prevents daughters from inheriting [the crown]. A small house might increase its possessions as a result, but in a great kingdom such as this one it can only lead to all sorts of misfortunes.

Several days after this marriage, or perhaps while it was still in negotiation, the territory of Artois was lost [by the duchess of Burgundy]. I wish only to make no error as to substance; if I fail to date [events] correctly, and I may err by a month or so, I beg the readers' forgiveness.[143]

143. The last three paragraphs of this chapter seem to be an attempt by Commynes to associate the themes introduced in chapters 1 and 2 of Book 6 (the English reaction to the death of their ally, Charles the Bold, and the German marriage of Mary of Burgundy negotiated between January and August, 1477) with the themes dwelt upon in chapters 11–17 of Book 5 (Mary of Burgundy's loss of Picardy, Boulogne, and the near-loss of Hainaut in January–June, 1477). Previous editors have not commented on Commynes' dating of the "loss" of the territory of Artois as occurring after August 19, 1477, date of Maximilian's marriage to Mary. Militarily, Artois was in Louis XI's power from early March onward, almost half a year before the marriage took place. (See, e.g., p. 333 for the fall of Saint-Omer; p. 342 for Hesdin; and pp. 341, 343, and 353 for Arras.) Juridically, Louis XI's demand to Mary in early February for control of all the cities in Artois was rejected. Thus, Commynes seems to date the "loss" of Artois either too early or too late, for juridically the first ratification of French control of Artois came in December, 1482, when the Peace of Arras was signed. (This "loss" was reversed in 1493, when Artois returned to Bur-

The king's affairs were prospering steadily, because he had no adversaries. He always took over one place or another unless there was a truce or some peace overtures were being made; but they could never come to an agreement because they were not at all reasonable and so their war continued.

Duke Maximilian and my lady of Burgundy had a son during the first year [of their marriage]—Archduke Philip [the Handsome (1478–1506)] who is the present ruler [of the Burgundian territories]. The second year they had a daughter named Margaret [of Austria (1480–1530)], who is our present queen.[144] The third year they had a son [who died in 1481 in infancy], named Francis in memory of Duke Francis of Brittany. The fourth year she died [on March 27, 1482] of a fall from her horse, or from a fever, but it is certain that she had a fall. Some affirm that she was expecting another child. Her death was a great loss for her people, for she was a very courteous and generous lady; her subjects had great affection for her and they respected and feared her more than her husband because the territory was hers by right of succession. She loved her husband very much and was a lady of good repute. Her death occurred in the year 1482.

In Hainaut the king held the towns of Quesnoy-le-Comte and Bouchain, but he returned them. Many were amazed at this because he had not been trying to make peace and he seemed to want to take everything without leaving anything to that house [of Burgundy]. And I believe that if he had been able to divide all these territories, distribute them to whomever he pleased, and destroy that house completely, he would have done so. But the reasons which moved him to return these places in Hainaut were twofold. First it seemed to him that a king has more authority and power in his own kingdom, where he has been anointed and

---

gundian control as a result of the Peace of Senlis; thus, Commynes probably wrote this passage of the *Memoirs* before 1493 and did not revise it after 1493.) In any case, it would seem that Commynes' purpose in these first chapters of Book 6 is not so much to achieve chronological exactitude as to tie together English-Burgundian actions and opinions in early 1477 with those French actions and opinions during the same period which were reported in Book 5.

144. Margaret (born January 10, 1480) was engaged to the future Charles VIII in 1482 and thus, when Charles succeeded to the throne of France in 1483, she was treated as "queen." Her engagement to Charles was broken in December, 1491, when Charles married Duchess Anne of Brittany instead, although the legality of this marriage and the breaking of the engagement to Margaret continued to be disputed, as Commynes reports in chapter 4 of this book. Presumably, however, Commynes would not call Margaret "our present queen" after December, 1491. Therefore, this passage was probably written before that date and after March, 1489, during Commynes' exile to his estates after his release from prison. See the end of n. 148 below for comment upon the general problem of dating Commynes' composition of the *Memoirs*.

crowned, than elsewhere. And these two towns were outside his kingdom; and they were given back in the year 1478.[145] The other reason
was that there had been solemn oaths and alliances between the kings
of France and the emperors, according to which they were not to in-
fringe on each other's territories; and the places which I mentioned were
situated in the Empire. For this same reason he gave up Cambrai or at
least put it in a state of neutrality, being content to lose it even though
they, feeling secure, had put the king in their town.

3

War was still being waged in Burgundy[146] and the king could not see
the end of it, because the Germans were to some extent helping the
prince of Orange, lieutenant for the above-mentioned Duke Maximilian
and my lady of Burgundy. But they did this because of the money
which the prince of Orange gave them rather than out of love for Duke
Maximilian; for no man was ever won to his side, at least during the time
with which we are concerned. But [these Germans, now] wandering
about [as mercenaries], had fought on the side of that league of Swiss
[against Charles the Bold], for they are no friends of the house of
Austria, nor do they wish them well.[147]

However, the Burgundians might have obtained much assistance, provided that they had paid for it; and no one was in a better position to
provide this help than Duke Sigismund of Austria, uncle of Duke Maximilian, who had his domains nearby, especially the county of Ferrette
which he had sold a few years before to Duke Charles of Burgundy
for 100,000 Rhenish florins and then had taken it back without returning

145. Louis XI and Maximilian signed a year's truce on July 11, 1478, one of whose
provisions was that Louis agreed to restore the areas which he had occupied not
only in Hainaut but in Franche-Comté, the latter fief also forming part of the Empire. He was probably prompted to pull back in this manner by at least one other
reason in addition to the two which Commynes mentions here: the revolt of towns
in the duchy of Burgundy and in Franche-Comté against his rule, which Commynes
describes in the next chapter. See p. 333, n. 124, for clarification of the juridical situation concerning the areas occupied by Louis XI's troops in 1477; as indicated in
this note (see especially the last paragraph on p. 335), it seems very questionable
whether Louis—let alone Commynes—took the imperial frontier seriously. See also
n. 155, p. 379.

146. "Burgundy" here refers to the duchy of Burgundy and the free county of
Burgundy (Franche-Comté) rather than to all the possessions of the duchess of
Burgundy. See p. 39, n. 84, for clarification of this distinction.

147. See pp. 176, 299 ff., and 354, for Commynes' earlier comments on the Swiss
leagues and on Swiss-Austrian relations. In this chapter and elsewhere in the *Memoirs*, Commynes sometimes seems to use the general word "Germans" to mean the
Swiss in particular (as indicated on p. 354, Commynes considered Switzerland part
of Germany).

the money; he still holds it today on that basis. There was never any great sense or great honor in him; and from such friends one can expect little help. And he is one of those princes whom I mentioned elsewhere; they are not interested in their own affairs except for what their ministers are willing to tell them. And they are always rewarded in their old age like this man was.

During these wars his advisers engaged him on whatever side they pleased; and he was almost always on the side of the king our master against his own nephew. In the end he wanted to leave his considerable inheritance to a foreign house and to disinherit his own family, for he had never had children although he was married twice. And finally, three years ago from now, under [the influence of] another set of ministers, he has transferred [at least] for the present all his territories to his nephew Duke Maximilian, of whom I have spoken and who is presently king of the Romans; and Duke Sigismund retained for himself only a pension worth about one-third of the revenue without any other authority or power, but I have been informed that he has regretted it many times since.[148] And if what was said to me is not true, it is still believable, for such is the end of princes who want to live stupidly.

148. See the map at the head of this volume where part of Maximilian's Hapsburg inheritance is indicated, including Ferrette and also Tyrol, which was the most valuable area which he received from Sigismund because of the vast silver mines found there in the earlier fifteenth century.

The French used at the beginning of this sentence ("et puis trois ans en ça") is obscure grammatically and entails a disturbing consequence chronologically. If, as we have translated it, it means the same as the modern expression "depuis trois ans en ça" ("three years ago from now"), then this passage was presumably written in 1493, since the cession to Maximilian of which this sentence speaks took place on March 16, 1490. Supporting this interpretation is the reading in the earliest edition of the *Memoirs*, cited by Mandrot, II, 20: "depuis trois mois [*sic*] en ça." Calmette, II, 261, n. 4 (see p. 82 for full citation of this edition of the *Memoirs*), points out that Commynes' statement about the cession of Ferrette to Maximilian in this paragraph does not contradict what he says in the previous paragraph about Sigismund "still" holding Ferrette "today" because the cession was a conditional and circumscribed one: Sigismund was to receive an annual pension of 52,000 Rhenish florins and to retain hunting and fishing rights in the county. Thus, Sigismund might be said by Commynes still to hold Ferrette in the sense that he had not given up all rights to it. (Commynes' additional assertion in the previous paragraph, that Sigismund sold Ferrette for 100,000 Rhenish florins and retook the county but never returned the money, is untrue in several respects, as Mandrot shows, I, 145, nn. 1 and 2. See also p. 176, n. 57.) Calmette, II, 261, n. 4, also says, however, that "it is not necessary to suppose, as B. de Mandrot does . . . , that Commynes rewrote this passage after 1493. . . ." Mandrot says, II, 20, n. 1: "This passage of the *Memoirs* would thus [in view of the cession of Ferrette 'three years ago from now'] have been written only in 1493, after all which preceded [this passage]." Calmette offers no evidence proving that this passage was not written in 1493, and indeed in I, xiv, his introduction to the *Memoirs*, he cites precisely this passage to prove that Commynes "probably reread it [the manuscript of the *Memoirs*] in 1493, to which time one passage at least must

What makes them so blamable is that God has given them a high position and much responsibility in this world. Those who are lacking in sense should not be reproached for anything; but those who have good sense and a favorable personal disposition, and yet waste their time in foolishness and idleness, do not deserve pity when misfortune befalls them. And those who divide their time, according to their age, sometimes in sensible things and in council, and sometimes in festivities and pleasures, are most worthy of praise, and their subjects are very fortunate to have such a prince.

The war in Burgundy lasted for a rather long time because of the limited assistance [which they received] from the Germans. However, the king's forces were too powerful for them. The Burgundians lacked money. People turned against them in one place after the other, through secret contacts [with the French].

Suddenly the lord of Craon besieged the town of Dole, chief town of the county of Burgundy. He was lieutenant by the king's appointment. There were not many people inside and he regarded them as insignificant. And this turned out badly for him; for owing to a sally which was made by those who were inside, he found himself very suddenly surprised and lost a part of his artillery and a few soldiers [October 1, 1477], which was shameful for him and he was blamed for it by the king.

The king, annoyed by this incident, began to consider appointing another governor in Burgundy, not only on account of this matter but also because of the great plunderings which he had committed in the region, which were in truth too excessive. Before he was dismissed from his office, however, he gained a small victory over a group of Germans and Burgundians, in which battle the lord of Châteauguion, the greatest lord of Burgundy, was captured [June 17, 1477]. Nothing important happened the rest of that day—and I speak of it only from hearsay—but the lord of Craon gained great personal reputation there.

As I began to say, for the above-mentioned reasons the king decided to appoint a new governor in Burgundy, without in any way interfering with the profits and benefits of the lord of Craon, except for the men-at-arms whom he took away from him, although he left him six men-at-arms

necessarily be ascribed." Calmette's earlier judgment is the better one, and Mandrot's words agree with it, except that it does not follow, as Mandrot supposes, that none of what precedes this passage may not also have been written in 1493. The whole question of the time of composition of various parts of the *Memoirs* should be left more open than Mandrot, Calmette, or I myself in Volume One, pp. 16 and 19, have done. Closer reading of the *Memoirs* would probably reveal many more passages which indicate the time when they were written than any students of Commynes' work have yet brought to bear on the question.

and twelve archers to escort him. The lord of Craon was quite a fat man and he was content enough, retiring to his estate where he was well provided for.

The king appointed in his stead Charles d'Amboise, lord of Chaumont, a very valiant, shrewd, and diligent man [October, 1477]. And this lord began to make intrigues in order to have all these Germans who were at war with him in Burgundy withdraw. This was not so much on account of their services as it was in order to be able more easily to conquer the rest of the territory and to engage them as his mercenaries. He also sent messengers to the Swiss, whom he called the gentlemen of the leagues, and he offered them fine and advantageous terms: first of all, twenty thousand francs a year, which he assigned for the benefit of the towns, which are four in number—Berne, Lucerne, Zurich, and I believe that Fribourg had its share; and their three cantons, which are villages near their mountains, also had their share—Schwyz, from which they all derive their name, Solothurn, and Unterwalden; secondly, twenty thousand francs a year, which he gave to private individuals and to persons whose help he made use of and who were useful to him in these bargains. He made himself their citizen and wanted written proof of this, and he made himself their principal ally. On this point they made some difficulty because from time immemorial the duke of Savoy had been their principal ally. They consented to grant his requests, however, and also to give the king six thousand men to be employed continually in his service, provided that he should pay them four and one half German florins per month. And that number [of soldiers] was constant until the king's death.[149]

A poor king would not have been able to bring this thing about; and everything turned to his profit. But I believe that in the end it will turn to their damage, because they have become so used to money, of which they knew so little before, especially gold money, that they have been very close to having divisions among themselves. Otherwise it is not possible to do them any harm, because their lands are rough and poor and they are good fighters; therefore few people will try to invade them.

After these treaties had been made and all the Germans who were in Burgundy had retired to the king's service and pay, the Burgundians' power was entirely broken. And in short, after several new exploits per-

---

149. According to Mandrot, II, 23, n. 2, at least some of these terms merely repeat those of the alliance to which the Swiss agreed in October, 1474 (see p. 256 ff. for Commynes' account of this period), ratified by Louis XI in January, 1475. It was only in August, 1480, however, that the first contingent of six thousand Swiss actually arrived in France, according to Mandrot, II, 23, n. 3.

formed by Governor de Chaumont, he besieged Rochefort, a castle near Dole where Claude de Vauldrey was, and he took it by means of a negotiated surrender.

Afterwards he besieged Dole, on account of which his predecessor had been removed, as I said before, and the town was taken by assault. It was said that some Germans among those who had recently come over [to the king's service] had expected to enter and defend it; but so many free archers mingled among them (not intending any harm but only to gain something) that as soon as they were inside everyone began to plunder, and the town was burned and destroyed [May, 1479].

Shortly after this capture he besieged Auxonne, a very strong town, but he had many informers inside, and he wrote to the king in order to obtain offices for certain persons whom he named before besieging the town; and his requests were willingly granted. Although I was not on the spot where these things were being done, I nevertheless knew this from the reports that were made to the king and from letters which I saw which were written to him about it, and I often wrote the replies to them by the king's command.

There were few soldiers in Auxonne, and their leaders, who had come to terms with the lord of Chaumont, the governor, gave it up after five or six days [June, 1479]. Thus nothing more was left to be gained in Burgundy except three or four castles on rocks, such as Joux and others, and the obedience of Besançon, which is an imperial town and owes nothing, or very little, to the county of Burgundy. But since it was an enclave within that territory, it made concessions to the prince of the region. The governor entered the town in the name of the king, and then left it. And they behaved in the same dutiful manner as they had been accustomed to do with the other princes who had possessed Burgundy.

Thus all of Burgundy was conquered. The governor employed great zeal there, and the king pressed him urgently, for he feared that the governor might always want to have one disobedient place in the region, so that he might be more indispensable, and so that the king would not dismiss him from there to make use of him elsewhere. For the territory of Burgundy is fertile and he managed it as if it belonged to him. The lord of Craon, of whom I have spoken, and the governor, the lord of Chaumont, both took care of their own interests very well there.

For some time the territory remained in peace under the government of the lord of Chaumont. A few places rebelled afterwards while I was there, however, such as Beaune, Semur-en-Auxois, and others. (And I was present at the time because the king had sent me there with the pensioned troops from his household. This was the first time that he had assigned a leader to these pensioned troops; since then this custom has prevailed to this day.[150]) These places were retrieved by the good sense and leadership of the governor, and by the lack of sense of his enemies. By this means one can see the difference between men, which proceeds from the grace of God; for He assigns the wisest ones to the regions that He wishes to support, or He gives the sense to choose them to the one who has authority over them. And He has made it plain from His actions up to now that in all things He has wanted to support our kings, our late good master as well as our present king, although He has sometimes sent them tribulations.

Those who lost these places were rather numerous, although they did not want to enter these places promptly, and that is why these places rebelled and revolted for them. But they gave the governor enough time to gather his troops, which they should not have done, for they were sufficiently informed of his situation, in view of the love which the territory had for them; therefore, they should have put themselves inside Beaune, which is a strong town, and they could well have guarded it. And the others they could not.[151]

150. Commynes' chronology is once again confusing. After accompanying Louis' pensioned troops (see n. 240, p. 511, for information about this corps) to Burgundy in early 1478, he was commanded by Louis XI to proceed to Florence in May, 1478. Thus, although Commynes has just reported events such as the fall of Dole and Auxonne which occurred in 1479, and although he says here that Beaune and other places rebelled "afterwards," nevertheless these rebellions took place in 1478. Events of 1478 occupy Commynes during the remainder of this chapter and throughout chapter 4. But at the beginning of chapter 5 Commynes returns almost exactly to the point in time at which he left off at the end of the preceding paragraph here: July, 1479. This entails a further confusion since it will be seen that the first paragraph of chapter 5 comments on how Commynes found Louis XI upon his return from Florence in October, 1478, while the first sentence of the second paragraph speaks of the siege of Thérouanne in July, 1479. Nevertheless Commynes says that the siege took place "ceste année-là": i.e., "that year" when he returned from Florence, 1478. See p. 324, n. 118, for a description of one of Commynes' earlier disruptions of chronology.

151. This paragraph offers another example of Commynes' confusing use of pronouns (see p. 83 for a general discussion of this problem in Commynes' writing). "These places" are "Beaune, Semur-en-Auxois, and others" mentioned at the beginning of the previous paragraph. "Those," "them," and the first "they" in our translation of the first sentence of this paragraph refer presumably to the local lords of the revolting towns; Commynes seems to mean that the revolts were premature because the local lords, who should have been energetically helping the towns revolt against their new overlord, Louis XI, were slow to gather troops to enter and defend the towns. Thus, although the towns went ahead and revolted in favor of the local Burgundian lords against the new French regime, the French governor still had time to gather his own troops and to develop a plan to reduce the revolt. The local lords developed no coordinated plan of revolt, such as to enter Beaune and fortify it rather than to try futilely to defend every tiny town. Calmette neglects to include in his variant readings the beginning of this paragraph in the Dobrée manuscript (see p. 81 for a description of this manuscript). It reads "Ceulx qui prindrent

Book Six

On the day that the governor set out to besiege a weak little town called Verdun-sur-le-Doubs—and he was well informed of their condition—the Burgundians entered it, as they expected to go to Beaune to place themselves inside. They were six hundred choice soldiers, both horsemen and infantrymen, Germans from the county of Ferrette, led by some wise gentlemen of Burgundy, and Simon de Quingey was one of them. They stopped at a time when they could well have gone and placed themselves inside Beaune, which no one could have recaptured from them, once they had entered it. For lack of good advice they remained one night too long [in Verdun], where they were besieged and taken by assault. After that Beaune was besieged and everything was recovered [by July, 1478]. Never again did the enemies regain any strength in Burgundy.

At the time I was in the territory of Burgundy with the king's pensioned troops, as I said before. And the king had me leave the place because of a letter which was written to him, according to which I had exempted certain burghers of Dijon when quartering the men-at-arms. That, together with some other small suspicion, was the cause of my being sent very suddenly to Florence. I obeyed, as was [only] right, and I left as soon as I received the letters.

4

The quarrel due to which the king sent me [to Florence] concerned a dispute between two great families of great renown. One was the house of Medici and the other the house of Pazzi; the latter were supported by the pope and by King Ferrante of Naples, and they intended to have Lorenzo de' Medici and all his followers killed. As far as he was concerned, however, they failed, but they killed his brother, Giuliano de' Medici, in the great church of Florence, as well as a person named Franceschino Nori, a servant of the house of Medici, who thrust himself in front of Giuliano. Lorenzo was severely wounded and withdrew to the vestry of the church, the doors of which are of copper and had been made by order of his father [April 26, 1478].

A servant, whom he had delivered from prison two days before, served him well in this need and received several wounds in his place. And this deed was committed at the time when High Mass was being sung. And they had their signals to kill, as it had been agreed, at the moment when the priest who sang the High Mass intoned the Sanctus.

...." ("those who took") instead of "Ceulx qui perdirent...." Either reading is consistent with the interpretation of the pronouns offered in this note.

It turned out differently from what had been expected by those who had undertaken this. For, believing that everything was won, some of them went up to the palace with the intention of killing the lords who were there—and these lords, who are in charge of the whole administration of the city, are renewed every three months, and they are about nine in number.[152] But those who undertook this were poorly supported, and after they had ascended the steps of the palace, a door was shut behind them, and when they reached the top there were only four or five of them, all struck with terror and speechless. The lords who were upstairs and who had already attended Mass saw this, as did the servants who were with them. From the windows they could see the uprising in the town, with Iacopo de' Pazzi and others in the middle of the piazza in front of the palace, shouting: "Liberty! Liberty!" and "The people! The people!", words which were intended to stir the people to take their part. But the people refused to do this and kept quiet. Therefore Pazzi and his companions fled from the piazza, as if they were confused about their enterprise. When they saw what was going on, the municipal magistrates or governors whom I mentioned, who were in the palace, seized at that very moment the five or six men who had come up, as I said before, poorly attended, with the intention of killing the governors in order to gain command over the city. Without further ado they had these men hanged and strangled at the palace windows. Among those hanged was the archbishop of Pisa [Francesco Salviati].

The governors, realizing that the whole town had declared itself for them and on the side of the Medici, immediately wrote to [those guarding the river] crossings that any man who might be found fleeing should be seized and brought to them. Iacopo de' Pazzi was taken at that very hour, as well as another man in the employ of Pope Sixtus [IV], who was in charge of the men-at-arms under Count Girolamo [Riario, the pope's nephew,] who was involved in this enterprise. Pazzi and the others were hanged immediately from the same windows. The other, the

---

152. The executive power in Italian city-states at this time was usually called the Signoria, or "lordship." Commynes uses it in reference to Florence and Venice where, in contrast to most late fifteenth-century city-states, the executive power was still vested in a committee rather than in a single man. The Florentine Signoria, elected by lot every two months, consisted of two representatives from the so-called lesser guilds and six representatives from the so-called greater guilds organized in the city, plus their chairman, the "standard-bearer of justice" (*gonfaloniere della giustizia*). The Venetian Signoria consisted of sixteen members: the Doge and his six councillors (one from each of the six regions or *sestieri* of the city), the three heads of the judicial body called the "council of forty" (*Quarantia*), and the six "great wise men" (*savi grandi*), a special committee of the Venetian Senate (see n. 273, p. 562).

pope's servant, had his head cut off; several people were taken in the town, and all of them were hanged on the spur of the moment, including Franceschino de' Pazzi; and it seems to me that all in all, fourteen persons of high rank were hanged, and several minor servants were killed in the town.

A few days after this occurrence, I arrived in Florence by the king's command [end of June–beginning of July, 1478]. And I did not take long to get there after leaving Burgundy, because I spent only two or three days with my lady of Savoy (who was the sister of our king), and she gave me a very kind reception. From there I proceeded to Milan, where I similarly stayed two or three days to ask them for men-at-arms to help the Florentines, whose allies they were at the time; and they granted them liberally, because the king had requested it, as well as because it was their duty. And thereupon they supplied three hundred men-at-arms, and they sent even more afterwards.

And to conclude this matter, after these things had happened the pope had the Florentines excommunicated [June 1, 1478]. He also sent an army as large as possible, composed of his forces joined with those of the king of Naples; it was a fine and large army and included a great number of men of high estate. They besieged Castellina in Chianti, near Siena, and took it, as well as several other places [July, 1478]. And it was mainly chance that these Florentines were not entirely destroyed, because they had been a long time without war and they were not aware of the danger in which they stood. Lorenzo de' Medici, who was the head of the city, was young, and he was governed by young men. His own opinion was very much listened to. They had few leaders and their army was very small.

For the pope and the king of Naples the leader [of the army] was [Federigo da Montefeltro,] duke of Urbino, a very wise man and a fine commander. With him were also Roberto [Malatesta], lord of Rimini, who has since become an important man, and similarly Lord Costanzo [Sforza, prince] of Pesaro, and several others, with the two sons of the aforesaid king, that is to say, the duke of Calabria [Alfonso] and the lord Don Frederick [prince of Taranto], both of whom are still alive, and a large number of gentlemen. Thus they took all the places which they besieged, but not as fast as we would do here, for they are not as well informed about the manner of holding a place and maintaining good order there; but as for provisions and other things which are necessary for camping in the fields, they understand it better than we do.

The [French] king's favor was important to them [the Florentines], but not as much as I should have wanted, for I had no army to help them;

I only had my retinue. I remained in Florence or in their territory for one year[153] and was very well treated by them and at their expense—better on the last day than on the first. And then I was summoned by the king to return. As I passed through Milan I received the homage of the present duke of Milan, named Gian Galeazzo, for the duchy of Genoa; at least his mother rendered the homage on behalf of her son to me as the king's representative [September 7, 1478]. From there I came to the king our master [mid-October, 1478], who gave me a warm welcome and a good reception and discussed his affairs with me more than he had ever done; and I slept in his room, although I was unworthy [of such an honor] and he had enough other more competent persons in his entourage. But he was so wise that one could not go wrong with him, provided that one simply obeyed what he commanded without adding anything of one's own.

5

I found the king our master somewhat aged; and he was beginning to become prone to illness. It was not immediately apparent, however, and he managed all his affairs with great sense. And he was still occupied with the war in Picardy, in which he took a very great interest. So did his enemies in this territory, but they were not in control of it.

The duke of Austria, who is now king of the Romans, having Flemings under his command that year, came to besiege Thérouanne [July 29, 1479]; and my lord of Cordes, the king's lieutenant in Picardy, assembled all the troops that the king had in that territory along all the frontiers and [also] eight thousand free archers, in order to relieve and guard the army. As soon as the duke of Austria found out that he was approaching, he raised the siege and went forward to meet him; and they met at a place called Guinegatte [August 7, 1479]. With the duke were a great number of people from the territory of Flanders, as many as twenty thousand or more, and also some few Germans, and three hundred Englishmen under the command of Thomas Aurigan, a knight from England, who had served Duke Charles of Burgundy.

The king's horsemen, who were far more numerous than the others, broke the duke's horsemen and pursued them as far as Aire, with Philippe

153. *Sic* in all manuscripts. Commynes was still in Florence on August 18, at which time a treaty was signed between Florence, Milan, and France. Commynes was in Asti on August 28. Thus, if he arrived in Florence in late June (he left Milan for Florence on June 22), and left Florence sometime between August 18 and 28, he must have spent about two months there. Mandrot, II, 30, nn. 2, 3, 4; 32, nn. 4, 5; and 33, nn. 1, 2, 3, gives the details of Commynes' movements on his Italian journey with admirable fullness.

lord of Ravenstein leading them. The duke joined his foot-soldiers. The king had about eleven or twelve hundred men-at-arms from his standing forces in this army.[154] All of them did not take part in the pursuit, but their leader, my lord of Cordes, did, and my lord of Torcy with him. And although they conducted themselves valiantly, it is not fitting that commanders of the vanguard should pursue. Some retreated under the color of going to guard their places, and others fled with full knowledge of what they were doing. The duke's infantrymen did not flee, even though they were in some trouble; but they had with them some two hundred gentlemen of good quality, on foot, who were leading them. And among them were my lord of Romont, son of the house of Savoy, and the count of Nassau, and several others who are still living. The courage of these men inspired these people to hold out, and it was marvelous, in view of the fact that they saw their horsemen flee. The free archers from the king's side began to plunder the duke's carts and those of the men who followed him, such as sutlers and others. Some of the duke's foot-soldiers made an attack on them and killed a certain number of them.

On the duke's side the loss was greater than on ours, and more men were killed or captured, but he remained master of the field. And I well believe that if he had been advised to return before Thérouanne, he would not have found a soul inside; and the same holds true for Arras. He did not dare undertake such an action, and it was to his disadvantage; but in such instances one cannot always know what is most necessary, and moreover he for his part had some fears. I speak of this matter only by hearsay because I was not there, but in order to continue with the subject I had to say something about it.

154. Calmette omits variant readings for this sentence, one from the Polignac manuscript and the other from the Sauvage edition (see pp. 81–82 for the value of this edition, which cites a manuscript now lost). These variants appear in Mandrot's text and apparatus, II, 35, as follows: the Polignac manuscript offers the figure "fifteen hundred men-at-arms" ("quinze cens hommes d'armes") and the Sauvage edition "five hundred men-at-arms" ("cinq cens hommes d'armes"). The variants are of some interest because of the criticism of Commynes' figures here and in the preceding paragraph by Ferdinand Lot in his *L'Art militaire et les armées*, II (Paris, 1946), 137–38. Commynes' account of the battle of Guinegatte is the clearest and his estimates the most sober among the chroniclers' stories, he says. But since there were only 16,000 free archers in all of France, Commynes' figure of 8,000 free archers appears "exaggerated." The 20,000 Flemish who, Commynes asserts, fought for Maximilian probably numbered no more than ten or eleven thousand men, for "it is probable," says Lot, "that only about 12,000 men were engaged on each side." Lot does not question Commynes' figure of "eleven or twelve hundred men-at-arms." A man-at-arms was a horseman equipped with lance, accompanied by five other men who together formed a lance-team, the basic unit of the *compagnies d'ordonnance* making up the French standing army. See nn. 14 and 23 on pp. 104 and 112 for more information on lance-teams and the standing army.

I was with the king when the news of this arrived, and he was very unhappy about it, because he was not used to losing; he had been so successful in all his affairs that it seemed that everything proceeded according to his pleasure. But also his sense helped bring about this good luck of his, for he did not leave anything to chance and did not want battles for anything; and this one was not fought by his command. He always made his armies so large that few people were able to fight them, and they were well equipped with artillery—better than under any other king of France. He also tried to take places suddenly, and especially those which he knew were insufficiently fortified. And once he had them he put so many soldiers and so much artillery inside that it was impossible to retake them from him. And if there was some commander or other person inside who would be able to hand it over for money and who was willing to bargain with him, he could be sure that he had found a buyer; and one could not have frightened the king by asking a high price, for he granted it liberally.

He was alarmed at first at this battle, believing that he was not told the truth about it, and that it was lost on all counts; for he well knew that if it were lost, then he had lost everything that he had conquered from the house of Burgundy in that border area [in the north], and that the rest was in great danger. When he learned the truth, however, he had patience and decided to give orders in such a way that such things would not be undertaken without his knowledge. And he was well pleased with my lord of Cordes.

From this very moment he decided to negotiate peace with the duke of Austria, but on condition that he might manage it entirely to his advantage, and that by transacting it he might restrain the duke so thoroughly by means of his own subjects (who he knew were inclined toward what he wanted), that he would never be in a position to do him harm.

During this time the king had a very singular desire, which came from all his heart, to be able to establish a new policy in this kingdom, principally in regard to delays in legal proceedings, and in this respect to put strong controls over the court of Parlement. He did not intend to reduce the number of its members or diminish their authority, but he resented several things which occasioned his hatred against them. He was also very anxious to see used in this kingdom one customary law and a single system of measures, and to have all the customary laws written in French in a beautiful book, so as to circumvent the ruses and robberies of lawyers, which are so great in this kingdom that none other can compare with it in this respect, as our nobility must well know. If

God had granted our king the grace to live another five or six years without being too handicapped by illness, he would have done much good for his kingdom. And he had pressed them [his subjects] more than any king before him. No man's authority, knowledge or remonstrance was able to make him more lenient; it had to come of his own accord, and it would have, if God had seen fit to preserve him from illness. Therefore it is best to do good while we are still at liberty to do so and God grants us health.

The arrangement which the king wished to make with the duke of Austria and those regions, by the intermediary of the officials of Ghent, was to bring about a marriage between my lord the dauphin his son, who is our present king, and the daughter of the duke and duchess. By this means they were to give him the counties of Burgundy, Auxerrois, Mâconnais and Charolais, and he would return Artois to them, with the exception of the city [*sic*] of Arras, which he would keep in the same position as he had put it in.[155] For the town was no longer of any consequence, in view of the cutting-off of the city [from the town] and the presence of large moats and strong walls between the two.[156] Thus

155. Ultimate suzerainty over the county of Burgundy (Franche-Comté) was held by the Holy Roman Empire. Thus for Louis to demand Franche-Comté and in return to offer Artois (which was held by the king of France, Louis himself, as ultimate suzerain) is a graphic example of how irrelevant the feudal theory of sovereign power had become (see nn. 124 and 145, pp. 333 and 385 for other comments on this question). For Louis—as later for the political theorist Jean Bodin and earlier for most of the many "illegitimate" rulers of Italian city-states—sovereignty meant effective politico-military control, not juridical legitimacy. The three counties called the Auxerrois, Charolais, and Mâconnais by Commynes adjoin the duchy of Burgundy on the west but were not part of it. They were not fiefs of the crown and thus did not revert in feudal law to the sovereign (Louis XI) upon the death of the last male heir (Charles the Bold), as did the duchy of Burgundy. Therefore, they had to be bargained for, like the county of Burgundy.

156. Scholarship is a cumulative discipline and so is a scholar's knowledge of that discipline. The second volume of these *Memoirs* is being completed two years later than the first, and at this point the editor of this work wishes he could eat the words in n. 127, p. 341, while the translator would like to take some nibbles at the paragraph to which the note refers. Commynes uses the word "city" ("cité") in that paragraph as in the paragraph here, and it does not mean "citadel." Nor does it mean what Littré, in quoting the passage from Commynes on p. 341, says it does: ". . . [the word] 'town,' more general than 'city,' expresses only [the idea of] a considerable agglomeration of houses and people. 'City' adds . . . to 'town' [the idea of] a political entity which has its own rights, duties, and functions." (See Emile Littré, *Dictionnaire de la langue française*, II, 354). On the contrary, as Mandrot, I, 416, n. 3, points out, "city" in this passage as in the passage on p. 341 refers to one kind of political entity, "town" to another. The "city" of Arras was a Roman foundation, a *civitas*. With the Christianization of Gaul in the early Middle Ages, bishops took up residence in the old Roman cities, including Arras. Later on many towns grew up on non-Roman sites, not infrequently in order to escape the jurisdiction of the bishop.

the city was well fortified and was held in the name of the king by the bishop. But the lords of the house of Burgundy have traditionally (or at least for one hundred years) selected whomever they liked to be made bishop, and have also chosen the commander of the city. The king did the opposite in order to increase his authority; he had the walls of the town demolished and others built around the city; for the city was closed off from the town by means of the large ditches which separated them; and thus the king [really] gave nothing.

Of the duchy of Burgundy, or the county of Boulogne, or the towns upon the river Somme, or the domains of Péronne, Roye and Mont-didier, he said not a word. These bargains were being transacted, and the people of Ghent were very much interested in them; and they were very rude to the duke and to the duchess his wife. Several other towns in Flanders and Brabant were rather inclined to have their own way, particularly Brussels, and this was a matter to wonder about, because Dukes Philip and Charles of Burgundy had always lived there and more-over the duke and duchess of Austria still resided there at that very moment. But the conveniences and pleasures which they had enjoyed under the above-mentioned lords had made them neglect God and their temporal lords, and so they went looking for trouble, and they eventu-ally found it, as you have seen.

In the case of Arras, a town began growing up outside the Roman walls about 650 A.D., centered around the Abbey of Saint Vaast. The city and town of Arras had as-sumed by Commynes' time the shape of a pair of rubber-rimmed goggles, the center of each "lens" being in the case of the city the cathedral and in the case of the town the abbey. The thick rubber rims of the "goggles" represent the large moats sur-rounding city and town, separating them from each other as well as from the sur-rounding countryside.

As Commynes informs us later in this paragraph, the dukes of Burgundy had developed control over the city of Arras through control of appointment of the bishop. Thus, when Commynes says that "the king did the opposite" he means that while the dukes of Burgundy did not bother to fortify the city of Arras (be-cause they controlled it by appointing bishops), and instead allowed the fortifica-tion of the town of Arras to proceed (because commercial-industrial activities in Arras, centered in the town, were important sources of revenue to the duke and warranted protection), the king tore down the town's fortification and augmented the city's. Commynes was wrong, however, to say that "the town was no longer of any consequence," and Louis XI's almost genocidal policy toward the town (he not only demolished the walls and changed Arras' name to "Franchise" but deported to France vast numbers of citizens, including most of the more important families, and replaced them with artisans from elsewhere) proved ill advised. In 1482 Louis was forced to allow the old families to return, the new ones to depart, and the old name, Arras, to be reinstated. See Jean Lestocquoy, *L'Histoire de la Flandre et de l'Artois* (Paris, 1949), pp. 15–60, for these and other details, and Lestocquoy, *Les Dynasties bourgeoises d'Arras du XIe au XVe siècle* (Arras, 1945), for a plan of the city in 1435 (unnumbered page at the end of the book).

6

At this time, which was March, 1479, a truce was concluded between the above-mentioned lords, and the king wanted peace, especially in the region I have mentioned, but on condition that it would be entirely to his advantage, as I said. He was already beginning to feel the effects of old age and illness, and [one day] as he was having dinner at Les Forges near Chinon he had a sort of seizure and lost his speech. He was taken from the table, placed near the fireplace, and the windows were shut. Although he tried to get to them, he was prevented from doing so by several well-meaning persons. And this illness came upon him in March of 1480;[157] he completely lost his speech as well as his understanding and his memory.

You arrived at once, my lord of Vienne, for at the time you were his physician. Thereupon he was given an enema and you had the windows opened to give him air. Immediately he regained some of his speech and sense, and then he mounted his horse and returned to Les Forges; for he was taken ill in a small parish town a quarter-league away, where he had gone to hear Mass.

The king was well taken care of, and he used sign language to express himself. Among other things, he called for the ecclesiastical judge of Tours[158] to hear his confession and he made signs that I should be sent for because I had gone to Argenton, which is about ten leagues from there. When I arrived at his castle, I found him at the table and with him were Master Adam Fumée, who formerly had been the physician of King Charles and was then *maître des requêtes*, and another physician called Master Claude. The king understood very little of what was said to him, but he felt no pain. He motioned to me to lie in his room: he hardly formed any words. I waited on his table for fifteen days and attended his person like a *valet de chambre*, which I considered a great privilege and was bound to do.

After two or three days he began to recover his speech and understanding and it seemed to him that no one understood him as well as

157. Calmette, II, 280, n. 1, points out that Louis XI's letters for this period show that this attack took place in March, 1479, not 1480, as indicated by Commynes himself in the first sentence of the paragraph. However, the truce mentioned in that first sentence did not take place in March, 1479, as Mandrot demonstrates, II, 39, n. 1. A year-long truce had been in effect until July 11, 1479, after which the siege of Thérouanne and the battle of Guinegatte took place. A new truce for seven months was finally signed on August 21, 1480.

158. The *officialis*, or ecclesiastical judge, was a person designated by the bishop of a diocese to exercise the bishop's judicial authority. Why Louis chose such a person to hear his confession is not clear.

myself; therefore he wanted me to stay with him at all times. He made his confession to the ecclesiastical judge in my presence, for otherwise they could not have communicated with each other. He did not have much to say, for he had made his confession only a few days before. When the kings of France want to touch the scrofulous, they first make their confession and our king never failed to do so once a week.[159]

When he felt a little better, he began inquiring as to who those were who had restrained him by force and had prevented him from going to the window. He was told their names. Thereupon he banished all of them from his house. He deprived some of them of their positions and never saw them again. From others, such as my lord of Segré and Gilbert de Grassay, lord of Champéroux, he took nothing, but he sent them somewhere else.

Many were astonished by this whim, and they blamed him for it, saying that these people had meant well and had done [what they thought was] for the best; and it was true. But the fancies of princes are of many kinds, and not everyone who tries to talk about them can understand them. He feared nothing so much as to lose his authority, which was very great, or to be disobeyed about anything whatsoever.

His father King Charles, on the other hand, when he contracted the illness from which he died, imagined that some people wanted to poison him at the request of his son; and this thought was so persistent that he refused to eat. Therefore it was decided by the advice of his physicians and of his closest and special servants that he should be fed by force. And so it was done, after much deliberation and by order of the persons who attended him. They put some broth into his mouth and shortly after this act of force King Charles died. King Louis, who had always condemned this procedure, took it very much to heart that, incredibly enough, he had been held by force; and he pretended to be more incensed than he really was, for the crux of the matter was that he feared that they might want to control, among other things, the way he managed his affairs and business, under the pretense that his judgment was impaired.

After he had severely dealt with those of whom I spoke, he inquired about the measures taken in council and the dispatches which had been sent during the last ten or twelve days. Those who were in charge of this business were the bishop of Albi [Louis d'Amboise], his brother the governor of Burgundy [Charles d'Amboise], Marshal de Gié, and the lord of Lude. For these men were present when he fell ill and they were all lodged under his room in two little rooms. He insisted on being

159. It was believed that a member of the French royal house, once anointed and consecrated as king, could cure scrofula by touching the afflicted person.

shown the letters which had arrived and which were arriving every hour. He was handed the most important ones and I read them to him. He pretended to understand them, took them in his hand and acted as if he were reading them, although he had no knowledge [of what they said]. And he said a word or two or made signs to indicate what answers he wished to be given.

We made few decisions while we waited for the end of his illness, for he was the kind of master with whom one had to play straight. This illness continued for about fifteen days, at the end of which he recovered his understanding and speech. But he remained weak and in danger of a relapse; for naturally he was inclined to discount the advice of his physicians.

As soon as he felt better he freed Cardinal Balue, whom he had kept a prisoner for fourteen years although the apostolic see and others had interceded in his behalf several times, and finally he had himself absolved of this imprisonment by a brief sent by our holy father the pope at his request.[160] When this illness struck him, those who were with him at the time believed him dead and they ordered several writs to be issued to abolish an excessive and very cruel tax which he had recently established under the influence of my lord of Cordes, his lieutenant in Picardy, in order to maintain twenty thousand regularly paid infantrymen and twenty-five hundred soldiers in charge of earthworks (the latter are called camp men): and to these he added fifteen hundred men-at-arms from his regular army to fight on foot if need be. He had a large number of tents and pavilions set up and many carts assembled to enclose them—a procedure which he had learned from the army of the duke of Burgundy. And this camp cost fifteen thousand francs a year. When it was ready, he went to inspect it, in a vast plain near Pont-de-l'Arche in Normandy [June, 1481]. The six thousand Swiss which I mentioned before were there. He saw them but once and returned to Tours, where he was taken ill again [September, 1481]. Once again he lost his speech, and for a good two hours everyone thought him dead. He was in a gallery, lying on a straw mattress, and several persons were with him.

My lord of Bouchage and I dedicated him to Saint Claude, and all the others present did the same. Thereupon he regained his speech and walked about the house, although he was very weak. This second illness took place in 1481. He went about the country as before. He was my

160. Cardinal Balue, imprisoned April 23, 1469, for treasonous relations with the duke of Burgundy (see p. 195), was released on December 20, 1480. Thus, Commynes has skipped a year and a half (March, 1479–December, 1480) somewhere in these pages, as well as exaggerating the cardinal's term of imprisonment.

guest in Argenton, where he stayed for a month and was very ill [November–December, 1481], and from there he proceeded to Thouars, where he was also very sick [December, 1481–February, 1482]. And then he undertook the trip to Saint-Claude [March–April, 1482], to which saint he had been dedicated, as you have heard.

When he left Thouars, he sent me to Savoy to oppose the lords of La Chambre, of Miolans and of Bresse (although he secretly aided them) because they had seized the lord of Illins in Dauphiné, whom the king had made a governor of his nephew Duke Philibert.[161] He sent a con-

161. Following the death in August, 1478, of Yolande, Louis XI's sister and wife of Amadeus IX, duke of Savoy (1465–1472), the young duke Philibert (1472–1482), still a minor, was through Louis XI's machinations put in the hands of the lord of Illins. Philip, the lord of Bresse mentioned by Commynes here, was the eldest brother of Amadeus IX and therefore had the strongest claim to be regent after the death of Yolande. He resented Louis' intrusions into the affairs of Savoy and may have had a hand in the seizure of the lord of Illins. Mandrot, II, 46, n. 1, maintains that the lord of La Chambre captured the lord of Illins by himself, without Philip of Bresse's authority to do so. In any case, Philip of Bresse decided, in view of the arrival of the French forces headed by Commynes, to come to terms with

---

The inscription, dated 1699, which appears at the top of this drawing, declares that the iron cage depicted is to be found, along with a second one, in the dungeon of the castle of Loches. (These cages were destroyed during the French Revolution.) Presumably, then, it was a cage like this which housed not only Cardinal Balue, as mentioned in the inscription (see also page 410 and note 160), and the bishop of Verdun (see page 422), but also Commynes himself. If the drawing is correct and if Commynes' estimate of the dimensions of the cage is fairly accurate, the apertures between the thick, ironclad wooden bars cannot have been larger than four inches square. It is hard to resist connecting Louis' apparent willingness to treat political prisoners of note as wild beasts with some kind of subconscious recognition of the character of his own political behavior. Whether or not Louis should be classed as afflicted by a zoophiliac displacement of normal human affection (see note 167, page 410), the evidence contained in this drawing should make it impossible to regard him as very prone to philanthropy. It seems obvious, too, that the distortions, gaps in sensibility, and fragmentation of religious insight which in my Introduction are called characteristic of Commynes' writing must have been strongly reinforced by being trapped for five months behind this closely woven grating.

La Cage de fer ou a este enferme le
Cardinal balüe, qui est dans le donjon du
Chasteau de Loches, ou il y en a encor une autre
pareille, elles ont 6 pieds et demie des 4 costez
1699.

siderable number of men-at-arms after me, and I led them to Mâcon against my lord of Bresse. However, he [the lord of Bresse] and I made a secret agreement, and he took my lord of La Chambre, who was sleeping in the duke's room in Turin in Piedmont, where he resided, and sent me word of it. And I immediately had the men-at-arms retire, for he took the duke of Savoy to Grenoble, where my lord the marshal of Burgundy, the marquis of Rothelin and myself went to receive him. The king sent for me to meet him at Beaujeu in the Beaujolais, and I was amazed to see him so thin and drawn; and I wondered how he could keep on travelling from territory to territory, but his great courage sustained him.

At Beaujeu he received letters informing him that the duchess of Austria had died of a fall from her horse, for she was riding a lively little pony. It threw her down and she fell against a big piece of wood. Some claimed that she did not die as a result of the fall, but from a fever. In any case, she died a few days after her fall, and it was most regrettable for her subjects and her friends, for they never again enjoyed prosperity nor peace. The people of Ghent and other towns had more respect for her than for her husband, because the territory had been hers by inheritance. This happened in the year 1482 [March 27].

The king told me the news and was very pleased about it. Besides, the two children had remained in the care of the people of Ghent, who were inclined to make trouble and to promote dissension against the house of Burgundy, as he knew; and it seemed to him that the [right] moment had come because the duke of Austria was a young foreigner and his father the emperor, who was still alive, was involved in wars everywhere and was very stingy.

Immediately the king began to negotiate with the governors of Ghent by the intermediary of my lord of Cordes, and to discuss the possibility of a marriage between his son, my lord the dauphin, and the duke's daughter, named Margaret, our present [prospective[162]] queen. Transactions were made with one of the councillors of the town, named Guillaume Rim, a shrewd and malicious man, and another named Coppenhole, clerk to the aldermen, who was a hosier and enjoyed great

---

Louis: He took La Chambre captive in the name of King Louis (end of January, 1482) and brought Duke Philibert to Lyon (March 9, 1482) where Philibert died in what amounted to French custody on April 22, 1482. Louis' interference in Savoyan affairs was ill founded in feudal law, most of the fiefs of the duke being held ultimately from the Holy Roman Emperor rather than from the French king. (See the line indicating the imperial-French boundary on the map at the head of this volume.)

162. See n. 144, p. 384.

credit with the people, for persons of his stamp have such credit there when things are in disarray like that.

The king returned to Tours [June 2, 1482]. He shut himself in for so long that few people saw him. He began to suspect everybody in an extraordinary way and worried greatly because he feared that his entourage might deprive him of his authority or curtail it. He removed from his presence all those who were used to attending him and the closest friends he ever had, but he took nothing away from them. They proceeded to their positions or charges or to their estates; but the situation did not last long, for he did not live long. He did some rather strange things, which made those who did not understand him believe that his mind was impaired; but they did not understand him.

As for being suspicious, all great princes are so, especially the wise ones and those who have had many enemies and have offended many people, as was the case with the king. Furthermore he knew that he was not well loved by the high-ranking persons of his kingdom, nor by many of the common people. And he had taxed them more than any of his predecessors, although he now had good intentions of unburdening them, as I said; but he should have started sooner.

King Charles was the first (by the assistance of many wise and excellent knights who had helped and served him in his conquest of Normandy and Guyenne, which were held by the English) to gain that point of imposing taxes in his country according to his pleasure, without the consent of the estates of his kingdom. And at the time there was much to be done because it was necessary to put garrisons in the conquered lands as well as to disperse the soldiers who were pillaging the kingdom. And the lords of France consented to this in return for certain pensions which were promised to them [in compensation] for the taxes which were levied in their territories.

If that king [Louis] were still living as well as those who were then with him in his council, he would have greatly advanced by now. But judging from what has already happened and will happen, he has charged his soul and the souls of his successors with a great burden and has inflicted a cruel wound upon his kingdom, which will bleed for a long time, and he has put upon it a terrible bridle of paid men-at-arms which he established in the manner of Italian lords.

At the time of his death King Charles VII levied taxes amounting to 1,800,000 francs on all things in his kingdom, and he maintained a regular army of only about seventeen hundred men-at-arms, who were kept in good order to guard the provinces of his kingdom; and for a long time before his death they had stopped riding up and down the kingdom, which was a great relief to the people. Our master the king at the hour of his death raised [an annual] 4,700,000 francs and had about four or five thousand men-at-arms and more than twenty-five thousand foot soldiers, including the camp men and the *mortes payes*.[163]

Thus one should not be amazed if he had several conflicting thoughts in his mind and if he suspected that he was not well liked, although among those who had been brought up and who had received benefits under him he would have found many who would have been faithful to him to death.

First of all, nobody was allowed to enter Plessis-du-Parc [i.e. Plessis-lez-Tours], which was his place of residence, except the domestic servants and his four hundred archers, who in good numbers patrolled and walked around the place every day and kept guard at the gate. No lord or high ranking person lodged in the castle, nor did any group of important lords enter, except once in a while. No one was admitted except my lord of Beaujeu, now duke of Bourbon, who was his son-in-law. Around the castle of Plessis he had a lattice of large iron bars set up and spikes of iron planted in the wall with several points protruding, especially at the entrance near the moat where it might have been possible to penetrate. He also had four cabins made of very thick iron with openings through which it would be convenient to shoot; this was a very grandiose thing, and it cost him more than twenty thousand francs. Finally he put forty crossbowmen in this moat, day and night, with orders to shoot any man who might approach during the night before the opening of the gate in the morning. It seemed to him more and more that his subjects might be inclined to take authority when they saw the [right] moment.

It is true that there was some talk among several people about the possibility of entering Plessis and taking over the management of affairs according to their own ideas, because nothing was being done; but they

---

163. See p. 401 above for mention of the camp men. The *mortes payes* had less complete armament and were paid less than the men-at-arms of the *compagnies d'ordonnance*. Mandrot, II, 49, nn. 2 and 3, and 50, nn. 1 and 2, adjusts the figures given here and in the preceding paragraph only slightly: Charles VII received in 1461 from the *taille* (the chief direct tax) 1,200,000 livres and had 1,500 men-at-arms; Louis XI in 1483 received 3,900,000 livres from the *taille*, 700,000 livres from *gabelles* and *aides* (indirect taxes), and 100,000 livres from the royal domain. But as Daviso, *Memorie*, p. 348, n. 1, points out, comparisons between Charles's and Louis' finances, let alone between either of them and later state budgets, tend to be subject to error because economic movements of inflation and deflation in all their local variation have not yet been worked out for fifteenth-century France and also because many sources of royal income and expense have not been recorded in extant documents.

did not dare put their plan into execution, and they were wise to refrain from attempting anything, for the king had provided well against any enterprise. He often changed his *valets de chambre* and other servants, saying that fear of him and respect would be maintained by changing things so.

In order to maintain his authority, he kept with him one or two men of low condition and of no great reputation, who should have foreseen, if they had been wise, that as soon as he was dead they would be deprived of all their offices; and that was the least that could happen to them. And this is what happened to them. These men did not report to him anything that was told or written to them, except what concerned the preservation of the state and the defense of the kingdom, for he was not interested in anything else.

At that time he was at peace or in a state of truce with everyone. He gave his physician ten thousand *écus* a month, and in the space of five months this physician received fifty-four thousand *écus*.

He rested his hopes of life in God and the saints, because he realized that he could hardly survive without a miracle; and remembering that Our Lord had prolonged the life of some king because of his humility and repentance, as well as by the prayer of some holy prophet, our king, who surpassed all the other princes in the world in humility, searched for a monk or other worthy man who lived an austere life, so that he might serve as mediator between God and him, and so that his life would be prolonged; and from everywhere in the world persons were suggested to him. He sent for several of them. Some of them came to speak to him and he spoke of nothing except this prolongation of his life. Most of them answered wisely that they did not have this power. The king offered important gifts—too many, according to the archbishop of Tours, a good and holy man, a Franciscan and a cardinal [Hélie de Bourdeille], who wrote him, among other things, that he would do better to take away the money from the canons of the churches where he gave his great presents and to distribute this to the poor plowmen and others who are paying so many taxes, rather than to raise money from them to give it to the rich churches and the rich canons to whom he offered these funds. His vows and offerings increased greatly in the course of one year; they included reliquaries and shrines, including the silver grille of Saint-Martin de Tours which weighed almost eight[een] thousand silver marks, the reliquary of Saint Eutropius at Saintes, and other shrines which he donated in Cologne at the Dreikönigen [chapel or shrine in the cathedral], in Aachen at the Liebfrauenkirche in Germany, in Utrecht at Sint Servaas, the reliquary of Saint Bernardino in Aquila in the kingdom of Naples, and the golden chalices sent to San Giovanni in Laterano in Rome, and several other gifts of gold and silver to various churches in his kingdom; the total amounted to around 700,000 francs.

He also gave many estates to the churches; but these gifts of land never went through. Anyway, there were too many of them.

7

Among the men renowned for their devotion he sent for a man from Calabria called Brother Robert.[164] The king called him "the holy man" because of the holy life which he led. In his honor the present king [Charles VIII] had a monastery built at Plessis-du-Parc [i.e. Plessis-lez-Tours], in compensation for the chapel [which he occupied in Louis' time] near Plessis at the end of the bridge. This hermit at the age of twelve went to live under the edge of a cliff and stayed there until the age of forty-three or so, when the king sent for him by a major-domo of his household who was accompanied by the prince of Taranto, son of the king of Naples; for the hermit did not want to leave without permission from the pope and from his king, which showed the sense in that simple person, who had built two churches in the land of the Moors.

He had never eaten meat, nor fish, nor eggs, nor milk products, nor any fat, nor has he since he began to lead this austere life; and I have never seen a man who lived such a holy life, nor through whose mouth it seemed more that the Holy Spirit spoke, for he was learned, although he had never been to school. It is true that his Italian language aided him. The hermit passed through Naples, where he was honored and visited as much as if he had been an important apostolic legate, by the king of Naples as well as by his children, and he spoke with them as if he had been raised at court. From there he went to Rome, where he received visits from all the cardinals. He had a private audience with the pope at three different times, and sat next to him in a sumptuous chair; and their conversation lasted for three or four hours each time, which was a great honor for such a small man.[165] He gave such wise

---

164. *Sic.* All that follows pertains to San Francesco da Paola, founder of the extremely austere order of Minims, one of the mendicant religious orders of the Catholic church (died in 1507; declared a saint in 1519). Contrary to Commynes' statement later in this paragraph, Francesco was sixty-six years old when Louis XI sent for him. In the third sentence of this paragraph I have followed the Polignac manuscript, as does Mandrot, rather than the Dobrée manuscript, as does Calmette: under the edge of a cliff" ("soubz ung coing de roc"), not "under a cliff" (soubz ung roc").

165. For commentary on Commynes' use of "small" (and "big" or "great") to designate men socially see pp. 48–49.

408

answers that everybody marveled. Our Holy Father granted him permission to found an order called the hermits of Saint Francis.

From there he came to the king [in April, 1483], who honored him as if he had been the pope himself; he knelt before him and begged him to pray to God for him, so that He would deign to prolong his life. He replied as a wise man should. I have heard him speak many times with our present king, in the presence of all the great lords of the kingdom, and not longer than two months ago. And it seemed that he was inspired by God when he spoke and made remonstrances; otherwise he would not have been able to speak of the things which he did. He is still alive, and therefore he might well change for the better or the worse, and so I shall say no more about this. Many people made fun of the coming of this hermit whom they called the holy man, but they could not read the mind of this wise king, and they did not know what led him [to send for him].

Our king was at Plessis with very few people except his archers, and he still entertained the same suspicions as I mentioned earlier. He provided well against them because he left no person of whom he had any suspicion in the town of Tours or in the [surrounding] country; but he had them withdraw far away from him and made them go and be conducted by his archers.

He was not informed of anything except important matters that were of concern to him. Judging by his appearance, he seemed rather dead than alive, because he was so thin that no one would have believed it. He dressed richly, which he never used to do before; he wore nothing but gowns of crimson satin lined with fine marten fur. He gave many of them away and sent them without being asked, for no one would have dared ask him for any.

He inflicted severe punishments in order to be feared, and because he was afraid of losing his authority, as he told me himself. He made changes in officers, disbanded men-at-arms, reduced pensions, and cancelled some of them entirely, and he told me a few days before his death that he passed the time by making and breaking people. And thus he saw to it that he was more talked about in his kingdom than ever before, and he did this for fear that his subjects might think him dead; for as I have said several times few people saw him, but when they heard of his deeds they doubted and found it hard to believe that he was ill.

He sent ambassadors everywhere outside the kingdom to negotiate that marriage [between his son and the princess] of England, and he paid the English well with his gifts, including King Edward and other private individuals. In Spain he always gave the people fine words of friendship and negotiation, and distributed gifts continually in all directions. Everywhere he had this good horse or that mule bought for him, whatever it cost him; but this was in countries where he wanted to be considered healthy and not at all in this kingdom.

He sent for dogs from every region: in Spain he bought mastiffs, in Brittany little female greyhounds, male greyhounds, and spaniels, and he paid much for them; in Valencia he obtained little shaggy dogs and had them bought for more than the dealers asked for them. In Sicily he sent for mules, especially those owned by officers of the region, and he paid double their value; at Naples [he sought] horses. And [he looked for] strange animals everywhere, such as in Barbary, [where he obtained] some kind of small wolves which are no bigger than little foxes; he called them adils.[166] In Denmark he sent for two kinds of animals; the first type is called the elk, and it has the shape of a stag, the size of a buffalo, and short, thick horns; the other is called the reindeer, and is of the shape and color of a deer but with much larger horns. Indeed, I have seen a reindeer with fifty-four horns. In order to obtain six of these animals the king gave the merchants four thousand five hundred German florins.

When all these animals were brought to him, he took no notice of them and most of the time he did not speak to those who had brought them. And indeed he did so many such things that he was more feared by his neighbors and subjects than he had ever been before, for that is what he wanted and he acted in this manner for that reason.[167]

8

To return to our principal subject and to the chief conclusion of all these memoirs,[168] we must speak of the negotiation of the marriage treaty

166. The adil is a cross between a dog and a wolf, according to Calmette, II, 298, n. 2.

167. Louis XI's "zoophilia" has been given a different interpretation by Auguste Brachet in his *Pathologie mentale des rois de France* (Paris, 1903), pp. cvi–cxx. It was systematically related to Louis' "epilepsy," as Brachet calls the illness reported by Commynes here and in the preceding chapters, and more importantly to his withdrawal of affection from humans, a necessary corollary of his manipulative genius in politics. (Animals can hardly threaten humans by making demands commensurate with their devotion and service. They can be fondled or abused with relative impunity.) For reasons similar to those which prompted him to conceal and distort details of the interview at Péronne or of the circumstances surrounding the battle of Nancy (see the commentary on these reasons in the Introduction, p. 72), perhaps Commynes pretended that Louis' mania for collecting animals was political in purpose and occurred only at the end of his life. In fact documents cited by Brachet show that such collecting occurred as early as 1468 at the time of the Péronne interview.

168. Commynes originally intended to conclude the *Memoirs* with Louis XI's death. All early manuscripts except the Dobrée manuscript add at this point the

which was made between our present king [Charles VIII], who was then called my lord the dauphin, and [Margaret] the daughter of the duke and duchess of Austria; it was arranged by the intermediary of the people of Ghent to the great displeasure of King Edward of England, who then considered himself disappointed in his hopes of a marriage between his daughter and my lord the dauphin, the present king of France. He and his wife the queen had desired this match more than anything in the world, and they had never wanted to believe any person, whether a subject of theirs or anyone else, who told them the contrary. For the council of England had remonstrated with King Edward several times when King [Louis] was conquering Picardy which is near Calais, and they told him that after he had conquered that province, he might well try to conquer Calais and Guines. The ambassadors who were continually in England, representing the duke and duchess of Austria, the Bretons and others, said the same thing to him, but he did not believe a word of it. In my opinion this was not so much a question of ignorance with him as one of avarice, for he did not want to lose the fifty thousand *écus* which the king gave him, and besides he did not want to give up his comfort or pleasures, to which he was very much given.

A conference was held at Alost in Flanders to discuss the question of this marriage. The duke of Austria, who is now king of the Romans, was present, and with him were delegates chosen by the three estates of Flanders, Brabant and other territories belonging to the duke and his children. There the people of Ghent did several things against the will of the duke, such as banishing some people and removing others from the presence of his son, and they told him that they wanted to have the marriage of which I spoke materialize in order to have peace, and they forced him to agree to it, whether he liked it or not. He was very young and poorly provided with men of great sense; for all the members of the house of Burgundy were either dead or had passed over to our side, or almost all: I refer to high-ranking persons who would have known how to advise him and to help him. As far as his party was concerned, he had come poorly accompanied. And since he had lost his wife, who was a princess native to the country, he did not dare speak as boldly as he had done formerly.

And to summarize, the king was informed of this by the lord of

---

words, "et de tous ces affaires des personnaiges qui vivoient du temps qu'ils ont esté faictz" ("and [to the conclusion] of all the affairs of those who lived at the time when they took place"), an addition which, if it is not authentic, nevertheless might be said to describe Commynes' achievement better than his own stated intentions. See pp. 16–17 for discussion of Commynes' purposes.

Cordes and was extremely pleased about it. And a day was appointed for the duke's daughter to be brought to Hesdin. A few days before, and this was in the year 1481 [*sic*: July 28, 1482], Aire had been given up to the lord of Cordes for a certain sum of money by the lord of Cohen from the territory of Artois, who had held it for the duke of Austria and for the lord of Bèvres, his commander. This town, which is situated in Artois, is very strong, and it was very useful to the Flemings in the advancement of their project because it is at the entrance of their province. And however much they wished to see their prince minimized, they would not have wanted to have the king at their frontiers nor so close to them.

After these things had been agreed upon, the ambassadors from Flanders and Brabant came to the king [December, 1482]. But everything depended on those from Ghent, owing to their strength and because they had in their hands the children [of Mary of Burgundy]; moreover, they were always the first ones ready to start some trouble. Some knights representing the king of the Romans, young like he was and badly advised, also came in order to make peace for their country. Jean de Berghes was one of them and Baudoin de Lannoy was the other and there was also a secretary.

The king was already very weak and was very reluctant to be seen. And so he made all sorts of difficulties before swearing to the treaties which had been agreed upon; but it was because he did not wish to be seen. He finally swore to them, however [January, 1483]. They were to his advantage; for he had often desired this marriage and he had wanted only the county of Artois or the county of Burgundy, either one of the two, but now my lords of Ghent (as he called them) had them both given to him, and the counties of Charolais, Mâconnais, and Auxerrois[169] also. And if they had been able to have him allotted Hainaut and Namur together with all the subjects of that house [of Burgundy] who are French-speaking, they would have done it willingly in order to weaken their lord.

The king our master was very wise and he understood well what Flanders was like and what a count of that province who does not possess the territory of Artois is up against. For Artois is situated between the kingdom of France and Flanders and it is like their [the Flemings'] bridle, for some very good soldiers are drawn from there to help chastise them [the Flemings] when they act like fools; and therefore by depriv-

169. Calmette, II, 302, and Mandrot, II, 61, retain the reading of the Polignac manuscript, "Auxonnois," instead of that of the Dobrée manuscript and the early editions of the *Memoirs*, "Auxerrois." The latter seems more probable, since Commynes has employed Auxerrois, not Auxonnois, in a similar list on p. 397 above.

ing the count of Flanders of the territory of Artois, he would leave him the poorest lord in the world and without any authority except by the consent of those of Ghent. The principal ambassadors to the conference of which I spoke were Guillaume Rim and Coppenhole, governor of Ghent, of whom I spoke earlier.

When the ambassadors had returned, [Margaret] the daughter [of the duke of Austria] was brought to Hesdin and put in the hands of my lord of Cordes; it was in the year 1483 [in late May]. My lady of Ravenstein, the natural daughter of the late Duke Philip [the Good] of Burgundy, conducted her there, and she was received by the present lord and lady of Bourbon [Pierre and Anne de Beaujeu], my lord of Albret and others who had been sent by the king. She was taken to Amboise, where the dauphin was residing.

If the duke of Austria had been able to take her away from those who were leading her [to Hesdin], he would have done so willingly before she left his territories; but those of Ghent had her well guarded. Anyway, he was beginning to lose all authority. Many others joined with the people of Ghent because they had the duke's son in their custody and they dismissed and appointed whomever they pleased among his attendants. The lord of Ravenstein, brother of the duke of Cleves, was with them and he was the principal governor of the child, named Duke Philip [the Handsome], who is still alive and who can expect a considerable inheritance if God grants him a long life.

Regardless of how many people were pleased about this marriage, it was the cause of bitter disappointment to the king of England, for he considered it a shame to and mockery of himself; and he strongly suspected that he would lose the pension which our king was giving him, or his tribute, as the English called it. Moreover, he feared that he would be greatly despised in England, and that this might lead to a rebellion against him, especially since he had refused to believe the council. And he realized that the king [of France] was quite strong and very close to his lands. This made him grieve so much that he became ill immediately upon hearing the news, and he died shortly after; according to some, it was of an apoplexy. Whatever the case may be, the sorrow which he experienced at the news of this marriage was the cause of the illness from which he died in a few days [on April 9, 1483].

It is a great fault in a prince to value his judgment more than the opinion of several people, and this sometimes leads to great sorrows and irreparable losses. King Edward's death occurred in the year 1483 in the month of April. As soon as the king died, the king our master was notified about it and he did not express any joy upon hearing it. A few days later he received letters from the duke of Gloucester, who had proclaimed himself king of England under the name of Richard and who had had the two children of his brother, King Edward, murdered.

King Richard sought the friendship of our king and I believe that he would have been happy to have had the above-mentioned pension, but the king refused to reply to these letters or to hear the message. He considered King Richard a very cruel and evil man; for after the death of King Edward the duke of Gloucester had rendered homage to his nephew as his king and sovereign lord; and immediately he committed this deed and in a plenary session of the parliament of England he had the two daughters of Edward degraded and declared illegitimate under the pretense that he had obtained proof of this from a bishop of Bath in England; this man had once enjoyed great credit with King Edward, who later dismissed him, put him in prison, and then ransomed him for a sum of money. This bishop affirmed that King Edward had promised marriage to an English lady (whom he named) because he was in love with her and wanted to enjoy her favors, and he had made this promise in the hand of the bishop. And on the strength of this promise, which he had made only to deceive her, he slept with her. Such games are very dangerous, however, as this evidence demonstrates.

I have known many courtiers who, if they had had a chance at such a good and pleasant adventure, would not have let the occasion go by for lack of promises. And that bad bishop kept this desire for revenge in his heart for perhaps twenty years. But nothing good came of it, as far as he was concerned. For he had a son whom he dearly loved and to whom King Richard intended to grant many favors, including marriage to one of those two daughters [of King Edward] who were deprived of their dignities; she [Elizabeth, who married King Henry VII in 1486] is now queen of England and has handsome children. The bishop's son was on a warship by order of King Richard, his master. He was seized on the coast of Normandy and as a result of an argument which arose between his captors, he was taken before the Parlement and was confined in the Petit Châtelet in Paris; he was there so long that he died of starvation and poverty.

King Richard did not live to enjoy his glory for very long and neither did the duke of Buckingham, who had had the two children killed. For against King Richard God all of a sudden raised up an enemy [the future Henry VII] who had not a coin in his pocket nor any rights to the crown of England, as far as I know, nor any great reputation except that he was an honest man and still is. He had suffered greatly, for during most of his life he had been a prisoner in the hands of Duke Francis in Brittany (who treated him well for a prisoner) since the age of eighteen. And with a small amount of money which the king [of France] had given him, as well as some three thousand men which had been raised in Normandy—the worst kind which could have been found anywhere—he proceeded to Wales, where he was joined by his stepfather Lord Stanley with about twenty-five thousand Englishmen. After three or four days he encountered that cruel King Richard, who was killed on the battlefield; he was crowned king and has reigned to this day.

I spoke of this elsewhere, but it was useful to mention it here again, especially to show how God has paid back ready coin for such cruel acts in our time without any delay. He has punished many others too in our time, [as someone] who could recount them all [could show].[170]

9

After this marriage of Flanders was concluded [between the son of Louis XI and the daughter of Mary of Burgundy],[171] which the king had so earnestly desired, he had the Flemings under his thumb. Brittany, which he greatly hated, was at peace with him (but he held its subjects in great fear and apprehension because of the large number of men-at-arms which he kept quartered along its borders). Spain was at peace with him, and the king and queen of Spain desired nothing except his friendship, and he kept them in fear and expense because of the territory of Roussillon which he held from the house of Aragon; it had been given to him as security by King John of Aragon, father of the present king of Castile, pending certain conditions which have not yet been fulfilled.[172]

As for the powers in Italy, they wanted to have him as a friend, and they made certain alliances with him; they often sent ambassadors to his court. In Germany the Swiss obeyed him as well as if they had been his own subjects. The kings of Scotland and Portugal were his allies. One party in Navarre did everything that he wanted. His subjects trembled before him. Anything which he ordered was immediately executed without any difficulty or excuse.

As for things that were considered necessary for his health, they were sent to him from everywhere in the world. The late Pope Sixtus [IV (died August 13, 1484)], being informed that out of devotion the king desired to have the communion cloth which Saint Peter had used when he sang, sent it to him instantly, together with several other relics which were returned to him.

170. See p. 366 for Commynes' earlier account of these events, laced with the same materialistic moralizing.

171. *Sic.* See n. 144 on p. 384 above.

172. Charles VIII gave up his claim to Roussillon in the treaty of Barcelona in January, 1493, which indicates that this passage was written before that date.

The holy ampulla, which is at Reims and had never been removed from its place [in the cathedral there], was brought to him in his room at Plessis, and it stood on his dresser at the time of his death.[173] He had intended to be anointed with it again, as he had been at his coronation, although many people thought that he wanted to anoint his whole body with it; but that is not very likely, because the holy ampulla is very small and there is not much in it. I saw it at the time of which I am speaking, and also when the king was buried at Notre-Dame de Cléry.

The Turk who reigns today [Bayezid II (1481–1512)] sent him an ambassador, who came as far as Riez in Provence. But the king refused to hear him or to let him come any farther. The ambassador was bringing him a large roll of relics which had been left in Constantinople in the hands of the Turk. He offered them to the king together with a large sum of money, on condition that the king would have close guard kept over the Turk's brother, who was in our kingdom in the hands of the knights of Rhodes. At present he is in Rome in the custody of the pope.[174]

By all these things which I mentioned it is possible to judge the wisdom and greatness of our king and the great esteem and honor which he enjoyed in this world; and we can see how spiritual objects of devotion and of religion as well as temporal things were used [in an attempt] to prolong his life. All this was to no avail, however, and he had to follow the path of his predecessors. God had granted him some grace, for just as He had created him wiser, more liberal and more virtuous in all things than the other princes who ruled with him and in his time and who were his enemies and neighbors, so that he surpassed them in everything, so also he surpassed them in length of life, although not by very much. For Charles the duke of Burgundy, his daughter the duchess of Austria, King Edward, Duke Galeazzo of Milan and King John of Aragon all died a few years before him. As for the duchess of Austria, King Edward, and himself, they died almost at the same time. In all of them there was a mixture of good and bad, for they were human. But without resorting to any flattery, I will say that our master had far better qualifications for the office of king or prince than any of the others. I have seen almost all of them and I knew what they knew how to do and I am not merely making guesses.

173. According to Calmette, II, 308, n. 5, Louis XI received a special dispensation from the pope to bring the holy ampulla from Rheims to Plessis, together with certain other sacred relics. The holy ampulla was used to anoint French kings during their coronation ceremonies at the cathedral of Rheims.

174. Prince Jem contested the throne with his brother Bayezid II. Defeated, Jem fled first to Egypt and then to Rhodes where he was taken into honorable custody and eventually used by the pope to extort money from Bayezid.

Book Six

10

In the year 1482 the king desired to see his son my lord the dauphin, whom he had not seen for several years. For he feared to have many people see him, on account of the child's health as well as because he was afraid that he might be taken away from there, and that, using him as a front, some rallying-point might be made in his kingdom. For thus he had been used by some lords of the kingdom against his father King Charles VII when he was only a boy of thirteen [*sic:* sixteen]. And this war [in 1440] was called the Praguerie. But it was over very soon and was only a dissension of short duration. Above all things he recommended some of his servants to his son the dauphin, and expressly ordered him not to change any of the officers, pointing out that when his father King Charles VII had gone to God and he had acceded to the throne, he had revoked the offices of all the good and notable knights of the kingdom, who had served and helped his father to conquer Normandy and Guyenne and to chase the English out of the kingdom and to restore peace and good order throughout the realm; for he found it in that condition, and in addition very rich. This action on his part turned out to be badly mistaken, for it resulted in the war called the Public Good, of which I spoke elsewhere, and which almost cost him his crown.

Very soon after the king had spoken to his son, my lord the dauphin, and had made the final arrangements for the marriage which I mentioned, he contracted the illness which caused him to leave this world.[175] It began on a Monday and lasted until the following Saturday, the next to the last day of August, 1483. I was present at the end of his illness, and therefore I wish to say something about it.

As soon as he was seized with his final attack, he lost his speech, as he had done formerly. And when he recovered it, he felt weaker than ever before, even though earlier he had been so feeble that he could only with great difficulty lift his hand to his mouth and was so thin and drawn that he inspired pity in all who saw him.

The king judged that he was about to die and he immediately sent for my lord of Beaujeu, his daughter's husband, who is now duke of Bourbon, and commanded him to go to his son the king (as he called him), who resided at Amboise. He recommended the king his son to him, as well as those who had served him, and put him in charge of the young king as his governor, and ordered him to see to it that certain persons

175. *Sic.* As Commynes indicates in the first sentence of this chapter, the king's interview with his son took place in 1482: instructions to Charles at Amboise dated September 21, 1482, have been preserved. Eleven months later, on August 25, 1483, the king was struck by a fatal illness.

would not approach him, and gave him several good and notable reasons. If the lord of Beaujeu had observed all of his commands, or at least part of them (for there were some extraordinary orders which did not deserve to be observed), but if he had preserved them in general, I believe that it would have been to the profit of this kingdom as well as to his own, judging from what has happened since.

After this the king sent the chancellor and all his men to take the seals to the king his son. He also sent him part of the archers of his guard, certain commanders, [the officers in charge of] the royal hunt and falconry and everything else. All those who came to him he sent to Amboise to [pay their respects to] the king (as he called him), and he begged them to serve him well. With everyone he sent some message or other, but especially with Etienne de Vesc, who had raised the new king and had served him as first *valet de chambre*; and already the king our master had made him bailiff of Meaux.

His speech never again failed him after he recovered it, and his sense had never been so good; for he had almost constant diarrhea, and this released all the vapors from his head. Never once during his illness did he complain, as all sorts of people do when they do not feel well. At least I am of that nature, and I have known many other similar people; and it is said that to complain alleviates the pain.

11

He always said something sensible; and his illness, as I said, lasted from Monday until Saturday night.

And now I want to make a comparison between the hardships and afflictions which he had inflicted on many people and those which he suffered himself before he died; for I hope that they will have served to lead him to paradise and that they may have been part of his purgatory. And if his torments have not been as great nor as long as those which he brought upon many, [one must consider that] he had another position in this world and a higher place than they had. He had never suffered physically; and he was obeyed to such an extent that it seemed as if all of Europe had been made merely to bring him obedience. Therefore the little which he suffered was so contrary to his nature and custom that it was more grievous for him to bear.

He still rested his hopes in the good hermit [Francesco da Paola] of whom I spoke, who was at Plessis and whom he had called there from Calabria; he continually sent messages to him, saying that if he wanted to, he could surely prolong his life. For nothwithstanding the recommendations which he had made to those whom he had sent to my lord the dauphin, his son, he regained hopes [of recovery] and very much counted on escaping [death]. And if it had turned out this way, he would quickly have disbanded the groups of people whom he had sent to Amboise to the new king. And because of the hope which he placed in this hermit, it was advised by a certain theologian and by others that he should be told that he was deceiving himself and that for him there was no hope left except in the mercy of God. It was agreed that his physician, Master Jacques Coictier, in whom he had great faith and to whom he gave ten thousand *écus* a month in the hope that he would prolong his life, should be present when this statement was made to him. This decision was made by Master Olivier and Master Jacques, the physician, so that the king would thoroughly examine his conscience and would put aside all other thoughts, including those of the holy man whom he trusted.

And just as he had raised them too suddenly and without reason to dignities which were beyond what was fitting for them, so they took it upon themselves without any fears to say this to such a prince, although it was not proper for them to do so; and they did not observe the reverence and humility which was proper in such a situation and which would have been shown by those whom he had raised at his court for a long time and whom he had banished from his presence not long before, on account of his imaginations about them. But just as in the case of two important persons whom he had executed during his lifetime—and on his deathbed he expressed remorse in relation to one but not the other (they were the duke of Nemours and the count of Saint-Pol)—whom he had informed of their lot by commissioners who were delegated to do this, who told them about their sentence in brief words, and who provided confessors to prepare their consciences in the few moments which were allowed for them to do this, similarly the three above-mentioned men[176] came to announce his death to the king in brief, blunt terms. They said: "My lord, we must do our duty. Do not place your hopes any longer in this holy man or in anything else, for surely this is the end of you; therefore examine your conscience, for there is no remedy left." And everyone added a few rather brief words to which he replied: "I have hope that God will help me, for perhaps I am not so ill as you think."

What sorrow it was for him to hear such news and such a sentence!

---

176. Presumably Olivier le Dain (Commynes' personal disdain for whom is expressed again here, as in chapters 13 and 14 of Book 5), Jacques Coictier, and the "certain theologian" mentioned in the preceding paragraph whom Calmette, II, 311, n. 5, identifies as "Philippe," a monk from the monastery of Saint-Martin de Tours.

For no man feared death so much or did so many things to try to prevent it. Throughout his lifetime he had requested his servants and myself that if we should see him in need, we should not tell him, but simply persuade him to confess himself, without mentioning that cruel word "death." For it seemed to him that he would not have the heart to hear such a cruel sentence. However, he endured it with courage, as he did everything else up to the time of his death, and he endured it better than any man whom I have ever seen die.

To his son, whom he called king, he sent several messages. He made a very good confession and he said several prayers appropriate to the sacraments which he was receiving and which he himself had requested. And as I said, he spoke as succinctly as if he had never been ill, and he spoke of everything which might be useful to his son the king. Among other things he said that he wanted the lord of Cordes to remain with the king his son constantly for six months, and that he should be asked not to attempt any action against Calais or any other place; although he had agreed with him [earlier] to undertake such projects for the good of the king and the kingdom, they were dangerous, especially the enterprise against Calais, and he was afraid that it might antagonize the English. Above all he wished that the kingdom should be preserved after his death in a state of peace for five or six years, which was more than he himself had ever been able to stand in his whole life. And to be truthful, the kingdom was in need of a rest; for although the realm was large and extended far, it was very meager and poor, especially owing to the passage of the men-at-arms who marched from one end of the kingdom to the other; for they have done it since and have done much worse.

He ordered that nothing should be attempted against Brittany and that Duke Francis should be allowed to live in peace without being given subject for doubts or fears. The same should apply to all the neighbors of the kingdom, so that the king his son and his kingdom might live in peace until the king should be grown up and old enough to manage his affairs according to his own pleasure.

In a preceding section I started to make a comparison between the hardships which the king had inflicted on some people and on many who lived under him and his authority, and those similar in nature which he himself endured before his death (and if they were not as great and did not last as long, as I mentioned in that section, they were still very great, considering his nature, which demanded more obedience than anyone else did in his day, and had obtained more of it; thus a very slight word of opposition against his will was a very great torment to him, which was hard [for him] to endure). I mentioned how his death was announced to him with little discretion. But some five or six months

420

earlier the king began to suspect everyone, especially those who were worthy of having authority. He was afraid of his son and had him closely guarded; no man saw him or spoke to him except by his command. At the end he feared his daughter and his son-in-law, who is at present duke of Bourbon, and he wanted to know who came to Plessis with them; and finally he broke up a council meeting which the duke of Bourbon was holding in the castle by his command.

At the time when his son-in-law and the count of Dunois returned from conducting the ambassadors who had been at Amboise to attend the wedding [*sic*] of his son the king and the [prospective] queen [Margaret of Austria], and they were entering Plessis with many people, the king, who had the gates strongly guarded, was in the gallery facing the courtyard of the castle, and he called for one of the captains of the guards and ordered him to feel the clothes of the servants of these lords to see whether they had coats of mail under their robes; he asked them to do it by such means as entering into a conversation with them and he asked them not to be too obvious about it.

Consider then, if he had made many people live under him in suspicion and fear, whether he was not well repaid for it; and whom could he trust if he mistrusted his own son, his daughter and his son-in-law? I do not say this only regarding him, but regarding all other lords who want to be feared. They never feel the effects of revenge until their old age, but then as their penance they are afraid of everyone.

What grief it must have been to this king to experience such fears and such anguish. He had his physician, named Master Jacques Coictier, to whom in five months he gave fifty-five thousand *écus* in cash, at the rate of ten thousand *écus* per month, in addition to the bishopric of Amiens for his nephew and other offices and domains for himself and his friends. The physician was so very harsh with him that one would not dare speak to a valet in such an outrageous and harsh manner as he used with the king. And our master feared him so much that he would not have dared dismiss him, although he complained about him to those in whom he confided; yet he did not have the courage to replace him, as he did all the rest of his servants. And it was because the physician had boldly told him: "I well know that one of these days you will dismiss me as you have others, but by the . . . (and here he swore a great curse) you will not live eight days after it." The king was so terrified by this expression that after this he flattered him continuously and gave him presents. And this was a great purgatory on earth to him, considering the great obedience which he had always obtained from everyone, including high-ranking men.

It is true that the king our master had ordered some rigorous prisons

421

to be built, such as cages of iron or of wood covered with iron plates on the inside and on the outside, and with terrible locks, about eight feet wide and higher than a man by one foot. The first to invent them was the bishop of Verdun, who was put straightway into the first cage that was made and spent fourteen years in it. A number of people have cursed him since then, including me, for I tried one of them out for a period of eight months under our present king.[177]

[King Louis] had once ordered from the Germans some very heavy and very terrible chain links to be put around the feet; and there was a ring to be put on one foot only, which was hard to open and fitted like an iron collar, with a thick and heavy chain attached to a large iron ball, which was much heavier than was reasonable or proper. These things were called the king's nets. However, I have seen many high-ranking persons wear them on their feet who later were freed from prison with great honor and great joy, and who have since obtained important benefits from him. Among the rest was a son of my lord of Gruthuse from Flanders, who was taken in battle; the king later arranged a marriage for him, made him his chamberlain and seneschal of Anjou, and gave him the command of one hundred lance-teams. The same happened to the lord of Piennes, a prisoner of war, and the lord of Vergy; both have been given men-at-arms and have been his or his son's chamberlains, and have received important estates from him. This was also true of my lord of Richebourg, the brother of the constable, and of a certain Rocaberti from the land of Catalonia, also a prisoner of war, to whom he granted many favors, and several others from various countries who are too numerous to be mentioned.

This is not our main subject but I must say once again that just as these various evil prisons were invented in his time, so he before he died found himself in comparable prisons, and in greater ones, and in as great fear as those whom he had kept there. I hold this to have been all the greater grace for him and part of his purgatory. And I say this to show that there is no man, of whatever dignity he may be, who does not suffer either secretly or publicly, especially if he has made others suffer.

The king toward the end of his life had everything around his res-

177. *Sic.* Guillaume de Harancourt, bishop of Verdun, was not the inventor of these cages, which had been used long before, according to Mandrot, II, 77, n. 2. Commynes was arrested in January, 1487 (not 1488, as Calmette, II, 320, maintains). He was transferred after some five months, not eight, from the iron cage he inhabited in Loches to a small room in Paris overlooking the Seine (see p. 125). He remained imprisoned in Paris from July, 1487, to March, 1489, when his case came to trial. Dupont's edition of the *Memoirs* (Paris, 1840–47, 3 volumes), III, 141 ff., reproduces documents which describe the conditions of Commynes' imprisonment. The document transferring him from Loches to Paris is dated July 17, 1487.

idence of Plessis-lez-Tours enclosed with large iron bars in the shape of a thick grating, and at the four corners of the house he had four iron cabins built, which were solid, large and thick. The grates were against the wall on the outside; they also were adjacent to the moat, for it had no talus. He had many iron spikes put in the wall; each one had three or four points and he had them planted very close together. Furthermore he placed ten crossbowmen in the moat at each one of the iron cabins, so that they could shoot at anyone who might approach before the opening of the gate. He wanted the crossbowmen to lie in the moat and to retire to the iron cabins [when the occasion demanded it].

He understood very well that this fortification was not strong enough to resist a large number of invaders or an army, but he was not afraid of that [kind of assault]. He only feared that one or more lords might make an attempt to take the place by night, partly by love and partly by force, by means of some connivance [with those inside], and that these men might take over authority and force him to live like a man without sense and unfit to govern. The gate of Plessis was not opened before eight o'clock in the morning nor was the bridge lowered before. Then the officers entered and the captains of the guards posted their ordinary gate keepers and ordered their archers to keep watch at the gate and in the middle of the courtyard, as in a frontier town that is closely guarded. No one was allowed to enter except by the wicket and with the king's knowledge; only major-domos and persons of that sort did not present themselves before him.

Is it then possible to confine a king, in order to guard him fittingly, in a closer prison than that in which he kept himself? The cages in which he had kept others were about eight feet square; and he, although he was such a great king, had [only] a small courtyard of a castle in which to walk. And he hardly ever used it, but he generally stayed in the gallery without stirring from there, unless he went through the rooms, and he went to Mass without passing through the court.

Would anyone say that the king did not suffer, considering that he locked himself up and had himself guarded, that he was afraid of his children and of all his close relatives, that he changed and transferred from day to day his servants and those whom he had nourished, who owed all their goods and honors only to him? Yet he did not dare trust any of them but fettered himself in such strange chains and enclosures. It is true that the place was larger than a common prison, but then he was greater than common prisoners.

It might be argued that there have been others more mistrustful than he was. But this has not happened in my time, and perhaps the other princes were not so wise, nor did they have such good subjects; and besides they may have been cruel tyrants. But our king did not do harm to anyone who had not offended him.

I have not spoken about these things merely to point out the mistrustful character of our king, but to show that the patience with which he endured his sufferings, which were similar to those which he had inflicted on others, is attributable in my opinion to the punishment which Our Lord sent him in this world so that he would have less of it in the next, such as the things which I mentioned earlier, like his illnesses, which were very great and painful to him and which he very much feared before they came upon him. I also say these things so that those who may succeed him will have a little bit more pity on the people and will be less severe in punishing than he was, although I do not want to accuse him or to say that I have known a better prince. It is true that he overburdened his subjects, but he would not have suffered anyone else to have done it, whether friend or stranger.

After so many fears and suspicions and sorrows Our Lord accomplished a miracle for him and cured his soul as well as his body, as it is always His custom when He performs His miracles, for He took him away from this miserable world in excellent health of sense and understanding and with his memory in good state. After receiving all the sacraments and without suffering any pain to anyone's knowledge, he continued to speak, finishing with a Paternoster just before his death. He gave orders for his burial, named those whom he wished to accompany his corpse, and the route. He said that he hoped not to die before Saturday, and that Our Lady would grant him this grace, since he had always placed his trust in her, was very devoted to her and had prayed to her; and he wanted to be buried on the following Saturday. And so it happened as he had wished it, for he died on Saturday, the next to the last day in August, 1483, at eight o'clock in the evening at Plessis, where he had taken ill the previous Monday. May Our Lord have received him in His kingdom of paradise. Amen!

12

Poor people and those of low estate should have little hope in this world, since such a great king, who had suffered and worked so much, had to leave everything and was not able to ward off death for a single hour, however diligently he tried. I have known him and I became his servant in the flower of his age and at the height of his prosperity; yet I have never seen him without troubles and care. His sole pleasures were hunting and hawking during the proper seasons, but he did not enjoy these as much as dogs. He was not involved with ladies during the period that I was with him, for at the time of my arrival he lost a son [Francis (September, 1472–July, 1473)], which caused him great sorrow, and then he made a vow to God in my presence never to touch any woman except the queen his wife. This was no more than what he should have done, of course, according to the laws of matrimony, but it still was particularly commendable to have had so much will power as to persevere so firmly in this promise, especially considering that the queen [Charlotte of Savoy] was not the kind of person in whom one might take great pleasure, although she was a good lady.

When he went hunting, he had almost as much trouble as pleasure, for he took great pains in his enterprise. He pursued the stag energetically, getting up early in the morning; sometimes he rode very far and did not abandon the chase, regardless of what the weather might be. And thus he often returned very tired, and he was almost always angry at someone, for it is a sport which is not always managed according to the pleasure of the leaders. However he was more of an expert on the subject than any man who lived in his time, in everyone's opinion.

He went hunting continually, lodging in villages, until some news of war was brought, for during almost every summer some fighting was going on between Duke Charles [of Burgundy] and him, and during all winter they made truces.

He also had much trouble over the county of Roussillon with King John of Aragon, father of the present king of Spain. Although father and son were poor and were having much trouble with their subjects, such as those of Barcelona and other places, and although the son had nothing (except that he was waiting [to receive] the succession [to the throne] of Don Henry of Castile, his wife's brother, which he eventually obtained), they still made considerable resistance; for the hearts of the subjects of the territory of Roussillon were for them, and this cost our king and our kingdom very much, for many worthy men died and were lost there and much money was spent there.

Thus the pleasure which he took from time to time was brief and it took great toll of his person, as I said. When he was resting, his mind was at work, for he had dealings in so many places that it was amazing, and he willingly became involved in his neighbors' affairs as well as his own, placed some of his men in their houses and divided their authority. When he was at war, he wished for peace or a truce; when he was at peace or in a state of truce, he could hardly bear it. He became concerned with many minor matters in his kingdom, although he would have done better to leave a good many of them alone. But such was his character and such was the life he led. Anyway, his memory was so great that he retained everything and knew everybody, in all regions as well as in those around him. And indeed he seemed more suitable to rule a world than to reign over a mere kingdom.

I shall not speak of his youth, because I was not with him [at the time]. But at the age of eleven [*sic*: sixteen] he became embroiled by some lords and others of the kingdom in a war [in 1440] against King Charles VII his father, which was of short duration and was called the Praguerie. He was married [in June, 1436] to a princess of Scotland [Margaret, daughter of James I Stuart], much to his displeasure, and as long as she lived [i.e., until August, 1445] he regretted this marriage. Later, owing to the divisions and quarrels in the household of the king his father, he withdrew to Dauphiné [in 1446], which belonged to him and where many high-ranking persons followed him, even more than he could support. During his stay in Dauphiné he married the daughter of the duke of Savoy [in 1451]. Soon after this marriage he had arguments with his father-in-law and they fought a very bitter war against each other [in 1454].

King Charles, seeing his son in too numerous a company of noblemen and men-at-arms for his taste, decided to proceed there in person with a large number of soldiers, and to drive them out. He went forth and did his best to have many persons withdraw from there, and he commanded them, as his subjects and under the usual penalties, to come to him. And many of them obeyed, to the great displeasure of our king, who upon finding his father to be so angry, and although he was strong, decided to leave the area and let him have that territory. And he proceeded with a small retinue to Burgundy to the court of Duke Philip of Burgundy [in 1456], who received him with great honor, distributed benefits to him and to his principal servants, such as the count of Comminges, the lord of Montauban and others, by means of annual pensions. And during our master's stay at court the duke gave presents to his servants. However, the king had so many expenses and supported so many people that he often lacked money, and this was a source of great hardship and annoyance to him. And so he was forced to look for money and to borrow some; otherwise his partisans would have left him, and this is a great affliction for a prince who is not used to it. Also he was not without his troubles [during his stay] at the court of Burgundy: he had to keep good relations with the prince and his principal governors, for fear that they might become weary of him for staying there so long, for he remained there for six years.[178] And the king his father was constantly sending ambassadors to the duke of Burgundy to request that his son should be expelled or returned to him. And you can well imagine that

178. *Sic*. Louis remained less than five years at Philip the Good's court (September, 1456–July, 1461).

our master was not idle nor without great worries and troubles about this.

At what time, therefore, can he be said to have had joy or pleasure, in view of all these things? I believe that since his childhood he never had anything but trouble until his death, and I am certain that if all the good days of his life during which he had more joy and pleasure than pain and trouble were to be carefully counted, there would be very few; and it seems to me that there would be at least twenty of sorrows and hardships against one of pleasure and ease. He lived for about sixty-one years. However, he had always imagined that he would never live beyond sixty, because he claimed that for a long time no king of France had lived longer, and some say not since Charlemagne. Nevertheless the king our master was well advanced into his sixty-first year.[179]

As for Duke Charles of Burgundy, what ease or what pleasure might one say that he enjoyed more than our king, of whom I spoke? It is true that in his youth he had had some, for he did not undertake anything before the age of about thirty-two, and before that time he had lived in good health and was without troubles. Then he began to have disagreements with his father's governors and his father took their part.[180] Therefore he left the court and went to reside in Holland, where he was well received; and he made contact with the people of Ghent and occasionally visited there. He received nothing from his father, but Holland was a very rich country and gave him large presents, as did several large towns from other regions, in the hope of acquiring his good graces in the future; for it is customary everywhere to try to please those whose power and authority are likely to increase in the future, rather than to please those who are already in such a high position that they cannot rise any more. And their love for the former is all the greater, especially among the people. And that is why Duke Philip, when he was told that the people of Ghent liked his son so much and that he knew so well how to manage them, replied that they had always loved their future lord, but as soon as he became their [actual] lord, they hated him. This proverb proved to be true, for after Duke Charles had become their lord, they did not like him and they showed it openly, as I said elsewhere. And he for his part did not like them either. Yet they did more harm to his descendants than they [ever] could have done to him.

To continue with my subject, since the time when Duke Charles undertook the war over the places in Picardy which our king had repur-

179. Louis lived some two months into his sixty-first year (born July 3, 1423; died August 30, 1483).

180. *Sic.* Charles was thirty, not thirty-two years old in 1463, when he began to dispute the Croy family's control of his father's policies (see pp. 97–98).

chased from his father Duke Philip, and when he made an alliance with the other lords of the kingdom in the war for the Public Good, what comfort did he enjoy? It was always trouble with no pleasure either of the body or of the mind, for glory went to his heart and spurred him to acquire everything which attracted him. Every summer he was in the field, exposing himself to great danger, and he took entire charge and care of the army; and still that was not enough to satisfy him. He was the first to get up and the last to go to bed; and he stayed fully clothed, like the poorest man in his army.

When he stopped fighting during some winters he made haste to raise money. And to do this he worked from six in the morning on and this was no great pleasure; he derived no satisfaction from this except that he was proud to take this trouble and to receive and hear a great number of ambassadors. In this state of trouble and misery he ended his days and was killed by the Swiss before Nancy, as you have heard earlier. And one could not say that he ever had a good day since he began to undertake to make himself more and more powerful, until his death. What did he gain from all this hard work, and what necessity was there for him to do it, considering that he was such a rich lord and that he had so many beautiful towns and territories in his possession, where he could have been so happy if he had wished it?

We should now speak of King Edward of England, who was a very great and powerful king in England. In his extreme youth he saw his father the duke of York discomfited and killed in battle, and with him the count of Warwick's father. The count of Warwick had been King Edward's governor in his youth and had managed his affairs. To be truthful, he had made Edward king and was responsible for depriving King Henry [VI (1422–1461)] of his position; Henry had reigned for many years in England and, in my estimation and the judgment of every-one else, he was the lawful king. But such things as kingdoms and large territories are in the hands of Our Lord, who disposes of them, for everything comes from Him.

The reason why the count of Warwick served the house of York against King Henry of Lancaster was that partisanship and dissension had taken place in the house of King Henry, who was not very wise; and the queen his wife, who was from the house of Anjou and the daughter of King René of Sicily, took the part of the duke of Somerset against this Warwick. For all of them had acknowledged King Henry, his father, and his grandfather as their kings. The lady would have done much better to have acted as a judge or mediator between the parties than to have said: "I shall support this side," as it became ap-parent, because many battles resulted from this; and in the end almost everyone died there on both sides. But princes are persuaded that by means of such questions and quarrels they will obtain information and will keep both sides fearful.

I should rather willingly agree that a young king may encourage dissension among ladies, because it is a pleasant pastime and he may learn some things from them; but among men, such as princes and persons of virtue and courage, nothing is more dangerous. It is like setting one's own house on fire, for someone or other will soon say: "The king is against us," and so he will think of making himself strong and of making intrigues with his enemies. And certainly the parties of Orleans and Burgundy should have made princes wise. For the war which resulted from this lasted sixty-two years, during which the English became involved in the fighting and believed that they could obtain the whole kingdom.

To return to King Edward, he was a very young prince and one of the most handsome among the elegant men of the world at the time when he was in every respect at the height of his power. Moreover, no other man was so fond of pleasure, especially of ladies, feasts, banquets and hunting. And it seems to me that this state of affairs lasted for sixteen years or so, until his dissension with the count of Warwick began.[181] And although the king was expelled from the kingdom, this dispute did not last too long, because he returned and obtained victory. And afterwards he took to his pleasures more than before, since he feared no one, and he became quite fat and heavyset. And at the flower of his age his excesses affected his kidneys and he died rather suddenly from an apoplexy, as I said before, and his descendants perished after him, as you have heard.

In our time two valiant and wise princes have also reigned—the king of Hungary, Matthias [Corvinus (reigned 1458–1490)], and Octavian [*sic*: Mohammed II (reigned 1451–1481)], emperor of the Turks.

King Matthias of Hungary was the son of a very fine knight [John Hunyadi] called the white knight of Walachia, a noble [of no great rank] but a person of great sense and virtues who had governed that kingdom of Hungary for a long time and had gained many victories against the Turks, who are neighbors of that kingdom because of the territories which they had usurped in Greece, Slavonia and Bosnia.

And soon after his death [in 1456], King Ladislaus [V (1439–1457)]

---

181. *Sic*. Edward fell out with Warwick in 1470. In 1454, sixteen years earlier, Edward was but twelve years old. See pp. 122 and 211 ff. for Commynes' earlier accounts of the vicissitudes in Edward IV's life. The date which Commynes mentions at the end of the preceding paragraph—sixty-two years for the duration of war between France and England—makes no sense, as Calmette and Mandrot in their notes on this passage agree.

reached manhood; that kingdom belonged to him, as did also Bohemia and Poland. This king was advised by certain people, as it is reported, to seize the two sons of the white knight, under the pretense that their father had had too much authority and power in the kingdom during the king's infancy, and that the children, who were fine persons, might eventually want to follow his example. Therefore King Ladislaus decided to have both of them taken into custody, and it was done. Immediately he had the eldest son put to death and had the second one, Matthias, put in prison in Buda, the principal town in Hungary. But he did not stay there long, and perhaps it was because Our Lord had been pleased with the services of his father, for shortly afterwards King Ladislaus was poisoned in Prague in Bohemia by a woman of good family. And I have seen the brother of this woman, with whom the king had been in love, and she with him so much so that she was very unhappy when she learned that he was going to be married in France to [Madeleine] the daughter of King Charles VII, who is now called the princess of Viane, because this was contrary to the promise which he had made to her. She poisoned him in a bath by giving him an apple to eat and by putting poison into the handle of a knife.

As soon as King Ladislaus died, the barons of Hungary assembled at Buda to elect a king, according to the custom and privilege which they have of electing [a ruler] when their king has died childless. And there was hatred and division among them concerning this dignity. The widow of the white knight and mother of Matthias unexpectedly appeared in the town with a very fine retinue, for she was a rich woman and possessed much ready cash which her husband had left her. With this she was able to assemble quickly a large number of soldiers, and I believe that she had good contacts among the electors and in the town, owing to the credit and authority which her husband had had in the kingdom. She proceeded directly to the prison and took her son out of it. Some of the barons and prelates who had assembled there to choose a king fled in fear. Those who remained made Matthias their king, and he reigned in the kingdom in great prosperity, with as much praise and approval as any king who had ruled for a long time.[182] He was one of the most valiant men of his time and he won important battles against the Turks. During his reign there were no ravages whatsoever in his kingdom, which he enlarged on the Turkish as well as on the Bohemian side. He held most of Bohemia and augmented his holdings in Walachia,

182. The stories of King Ladislaus' death (he seems to have died of the plague) and of King Matthias' election (he was released from prison only after his election) reflect Commynes' tendency to accept court gossip uncritically when it agrees with his moral prejudices.

where he was born, and in Slavonia; and on the German side he took most of Austria from Emperor Frederick, who still lives, and kept it until his death, which occurred in the city of Vienna, the chief town of Austria, in the year 1491 [*sic*].

He was a king who managed his affairs as wisely in time of peace as in time of war. Toward the end of his days, finding himself with no enemy to fear, he began to live with great pomp and in a triumphal style; he gathered great quantities of beautiful furniture, jewelry and dishes to adorn his household. He attended to all business personally, or had it managed according to his orders. He saw to it that he was greatly feared, for he became cruel; and eventually he suffered from several incurable diseases, from which he died at a rather early age, after having had a life of hard work and trouble more than one of pleasure.

The Turk whom I mentioned earlier was a wise and valiant prince, who made more use of sense and cunning than of valor and boldness. It is true that he was left in a strong position by his father, who had been a valiant prince and had taken Adrianople, which means the city of Adrian. The son, of whom I am speaking, took Constantinople, which means the city of Constantine, at the age of twenty-three. I have seen his portrait, and indeed he seemed to be a man of great intelligence.

It was a very shameful thing on the part of all the Christian princes to allow that city to be lost. He took it by assault; and the emperor of the East, whom we call the emperor of Constantinople, was killed in the breach. Many other worthy men were also killed and many women of great and noble families were raped. No cruel act was omitted. And this was his first exploit. He continued to perform great actions and so many that I once heard a Venetian ambassador say in the presence of Duke Charles of Burgundy that the prince had conquered two empires, four kingdoms and two hundred cities. He meant the empires of Constantinople and Trebizond and the kingdoms of Bosnia, Serbia and Armenia; I do not know whether he considered Morea to be one of these kingdoms. He conquered many a beautiful sea island, where the Venetians still own several places, and also the islands of Negropont and Mytilene. In addition he conquered almost all of Albania and Slavonia. And if his conquests over the Christians were very great, they were no less considerable over those of his own religion, and he destroyed many great lords, such as the prince of Karaman and others.

He managed most of his affairs himself and according to his own judgment, as was also the practice of our king and of the king of Hungary; and these were the three greatest men who had reigned for the past one hundred years. But the courtesy and manner of living of our king, and the good behavior which he maintained toward persons close

431

to him as well as strangers, were completely different from and better than those of the two others. And besides he was a most Christian king.

As for worldly pleasures the Turk certainly enjoyed his share of them and spent a great part of his time in them. And he would have caused even more hardships than he already had if he had not been so consistently occupied with carnal pleasures. He was a gourmand beyond all measure. And illnesses came upon him at an early age, as a result of the life [which he was leading], for his legs began to swell, as I heard from those who had seen him; and this affliction used to start at the beginning of summer, at which time his legs became as large as a man's body. They never broke open, and eventually the swelling subsided and the legs decreased to their normal size again. No surgeon ever understood this case, but people said that it was the result of his great gluttony or that it might have been a punishment from God.

He died at the age of fifty-two or thereabouts, and rather suddenly. However he had made a will, and I saw it. In it he expressed remorse for a tax which he had recently imposed (if the will is authentic). Consider therefore what the duty of a Christian prince is who has no authority founded in reason to raise any money without the consent of his people.

Thus you have seen the death of so many great men within a short time; they had worked very hard to aggrandize themselves and to acquire glory, and as a result they suffered anguish and afflictions and shortened their lives. And perhaps their souls may have suffered from this. In this respect I am not referring to the Turk, for I consider that question settled and [I suppose] that he is now lodged with his predecessors. But as for our king, I am hopeful, as I said, that Our Lord has had mercy on him, and that He will have pity on all others, if it is His pleasure.

But to speak naturally, as a man who has no learning but only a bit of experience, would it not have been better for them and for all other princes, as well as for persons of middle estate who have lived under these great men and who will live under those who reign [at present], to have chosen the middle way in these matters? That is to say, should they not have worried less and have been less concerned, and have undertaken fewer things, and have been more fearful of offending God and of persecuting the people and their neighbors in so many cruel ways, which I have sufficiently explained earlier, and should they not have spent more time upon their own comfort and in honest pleasures? Their lives would have been longer, their illnesses would have come upon them later, and their deaths would have been regretted by more people and less desired by them. And they would have had less reason to fear death.

Could one have better examples to show what a petty thing man is, how short and miserable his life is, and how empty the differences between the great and the small are, as soon as they are dead? For everyone is horrified by a corpse and vituperates it, while the soul must immediately go to receive God's judgment. Sentence is given at that very moment in accordance with the works and merits of the corpse.

Fat-faced, with nose, chin, and fleshy underchin thrust slightly forward and upward, Lodovico Sforza, the duke-usurper of Milan, appears here full of that sovereign self-satisfaction which made him seem to himself and others for a few years in the 1490's the very arbiter of Europe. "The pope is my chaplain, Venice my treasurer, the emperor my chamberlain, and the king of France my courier:" such was his reported boast. Originally named Lodovico Maurus rather than Lodovico Maria Sforza, his adoption of Maurus as a nickname (the word means both "Moor" and "mulberry") resulted in a considerable increase in black slaves at Milan as domestic servants; no courtier could be without one. Lodovico loved splendor: below the embroidered M on his cape is a pendant jewel, while his doublet of mulberry hue is embroidered with another personal emblem, the scoppetta *or whiskbroom. There does seem to be something brisk and clean about his unctuous calm. This is expressed by the starched, straight line of his white collar, the sleek smoothness of his hair, and the neat little crease in the corner of his mouth. His stance is very erect, counterpointing the portliness of his physique. Unlike Louis XI, Lodovico seems to have been imposing as well as devious.*

BOOK SEVEN

The French Invasion of Italy, 1494-1495

1

To continue the memoirs I have begun, I wish to tell you how it came about that King Charles VIII, who rules at present, undertook his journey to Italy, in which I took part, and left from the town of Vienne in Dauphiné on the twenty-third day of August, 1493, and returned to his country about the month of October, 1495.[183] There was much discussion about whether or not he should go, because the enterprise seemed most unreasonable to all those who were wise and experienced, and he was the only one to approve of the plan, aside from a person named Etienne de Vesc, a native of Languedoc, a man of petty lineage who had never heard or seen anything. Also involved with this affair up to that time was a man who lacked courage—a collector of taxes called the [receiver-]general Briçonnet, who on account of this trip has

183. The opening sentence of what is often called the "second part" of the *Memoirs* is puzzling in several respects. It contains what is probably a scribal error, yet one which all manuscripts and early editions respect (Charles VIII left Vienne on August 22, 1494, *not* 1493, returning to French soil on October 23, 1495). It mentions the town of Vienne but does not mention the archbishop of Vienne, Angelo Cato, to whom earlier books were addressed. Since Cato died about March, 1496, and since he is not mentioned, it would seem that this sentence was written after March, 1496. (Indeed the last sentence of this chapter says specifically that Commynes is dictating these words in 1497, although this need not imply that the first sentence of the chapter was also dictated in 1497.) Nevertheless, Commynes addresses Cato midway in chapter 5 of this book as if he were alive, and this is puzzling in the light of the omission of any mention of Cato here. (Commynes' address in chapter 5 seems to me to be an apostrophe to a dead man, as I try to show in n. 201.) In any case these first words of the second part of the *Memoirs* were written before the death of Charles VIII on April 7, 1498, an event which Commynes describes in Book 8, chapter 25. Calmette, I, xiv-xv, believes that Books 7 and 8 of the *Memoirs* were written partly in 1495 and partly in 1496-1497, and that they were "finished or revised" in 1497-98. Whether or not that is true, this sentence was clearly not revised after Commynes wrote the end of his *Memoirs* or Commynes would have deleted the phrase, "who rules at present." There is in fact no unequivocal evidence in Books 7 and 8 to indicate that Commynes made revisions. The evidence which Calmette cites in favor of such revisions is the same as that which leads him to declare that composition of Book 7 began in 1495, and it is not sound (see n. 201). Commynes himself refers only to the years 1497 and 1498 as the time of his writing this continuation of a set of memoirs originally undertaken in order to explain (and defend) Louis XI's politics (and Commynes' own).

since obtained high positions in the church, such as the cardinalate, and many benefices. The other [Etienne de Vesc] had already acquired many inheritances, and he was seneschal of Beaucaire and *président des comptes* in Paris, and he had served the king very well as *valet de chambre* during the latter's childhood; and this man attracted the said [receiver-]general to the project.[184] And the two of them were the cause of the above-mentioned enterprise, for which few people praised them and many blamed them; for all the things necessary for such a great enterprise were lacking.

For the king was very young; he was feeble in person [but] very willful.[185] He had few wise persons or good leaders around him. He had no ready cash; for before they left, they borrowed 100,000 francs from the bank of Sauli in Genoa at the rate of fourteen percent interest [computed] from fair to fair, and from several other sources, as I shall explain later. They had neither tents nor pavilions, and it was in winter that they began to march into Lombardy. One good thing they had, and that was a bold company full of young gentlemen, though [they were] little inclined to obedience. Therefore one must conclude that this trip, both going and returning, was led by God, because the judgment of the leaders whom I mentioned was hardly of any use to the expedition. However, they can well assert that they were the occasion of bringing great honor and great glory to their master.

When the king of whom I have been speaking was of the age of his coronation [May 30, 1484]—that is, fourteen or fifteen years old—the

184. Commynes has referred to de Vesc's position as Charles VIII's favorite on p. 418 above. Receiving inheritances from the king had political as well as economic significance in a society where such inheritances usually consisted of fiefs. The offices of bailiff of Meaux (see p. 418) and seneschal of Beaucaire which de Vesc exercised were those of prominent royal officers in the regions named. De Vesc's position as the first or chief of the two *présidents des comptes*, or heads of the *chambre des comptes*, the royal accounting bureau, meant that he often came in contact with those in charge of collecting taxes in the various provinces of France. Briçonnet was chief tax collector or "receiver-general of finances" in the province of Languedoc. He later took holy orders, was appointed bishop of Saint-Malo, and was finally made cardinal of Saint-Denis, as Commynes explains later in this book.

185. In spite of the fact that the Dobrée manuscript and the earliest editions of Book 7 read "plein de bon vouloir" ("full of good will"), both Mandrot, II, 99, and Calmette, III, 3, emend this passage to read "plein de son vouloir" ("full of his own will" or "very willful"). Calmette, but not Mandrot, asserts that the Sauvage edition of 1552 (see p. 82 for a brief description of it) reads "son vouloir." The emendation is almost certainly correct, in view of Commynes' statement on page 543: "The king was young and willful, as was said elsewhere." On the other hand, Commynes refers several times to Charles VIII's "bon vouloir" later in the *Memoirs* (see, e.g., p. 481, where Commynes tells us that Charles's intentions —i.e., "vouloir"—were good) so that there is nothing incongruous about the manuscript reading, either.

duke of Lorraine [René] came to him to demand the duchy of Bar, which King Louis had held, and the county of Provence, which his first cousin King Charles of Anjou had left after his death by will to King Louis XI, for he died childless. The duke of Lorraine claimed it as his own because he was the son of [Yolande,] the daughter of King René of Sicily, duke of Anjou and count of Provence, and he said that King René had done him wrong, and that King Charles, of whom I spoke, was only his nephew, son of the count of Maine; but the other [King Charles VIII] maintained that Provence could not be handed down by their wills to daughters. As a matter of fact, Bar was restored [to René] and the king requested only a sum of money. And since the duke enjoyed great favor and had many friends (and particularly Duke John of Bourbon, who was old and wanted to marry his [Duke René's] sister [Margaret of Anjou]), he obtained an important position from the king, as well as the command of one hundred lance-teams; in addition he was to be paid thirty-six thousand livres annually for four years, during which time the law [of succession] pertaining to the above-mentioned county [of Provence] would be investigated.[186] And I was present when this discussion and this decision were made, for I took part in this council, which had been established at the time by the king's close relatives as well as by the three estates of the kingdom.[187]

Etienne de Vesc, of whom I spoke and who had already acquired something in Provence, and who had taken it into his head to promote this Neapolitan affair, had the king, young as he was at the time, tell my lords of Comminges and of Lau (for both of them were also members of the council) and myself, in the presence of his sister [Anne de Beaujeu], duchess of Bourbon, to see to it that he should not lose the county of Provence. And this was before the arrangement of which I spoke.

Before the four years had elapsed some lawyers arrived from Provence and advanced certain wills of King Charles I, brother of Saint Louis, and of other kings of Sicily who were from the house of France, and other reasons, claiming that not only did the county of Provence belong to the king, but also the kingdom of Sicily and other lands possessed by the house of Aragon, and that the duke of Lorraine had no rights to them (although some wished to maintain that it was otherwise). And all these people addressed themselves to Etienne de Vesc, who influenced his master along those lines, and they insisted that the late King Charles,

186. See Appendix B for an explanation of the house of Anjou's rights of inheritance to the duchy of Bar and county of Provence.

187. The council of regency formed after Louis XI's death to govern France during the childhood of Charles VIII included Commynes from October 27, 1483, onward. This council was presented to and approved by the Estates-General of France which met at Tours in February, 1484.

count of Provence and son of Charles of Anjou, count of Maine, and nephew of King René, had left it to him by his will. For King René had put him in his place [as his successor] before he died, and in preference to the above-mentioned duke of Lorraine, who was his daughter's son; and this was on account of the wills made by this *Carlo primo* [*sic*, i.e., Charles I Anjou] and his wife, countess of Provence, which stated that the kingdom and the county of Provence could not be separated, nor could they be handed down to daughters as long as there was a son of their line. And their immediate successor to the kingdom, that is, Charles II, made a similar will.

During these four years those who governed the king, who were the duke and duchess of Bourbon and a chamberlain named the lord of Graville, as well as other chamberlains who had great influence at the time, called the duke of Lorraine to court and put him in a position of authority and consideration in order to obtain support and aid from him, for he was a bold man, more so than courtiers are; and it seemed to them that they would surely get rid of him in due time, as they did when they felt strong enough and the power of the duke of Orleans and of several others of whom you have heard was weakened.[188] Moreover, they could no longer have the duke of Lorraine stay after the four years had elapsed without either giving him the county [of Provence] or assuring him in writing [that he would have it] within a certain time and [that meanwhile] they would continue to pay him the thirty-six thousand livres. To these terms they could not agree, and because of this he left court very displeased with them [August, 1486].

Four or five months before his departure from court [*sic*, in June, 1485] a good opportunity came to him, if he had understood it. The whole kingdom of Naples rebelled against King Ferrante because of his great tyranny and that of his children, and all the barons as well as the three parts of the kingdom gave themselves up to the church.[189] How-

188. In these laconic terms Commynes refers to the feudal coalition directed against Anne de Beaujeu's domination of the council of regency and government of France. This coalition, whose leader was the duke of Orleans (the future Louis XII), included Commynes and led to his removal from the offices of seneschal of Poitou and of captain of the castle of Poitiers. It also brought about his banishment from court, as he tells us at the end of this chapter (see also my Introduction to the *Memoirs*, p. 13). Unsupported by large sections of the population, the "Foolish War" ("guerre folle") of 1485 begun by the coalition strengthened Anne de Beaujeu's hand in the council or regency, as Commynes indicates.

189. To "give themselves up to the church" meant that the feudal lords and other public authorities of the kingdom of Naples withdrew their fealty from the king, asserting that he had broken his feudal oaths to them, and gave their fealty back to the king's suzerain, the pope, from whom Ferrante (1458–1494) held the kingdom in fief. The "conjuration of the barons," as this revolt is called, began in

ever, King Ferrante, who was helped by the Florentines, moved against the rebels strongly and therefore the pope [Innocent VIII] and the lords of the kingdom who had rebelled sent for the duke of Lorraine to make him king of the land. For a long time galleys waited for him at Genoa, as did the cardinal of Saint Peter in Chains [Giuliano della Rovere, afterwards Pope Julius II], while he was involved with these dissensions at [the French] court and was ready to depart; and he even had with him messengers from all the lords of the kingdom who were pressing him to leave.

When all was said and done the king and his council expressed their desire to help him in all possible ways, and he was promised sixty thousand livres, of which he received twenty thousand (the rest was lost). He was allowed to take away the one hundred lance-teams which he had been given by the king, and ambassadors were sent everywhere in his favor. The king, however, was already nineteen years of age or older,[190] and he was raised by those whom I have named, and every day they told him that the kingdom [of Naples] ought to belong to him (and I say this frequently because persons of low rank kept agitating about this); he was also told this by some of these ambassadors who went to Rome, Florence, Genoa, and elsewhere for the duke of Lorraine, as I learned from several of them as well as from the duke himself when he passed through Moulins [about August, 1486], where I was staying at the time with Duke John of Bourbon because of the divisions at court, and his enterprise was already half lost because of the long delay. And I went to meet him, although I was not bound to do so; for he had helped to have me banished from court with harsh and foolish words.[191] He gave me the warmest greeting in the world as he complained about those who managed the government; he remained for two days with Duke John of Bourbon and then he proceeded to Lyon.

In sum, his friends were so tired and disappointed through having waited for him so long that the pope negotiated for peace and so did the barons; and on the strength of this agreement they went to Naples, where all of them were seized [December, 1486], although the pope, the Venetians, the king of Spain, and the Florentines had vouched for the observance of the agreement and had sworn and promised their security. The prince of Salerno escaped; he came here [to France] and refused

---

October, 1485, and ended with the signing of peace on August 11, 1486, as Commynes tells us in the last paragraph of this chapter.

190. *Sic.* Charles was born June 30, 1470, and was thus only fifteen or sixteen years old at the time of the "conjuration of the barons."

191. See n. 188, p. 440 above.

to be included in the peace agreement, since he knew Ferrante. The duke of Lorraine returned to his country, much ashamed of himself; never again did he enjoy authority in France. He lost his men-at-arms and the thirty-six thousand livres which he had for Provence, and to this very moment, which is the year 1497, he is still in that condition.

2

The prince of Salerno went to Venice because he knew many people there; and with him were three of his nephews, sons of the prince of Bisignano. They asked advice of the Signoria, as the prince told me, as to where they would rather have them go—toward the duke of Lorraine or the king of France or the king of Spain. He said that they answered him that the duke of Lorraine was as good as dead and that he would be unable to reestablish them [in Naples]; as for the king of Spain, he would become too powerful if he had the kingdom together with the island of Sicily as well as the other places which he possessed on the Gulf of Lion; and he was strong at sea. But they would advise him to go to France because they had been good friends and good neighbors with the kings of France who had reigned in the kingdom [of Naples]. And I do believe that they did not foresee that what happened later as a result of this would come to pass.

Thus these above-mentioned barons came to France, where they were well received but poorly endowed with goods. They pressed matters greatly for about two years, and in everything addressed themselves to Etienne de Vesc, who was at the time seneschal of Beaucaire and chamberlain to the king. One day they were full of hope and the next day the opposite. They were active in Italy, and especially in Milan where Gian Galeazzo was duke—not the great one [Gian Galeazzo Visconti, ruled 1378–1402] who is buried in [the church of] the Carthusians [called the Certosa] at Pavia, but the one who was the son of Duke Galeazzo [Maria Sforza] and Duchess Bona of the house of Savoy, who had little sense, for she was the children's guardian, and I saw her in a position of great power when she was a widow, directed by a secretary called Cicco [Francesco Simonetta]. He had been kept in that household for a long time and for the security of that lady and her children had driven away and exiled all of Duke Galeazzo's brothers, one of whom was named Lord Lodovico [il Moro], who has since become duke of Milan. She later recalled him, [although] he was her enemy and was at war with her; and she also recalled Lord Roberto di Sanseverino, a valiant commander, whom Cicco had similarly expelled [in 1477]. In the end, by means of a young man who was her squire-carver, a native of Ferrara

and of insignificant lineage who was called Antonio Tassino, she foolishly recalled them [in 1479], believing that they would do Cicco no
harm; and they had so sworn and promised. But the third day afterwards they seized him and carried him in a barrel across the town of
Milan, for he was related by marriage to some members of the Visconti
family, and it is said that if he had been within the town they would
not have dared take him. And Lord Lodovico wanted Lord Roberto di
Sanseverino, who was coming and who greatly hated Cicco, to meet
him in that condition. He was taken to prison in the castle of Pavia
where he eventually died [executed October 30, 1480].

They treated the lady with great honor, or so it seemed to her, and
they gratified her; but they held councils among themselves without
telling her anything except what they pleased. And they could give her
no greater pleasure than not to inform her of anything. They let her give
Antonio Tassino whatever she wished. He was lodged near her room
and he carried her on horseback behind him through the town; and
everything was feasting and dancing there. But it did not last long, perhaps half a year. She gave Tassino many presents and the couriers'
leather satchels were directed to him. Out of this came great envy; and
moreover, Lord Lodovico, the two children's uncle, greatly desired to
make himself ruler, as he did afterwards.

One morning [in October, 1480,] they took her two sons away from
her and put them in a dungeon which they call the *rocca* [i.e., the castle
of Milan]. And this was agreed upon by Lord Lodovico, Lord Roberto
di Sanseverino, a person named Pallavicini, who was the young duke's
governor, and the captain of the *rocca*, who had never left it since the
death of Duke Galeazzo nor for a long time after, until he was taken
by the deception of Lord Lodovico and by the folly of his master [the
young Duke Gian Galeazzo], who took after his mother's temperament
and was not very clever.

Now after the above-mentioned persons had put these children in
the *rocca* they laid their hands on the treasure, which was the greatest in
Christendom at the time, and they made her recognize this; and three
keys were made for it, of which she received one. But never again did
she touch it. They had her renounce the guardianship, and Lord Lodovico was made guardian. And furthermore they wrote letters to
several places, and especially to France, which I saw, to her great shame,
and which charged her with [the matter involving] Antonio Tassino and
something else. No harm was done to Tassino, but he was sent away
and Lord Roberto saved him, as well as his possessions. These two
great men did not enter the *rocca* as they pleased, for the captain had
his brother inside, as well as at least one hundred and fifty paid merce-

naries, and he had the gate strongly guarded when they entered; and he never let more than one or two men enter with them. And this situation lasted for quite a long time.

In the meantime a big disagreement arose between Lord Lodovico and Lord Roberto di Sanseverino, as is of course customary, for two great people cannot endure each other. Lord Lodovico gained the upper hand, and the other went into the service of the Venetians [1482]. However, two of his sons, Galeazzo and the count of Caiazzo, returned to the service of Lord Lodovico and the state of Milan. Some say it was with their father's knowledge and others say it was not, but whatever the case may be, Lord Lodovico held them in great affection and made profitable use of their services and still does today. And one should understand that their father, Lord Roberto, was from the house of Sanseverino, son of an illegitimate daughter;[192] but in Italy they do not make much distinction between an illegitimate child and a legitimate one. I say this because they helped us to manage our enterprise in Italy, both in order to favor the above-mentioned prince of Salerno [Antonello di Sanseverino], who is the head of the house of Sanseverino, and for other reasons which I shall explain later.

Lord Lodovico soon made it evident that he very much wanted to keep his authority; and he had money coined with the duke['s portrait] stamped on one side and himself on the other, which made many people murmur. The duke was married [in 1489] to [Isabella of Aragon,] the daughter of the duke of Calabria, who has since become King Alfonso after the death of his father, King Ferrante, king of Naples. The young lady was a woman of courage, and she would willingly have trusted her husband if she had been able to do so; but he was not very clever, and he repeated whatever she told him. Furthermore, the captain of the *rocca* in Milan, who never left it, was for a long time in a position of great authority. Suspicions began to arise; and when one of the sons went out, the other remained inside.

In short, about a year or two before we went to Italy [*sic*: in 1489] Lord Lodovico, coming from outside with the duke with the intention of doing ill, led him down to the *rocca*, as was their custom. The captain came on the drawbridge with his men around him in order to kiss the duke's hand, as is their custom. This time the duke was a small distance off the bridge, and the captain was forced to take a step off, or possibly two, so that those two sons of Sanseverino and others who were around

192. *Sic* in the manuscript and all early editions. As Calmette points out, the text should read "Sforza," not "Sanseverino," for the mother of Roberto di Sanseverino was Elisa Sforza, daughter of the same mother and father as Francesco Sforza, Lodovico Sforza's father. Lord Lodovico and Lord Roberto were thus first cousins.

them seized him. Those who were inside raised the bridge, and Lodovico had a piece of candle lighted, swearing that he would have their heads cut off if they did not give up the place before the candle burned out; which they did. And he provided the place with strong means of defense and made it secure for himself, although he always spoke in the name of the duke. And he started a lawsuit against this honest man, alleging that he had wanted to give the place up to the emperor.[193] And he had several Germans arrested, saying that they were engaged in this transaction; and then he let them go. He had one of his secretaries beheaded, charging him with managing this affair, and another because he claimed that he had delivered messages. He kept the captain prisoner for a long time; finally he set him free, saying that my lady Bona [the duke's mother] had once gained a brother of the captain over to her side in order to have him kill him as he entered the *rocca*, and that the captain had prevented him from doing so. Therefore at this time he would save his life. I believe, however, that if he had been guilty of such a charge as to have wanted to give up the castle of Milan to the emperor (who might claim rights to it both as emperor and as duke of Austria, for the house of Austria has claims there), he would not have forgiven him. Moreover, it would have provoked great commotion in Italy, for the whole state of Milan would have turned [against him] in a single day, because in the days of the emperors they paid only one ducat per hearth, whereas now the clergy, nobility, and people are most cruelly treated, in true tyranny.

3

When Lord Lodovico saw that he had taken the castle and that he had all the forces and men-at-arms of that house under his thumb, he decided to proceed further, for whoever has the command of Milan has absolute lordship; for the principal officials of the entire territory live there, as do those who are in charge and in command of other places. And as for what that duchy includes, I have never seen a more beautiful piece of land nor a more valuable one, for if its lord were satisfied with five hundred ducats per year, his subjects would be only too rich and the lord would live in perfect security. But he raises 650,000 or 700,000 ducats, which is great tyranny; therefore the people demand nothing other than a change of lord.

Since he saw himself so close to the fulfillment of his desire, as was said, Lord Lodovico (who was married [in 1491] to [Beatrice d'Este,] the duke [Ercole I d'Este] of Ferrara's daughter—and she had given him

193. Milan was in feudal theory a fief of the Holy Roman Empire.

several children) took pains to gain friends in the duchy as well as outside Italy. And first of all he entered into an alliance with the Venetians [1484], with whom he was very friendly, for the [mutual] preservation of their lands but to the prejudice of his father-in-law, from whom not long before the Venetians had taken a small territory called the Polesina [1482], which is entirely surrounded by water and which is marvelously abundant in all kinds of products. The Venetians hold this land, as far as a half league from Ferrara, and in it are two fine little towns which I have seen, namely Rovigo and Badia. And this land was lost when the Venetians alone were at war with King Ferrante, who was king of Naples at the time and had his son Alfonso, duke of Calabria, there with all his forces, [with] Lord Lodovico representing Milan, and [with] soldiers from the Florentines, the pope, and Bologna. However, when the Venetians were almost crushed, or at least were in the worse position and were extremely short of money and had lost several places, Lord Lodovico made a settlement [in August, 1484,] which was to the honor and profit of the Venetians; everyone regained what had originally been his except the poor duke of Ferrara, who had begun the war at his request and that of King Ferrante, whose daughter [Eleonora] he had married. And he had to abandon the Polesina to the Venetians who still hold it. It is said that Lord Lodovico obtained sixty thousand ducats from this arrangement; I do not know whether this was true, however, but I have seen the duke of Ferrara express the belief that it was. It is true that at the time Lodovico had not yet married his daughter. And thus the friendship between Lodovico and the Venetians was kept up.[194]

No servant or relative of Duke Gian Galeazzo of Milan presented any objection to Lord Lodovico's taking the duchy for himself, except the duke's wife, who was young and wise; and she was the daughter of the above-mentioned Duke Alfonso of Calabria, eldest son of King Ferrante of Naples. And in the year 1493 Lord Lodovico began to send ambassadors to King Charles VIII, our present ruler,[195] in order to arrange

194. This paragraph, which takes as its point of departure the year 1492 and moves to 1491, 1484, 1482, and back to 1484, shows how Commynes' chronological sense operates backward and sideways as often as forward, as if weaving a fabric rather than unfolding a narrative. Commynes' intent is fabric-like here: he wishes to provide a backdrop, a canvas before which the drama of the Italian invasion will unfold.

195. Commynes was wrong to date Lodovico's efforts to induce Charles to come to Italy only from 1493, according to Calmette, III, 19, n. 4, who follows Mandrot, II, 18, n. 5. Mandrot points out that Lodovico sent an embassy to Charles in February, 1492, in order to strengthen the existing alliance between Milan and France. In Mandrot's opinion the embassy also was sent to encourage the Neapolitan expedition. However, Mandrot's arguments are circumstantial only and a strong

that he should come to Italy and conquer the kingdom of Naples, so as to destroy and crush those who possessed it, whom I have named. For while these people were in power, he would not have dared undertake what he did since; for at this time Ferrante, king of Sicily, and his son Alfonso were strong and rich and they were well trained in warfare; and they were considered very valiant, although it appeared otherwise afterwards. This lord [Lodovico] is a very shrewd man but a very apprehensive one, and he is very dejected when he is afraid (and I speak as one who has known him and negotiated many matters with him); he is a man without faith if he sees profit in breaking it.

And therefore, as was said, in the year 1493 he began to suggest to this young king of twenty-two that praises and glory could be his in Italy, pointing out to him, as was said, the right that he had to this fine kingdom of Naples, which he well knew how to celebrate and praise. And in all these matters he addressed himself to Etienne de Vesc, who had been made seneschal of Beaucaire and who had become rich, though still not enough to suit him, and to the [receiver-]general Briçonnet, who was a rich man and well versed in finances and a great friend of the seneschal at the time. Lodovico had Briçonnet advised to become a priest, [saying] that he would make him a cardinal; to the other he dropped hints about a duchy.

And in order to get all these things under way, he sent a large embassy to the king in Paris that year [*sic*]; it was headed by the count of Caiazzo, eldest son of Roberto di Sanseverino, whom I mentioned. In Paris the count met the prince of Salerno, who was his cousin, as I said above, for he was the head of the house of Sanseverino, and he was living in France, having been banished by King Ferrante, as you have heard before; and he was pursuing the enterprise against Naples. With the count of Caiazzo were Count Carlo di Belgioioso and Galeazzo Visconti, both of them Milanese, and they were extremely well dressed and well attended. Their public statements were made simply on the occasion of visits and consisted of rather general words; and this was the first important embassy which Lodovico had sent to the king.

It is true that he had sent a secretary before, in order to obtain that

---

counterargument is formulated by Cecilia Ady, *A History of Milan Under the Sforza* (New York, 1907), p. 144, and by H. F. Delaborde, *L'Expédition de Charles VIII en Italie* (Paris, 1888), p. 236. Whether Mandrot and Calmette or Ady and Delaborde are right, however, Commynes is once again in error chronologically, for Caiazzo, Belgioioso, and Visconti, whom Commynes names two paragraphs further on as heading the embassy of 1493, came to France in February, 1492, and not in 1493.

the duke of Milan, his nephew, be given permission to render homage for Genoa to a proxy; and it was done, wrongly so. The king could indeed grant him the favor of assigning someone to receive this homage, for he was under his mother's tutelage and I, as ambassador by appointment of the late King Louis with the express commission to do this, received homage in the castle of Milan from the duke's mother, since she had tutelage over her son.[196] But at the time Genoa was out of their hands, and it was held by Battista di Campofregoso. Now at the time of which I am speaking Lord Lodovico had recovered it; and he gave some of the king's chamberlains eight thousand ducats in order to obtain the investiture. And they caused great damage to their master because they might have secured Genoa for the king shortly before, if they had wished. And if they did have to take money for the investiture, more should have been asked, for Duke Galeazzo once paid King Louis, my master, fifty thousand ducats for it, of which I received thirty thousand *écus* in cash as a gift from King Louis, to whom may God in His grace grant forgiveness. However, they said that they took the eight thousand ducats with the king's consent. And Etienne de Vesc, seneschal of Beaucaire, was one of those who took money, and I rather believe that he did so in order to better influence Lord Lodovico about the enterprise which was his aim.

When the ambassadors of whom I have spoken both in this chapter and in general had arrived in Paris, the count of Caiazzo had a private conversation with the king. The count was held in great esteem in Milan (and his brother Galeazzo di Sanseverino was even more so), especially in questions of soldiering. He began to offer the king large services and assistance in both men and money; for his master could already dispose of the state of Milan as if it were his, and he made the affair appear easy to manage. A few days later he and Galeazzo Visconti took their leave of the king and left. Count Carlo di Belgioioso remained to promote the project, dressing straight away in the French fashion and carrying the affair on most diligently, and many persons began to take an interest in this matter. And the king sent to Italy a man named Perron di Baschi, who was raised in the house of Anjou by Duke John of Calabria. He was in favor of this enterprise and he went to Pope Innocent, the Venetians, and the Florentines. These negotiations, coming and going, lasted for seven or eight months more or less, and those who knew about it talked in various ways about it, but no one believed that the king was going to go there in person.

196. See p. 394 above, where Commynes mentions this. It is as count of Provence (see Appendix B) that the French king is entitled to homage for the fief of Genoa.

4

During this period which I am talking about peace was negotiated at Senlis between the king and the archduke of Austria [Philip, son of Maximilian], heir to the house of Burgundy [January–May, 1493]. Although they were already in a state of truce, a grievance had come up. For the king had abandoned [Margaret] the daughter of [Maximilian] the king of the Romans and the archduke's sister; and since she was very young, there could have been no other obligations except verbal ones (but the words that were exchanged were such and so great that nothing more could have been said). And he took as his wife [Anne] the daughter of Duke Francis of Brittany in order to maintain the duchy of Brittany in peace. He possessed almost all of it at the time of the treaty except for the town of Rennes and the young lady [Anne] who lived there. She was guided [in her policies] by the prince of Orange, her uncle, who had negotiated the marriage between her and the king of the Romans and had her married by proxy, publicly, in the church. And all this took place about the year 1492.[197]

On behalf of the archduke and in his favor a large embassy was sent by Emperor Frederick, who wanted to serve as mediator of the agreement. The king of the Romans also sent ambassadors. The count palatine and the Swiss did the same in order to arbitrate and arrange for peace, for it seemed to all of them that great dissension would arise from this, and that the king of the Romans was extremely offended because not only was the lady whom he looked upon as his wife taken away from him, but his daughter, who had been queen of France for several years, was also returned to him.

In the end the matter was settled peacefully, for everyone was weary of war, particularly the subjects of Duke Philip, who had suffered so much because of the king's war and because of their own private divi-

197. *Sic.* See p. 384, n. 144, on the date of Charles VIII's marriage to Anne and the breaking of Charles's engagement to Margaret. Francis of Brittany (duke, 1458–1488) had negotiated with Maximilian of Austria since 1487 about a marriage between Maximilian and his daughter Anne (born 1476; duchess, 1488–1515), an alliance which would have threatened France even more than the alliance between Duke Francis and Charles the Bold had done at the time of the War for the Public Good. On December 6, 1490, a representative of Maximilian married Anne in his name, and Anne took the title of queen of the Romans (Maximilian was elected king of the Romans—that is, heir-elect to the Holy Roman Empire— in 1486). But in 1491 Charles VIII led an army personally to besiege Rennes, Anne's residence, and the principal ports of Brittany—Saint-Malo, Dinan, Brest, Vannes, Nantes—were gained by subversion for the French cause. Anne was thus forced to abandon her union with Maximilian. (See Mandrot, II, 121, n. 3, for further details and bibliography.)

sions that they could not stand any more. A peace was arranged for four years only, in order to have some rest and to recover their young lady [Margaret], for some people resisted having her returned to them (at least certain persons who were in the king's entourage did). I was present at this peace treaty, along with the negotiators, which included Duke Peter of Bourbon, the prince of Orange, my lord of Cordes, and several other great persons. It was promised that whatever the king held in the county of Artois should be returned to Duke Philip, as had been promised when the said marriage was negotiated (which was in the year 1482); [that is,] that if the marriage were not accomplished, then the lands which had been given to the young lady as a dowry would revert, along with her, to Duke Philip. But the archduke's men had already taken Arras [November, 1492,] and Saint-Omer [February, 1489,] without difficulty; and so there was nothing left to return except Hesdin, Aire, and Béthune. Their revenue and the direction of their government were given up to them on the spot, and they put officers in these places. But the king retained the citadels [in these towns] and was allowed to put garrisons in them up to the end of four years, which will expire on the feast of Saint John in the year 1498. At that time the king is to return them to my lord the archduke; and so it was promised and sworn.

Whether these marriages were thus changed in accordance with the ordinances of the church or not, I [for my part] will stick to what happened. But several doctors of theology have told me that they were not, and several have told me that they were. But whatever the case may be, all of these ladies have had some unhappiness as regards their children. Our queen [Anne] had three sons in succession in four years; one lived about three years and then died, and the other two also died. My lady Margaret was married to [Don Juan] the prince of Castile, the only son of the king [Ferdinand] and queen [Isabella] of Castile and several other kingdoms, and the prince died in the first year of his marriage, which was the year 1497. The lady was left with child, and she was delivered of a stillborn son immediately after her husband's death; and this caused great sorrow to the king and queen of Castile as well as to the whole kingdom.

Immediately after the changes of which I have been speaking, the king of the Romans married [Bianca Sforza] the daughter of Duke Galeazzo of Milan and the sister of Duke Gian Galeazzo, who has been mentioned earlier, and this marriage was arranged by Lord Lodovico. The marriage was most displeasing to the princes of the empire and to several friends of the king of the Romans because the lady was from a house which was not as noble as would have been suitable for him, as it seemed to them; for on the side of the Visconti, which is the name of those who rule in Milan, there is little nobility, and there is even less on the side of the Sforza, of whom Duke Francesco of Milan was a son, for his father was a shoemaker in a little town called Cotignola.[198] But he was a very virtuous man, and this was even more true of his son, who made himself duke of Milan through the help of his wife [Bianca Maria Visconti], who was the illegitimate daughter of Duke Filippo Maria. He conquered it and possessed it, not as a tyrant but as a true, good prince; and his virtue and goodness should certainly be esteemed equal to the qualities of the most noble princes who lived in his time. I say all these things to show what has ensued from these changed marriages, and I cannot tell what may still arise out of them.

5

To return to our main subject, you have heard how the count of Caiazzo and other ambassadors took leave of the king in Paris, and how several bargains were being transacted in Italy, and how our king, extremely young as he was, had his heart set on this; but he did not reveal his thoughts to anyone except these two [de Vesc and Briçonnet]. The Venetians were requested by the king['s representative, Perron di Baschi, in July, 1493,] to be so kind as to give him aid and advice in this enterprise; and they replied that he would be most welcome [in Italy] but that they could not give him aid because they mistrusted the Turk, although they were at peace with him. As for giving advice to such a wise king, who had such good counsel, it would be much too presumptuous of them, but they would rather aid him than make trouble for him.

Now notice that they thought they had spoken quite wisely, and indeed they had, because for the moment I believe that their affairs are managed more sagely than those of any prince or commune in the world. But God always wants it to be known that the judgments and the sense of men are of no avail wherever it is His pleasure to put in His hand. He managed the affair other than they expected; for they did not think that the king might come in person, and moreover they had no fear whatever of the Turk, regardless of what they said, because the Turk who now reigns [Bayezid II] is of small courage. But it seemed to them that they would take vengeance on the [members of the] house of Aragon, whom they greatly hated, both father [Ferrante] and son [Alfonso]; they said that they had [been instrumental in having] the

---

198. Muzio Attendolo Sforza (1369–1424) was the son of a family of well-off farmers, one of the chief families in the tiny town of Cotignola in the Papal States. He became a famous condottiere and was eventually created count of Cotignola—that is, he was raised to the nobility.

Turk come to Shkodër [or Scutari, Albania, in January, 1479]. I am referring to the father of the Turk [now reigning, that is, the one] who conquered Constantinople, named Mohammed [II] the Ottoman, who did much other great damage to the Venetians. About the duke of Calabria, Alfonso, they said many other things—among them that he had been the cause of the war which the duke of Ferrara had provoked against them, which cost them an incredible amount and which almost destroyed them. I have said a few words about that war. And they also said that the duke of Calabria had sent a man on purpose to Venice in order to poison the cisterns, at least those which he might reach, for some are locked; for in that place they use no other water because they lie entirely in the sea. And that water is very good; I drank it for eight months during a single voyage, and I have been there another time since then, in the period of which I am speaking.

But their principal reason [for hating the house of Aragon] was not related to these reasons, but was that these people prevented them from increasing their power in Italy as well as in Greece, for they had their eyes open on both sides. However, they had recently conquered the kingdom of Cyprus, although they had no title to it [1489]. Because of all this hatred it seemed to the Venetians that it would be to their profit that war should break out between our king and the house of Aragon. They had hoped that it would not be over as fast as it was, and that it would only weaken their enemies and not destroy them. And then, if worse came to worst, one party or the other would give them a few towns in Apulia, which is on the side of their gulf,[199] in order to obtain help from them. And so it happened, but they almost made a miscalculation. Moreover, it seemed to them that they could not be charged with having had the king come to Italy, since they had given him neither advice nor aid, as was apparent from the answer which they gave Perron di Baschi.

In this year 1493 the king proceeded to Lyon [*sic*: he arrived at Lyon on March 6, 1494,] in order to take care of these matters—not that anyone expected him to cross over the mountains. And there he met Galeazzo di Sanseverino, brother of the count of Caiazzo, of whom I have spoken, and he was well attended on orders of Lord Lodovico, whose lieutenant and principal servant he was; and he brought a large number of beautiful and fine horses with the proper harnessing for jousting. And he jousted and jousted well, for he is a young and very noble knight. The king honored him greatly, gave him a warm welcome,

199. Commynes seems to regard the Adriatic Sea as a gulf belonging, in effect, to the Venetians because of their extensive holdings along its coasts, as he explains on p. 570.

and awarded him the order of his kingdom.[200] And then he returned to Italy [in late June]. The count of Belgioioso still remained as ambassador in order to promote the expedition. A very great army was starting to be prepared in Genoa; and my lord of Urfé, grand equerry of France, and others were there on behalf of the king.

Finally the king proceeded to Vienne in Dauphiné about the beginning of August in that year, and every day news arrived from Genoa, where Duke Louis of Orleans, who reigns at present [as Louis XII], had been sent. He was a young man and handsome of person, but fond of his pleasures. A good deal has been said about him in these memoirs. And it was thought at the time that he would conduct the fleet in order to land in the kingdom of Naples by the aid and advice of the princes who had been banished from there whom I have named, that is, the princes of Salerno and of Bisignano. As many as fourteen Genoese vessels were prepared, as well as several galleys and galleons, and in this matter the king was obeyed as well as if he had been in Paris. For that city was under the state of Milan, which was governed by Lord Lodovico; and he had no competitor there except the wife of the duke his nephew, whom I have named [elsewhere], the daughter of King Alfonso (for at that time [January 25, 1494] his father King Ferrante died). But that lady's power was already much diminished, since one could see the king ready to cross over or to send men and declaring himself for the other party; moreover, her husband had little sense and he repeated everything she said to his uncle, who had already ordered a messenger to be drowned whom she had sent to her father. The expense of this fleet was quite great, and it is my opinion that it cost 300,000 francs, although it was useless. And all the liquid money that the king could procure from his finances was spent on it.

For, as I said, he was equipped with neither sense nor money nor any other thing necessary for such an enterprise; and yet it turned out favorably for him by the grace of God, Who thus clearly made it known. I do not mean to say that the king was not wise for his age, but he was only twenty-two [*sic*: twenty-four] years old and he was venturing for the first time outside the fold. Those who managed him in this affair, whom I have named, Etienne de Vesc, seneschal of Beaucaire, and [receiver-]general Briçonnet, at present cardinal of Saint-Malo, were two men of small estate, and they had no experience of anything. But in this Our Lord showed His power all the more; for our enemies were reputed to be very wise and experienced in matters of war, rich, well provided with wise men and good captains, and in possession of their

200. That is, Charles made Galeazzo di Sanseverino a member of the knightly Order of Saint Michael (see p. 146 for an illustration of the insignia of the order).

kingdom. I refer to King Alfonso, recently crowned by Pope Alexander [VI, Borgia] (born [a subject of the crown] of Aragon), who was on his side, as well as the Florentines, [and he also had] good relations with the Turk. He had a fine person for a son, named Don Ferrandino, who was twenty-two or twenty-three years old, [and already trained to] wear armor, and who was well liked in that kingdom, and he had a brother named Don Frederick, who later became king after the above-named Ferrandino, a very wise man who led their naval forces and who had been schooled for a long time in France; and concerning him, you, my lord of Vienne, speaking as an astrologer, assured me several times that he would be king. And thereupon he promised me an income of four thousand livres in the kingdom if it should come true; and it was twenty years before it came to pass.[201]

Now to continue, our king changed his mind due to pressure from the duke of Milan, who kept sending letters, and from his ambassador Count Carlo [di Belgioioso], as well as from the two whom I have named [Etienne de Vesc and Briçonnet]. However, the [receiver-]

201. Don Frederick became King Frederick of Naples on October 7, 1496. The sudden mention of Angelo Cato here is puzzling, as I have indicated in n. 183. Calmette, III, 34, n. 2, believes that this chapter was written in 1495 or early 1496, before Cato died (*ca.* March, 1496); then in 1498 additions were made, such as this one concerning the advent of Frederick to the throne and the one on p. 453, describing Louis XII as reigning "at present"—that is, after April 7, 1498, when Charles VIII died. Calmette's dating may be correct, but it is not necessarily so. It is strange, indeed, that Commynes should address Cato directly about a prediction which presumably came true some six months or more after his own death! Perhaps this is a rhetorical address to a man dead at the time Commynes dictated these words (the exact date of Cato's death has not been established). The reason this prediction stuck in Commynes' mind and found expression here probably had something to do with Frederick's offer to Commynes of a benefice in the kingdom of Naples, an offer which, however unrealistic, could not be forgotten by the avid memorialist. More importantly, the presumable occasion of Cato's utterance of the prediction and Frederick's response to it was of crucial importance to Commynes' personal feelings about the direction of events in his time: The prince had passed through France in late 1475 en route to join the forces of Charles the Bold in Lorraine. Cato was in his entourage. When, in June, 1476, Frederick applied for and received from Louis XI a safe-conduct allowing him to return to Italy, Cato presumably left with him. Commynes recounts these events in chapter 3 of Book 5 (see p. 307 ff.), stating that he learned of the state of Charles the Bold's army from Frederick himself. This, then, was presumably the time of Cato's prediction and of Frederick's promise to Commynes: the moment just before the catastrophic battle of Morat which destroyed Charles the Bold's power and led to the final destruction of Burgundy as a great power, with which Commynes' early career had been bound up. The changeability of fortune—"another name for Providence," as Commynes called it—was indelibly stamped on the chronicler's consciousness by this destruction, and a drastic change in Frederick's status as a younger son in the royal house perhaps seemed less unlikely to Commynes at that moment in 1476 than at any time in the ensuing twenty years until Cato's prediction came true.

general's sense[202] failed him when he saw that every wise and reasonable person blamed the king's expedition down there for a number of reasons, including the fact that they were to be there in the month of August without money, tents, or other necessary things. Only the seneschal maintained his confidence, and for this I esteemed him, and I still do. So the king frowned on the [receiver-]general for three or four days, and then he got back into line.

At this time one of the seneschal's servants died of the plague, or so it was alleged; therefore he did not dare present himself before his master, and this troubled him a good deal, because no one was pursuing the matter. My lord of Bourbon and his wife were there, doing everything in their power to try to break up this trip, and the [receiver-]general conversed with them about it. One day the expedition was called off and the next day it was taken up again. Finally the king decided to leave; and I was among the first to mount on horseback, hoping to pass across the mountains in small company. I was recalled, however, and was told that everything had been called off.

And that day fifty thousand ducats were borrowed from a merchant of Milan, but it was Lord Lodovico who gave them, by means of providing guarantors who pledged themselves to the merchant [to repay him in case of loss]. I pledged six thousand ducats for my share and others vouched for the rest. And there was no interest. Already before that 100,000 francs had been borrowed from the bank of Sauli in Genoa and within four months it had cost fourteen thousand francs in interest. But some people said that persons from our side had a share in this money and in the profit.

6

And so finally the king left from Vienne on the twenty-third day of the month of August, 1493, and proceeded directly toward Asti.[203]

202. *Sic* in the Polignac manuscript and in the first edition of 1528. Except for Calmette and Mandrot, most later editors and translators have emended "le sens" to read "le coeur."

203. Asti and the area around it (see map) passed into the hands of the Orleans family when Valentina Visconti, who married Louis d'Orléans (see n. 207), brought it to her husband as part of her dowry. Consequently, the king was still in "French territory," so to speak, when passing time at Asti. Commynes' chronological indications here as elsewhere are few and incorrect. As mentioned in n. 183, Charles VIII left Vienne on August 22, 1494, not August 23, 1493 (see Calmette III, 36, n. 1 for references), stayed at Grenoble August 24–29, arrived at Susa on September 3, at Turin on September 5, and at Asti on September 9. Later in this paragraph Commynes also mentions the king's visit to the marchioness of Monferrato, which took place October 7–10, 1494 (see p. 460 where this visit is further described).

Galeazzo di Sanseverino came posthaste to meet him at Susa. From there the king went to Turin, and he borrowed the jewels of my lady of Savoy, daughter of the late Marquis Guglielmo di Monferrato and widow of Duke Charles of Savoy, and he pawned them for twelve thousand ducats. And a few days later he went to Casale to see the marchioness of Monferrato, a young and wise lady who was the widow of the marquis of Monferrato. She was the daughter of the king of Serbia. The Turk had conquered the country, and the emperor, whose relative she was, had her married there after having taken care of her. She lent her jewelry, which was also pawned for twelve thousand ducats. So you can see what a beginning this war would have had, if God had not guided the enterprise.

The king remained at Asti for several days. That year all the wines of Italy were sour and our men did not like this any more than the air, which was so hot. Lord Lodovico and his wife came there with a very large retinue. He stayed there for two days and then withdrew to Castello d'Annone, a castle which belongs to the state of Milan and is located within a half league of Asti; and every day the council came to him.

King Alfonso had two armies in the field. One was in Romagna near Ferrara; it was led by his son, who was well attended; with him were Lord Virginio Orsini, the count of Pitigliano [Nicola Orsini], and Gian Giacomo Trivulzio, who is on our side at this moment.[204] And against them on the king's side was my lord of Aubigny, a good and wise knight, and with him were some two hundred lance-teams at least. And there were five hundred Italian men-at-arms paid by the king and led by the count of Caiazzo, whom you have heard mentioned often enough, who had been sent by Lord Lodovico. And he was not without fear that his army might be broken, for [if it had been], we would have turned back and he would have been left with his enemies on his hands;[205] and they had many informers in the state of Milan.

The other army was at sea and was commanded by Don Frederick, Alfonso's brother. It was stationed at Leghorn and Pisa, for the Florentines were still on their side and they had a certain number of galleys. With him [Don Frederick] were Obietto Fieschi and other Genoese, by means of whom he hoped to have the town of Genoa pass over to his

204. See p. 515 below, where Commynes mentions Trivulzio's change of sides.
205. King Alfonso's forces passed over the Apennines and descended into the Lombard plain near Ferrara on August 14. If d'Aubigny's and Caiazzo's armies had been defeated, the way to Milan would have lain open to the Neapolitans. Delaborde, *op. cit.* (see n. 195), pp. 324–26, estimates a total of 40,000 combatants in the French armies and their Italian allies exclusive of the sailors manning the ships in the French fleet.

side; and he came quite close to achieving this. They were also stationed at La Spezia, near Genoa, and at Rapallo, where he landed some one thousand men and some of their partisans. And they probably would have accomplished what they were trying to do if they had not been assailed so soon; but on that day or the next one Duke Louis of Orleans arrived there with some ships and a good number of galleys and a large galleass which was mine, whose captain was a man named Alberto Lomelino. The duke and the principal officers were on board. In this galleass there was much artillery and several large cannon, for it was strong; and it got so close to the shore that the artillery almost destroyed the enemy, who had never seen anything like it because it was new to Italy. And those who were in the ships landed.

A number of Swiss led by the bailiff of Dijon came by land from Genoa, where the army was stationed. And there were also soldiers of the duke of Milan, commanded by Obietto's brother, named Giovan Luigi Fieschi, and Giovanni Adorno; but they did not come to blows. However, they performed their duty well and they guarded a certain passage. Indeed, as soon as our men encountered them, the enemies were defeated and fled. One hundred or one hundred and twenty of them died, and eight or ten were taken prisoners; among them was a man called il Fregosino [Giovanni di Campofregoso], son of the cardinal of Genoa. Those who escaped were all stripped to their shirts by the duke of Milan's men; and they did them no other harm, for such is their custom.

I saw all the letters which were sent from there to the king as well as to the duke of Milan. Thus this fleet was repulsed [in the battle of Rapallo, September 5, 1494], and never since did it appear so close. Upon our return the Genoese almost revolted; they killed a few Germans in the town and some of their men were killed by them; but everything was quelled.

A few words are in order concerning the Florentines, who had twice sent ambassadors to the king before he left France in order to deceive him. Once I, along with the seneschal and the [receiver-]general, happened to be negotiating with those who came. They were the bishop of Arezzo and a person named Piero Soderini. They were asked only to give us passage and one hundred men-at-arms to be paid at the Italian rate, which was only ten thousand ducats per year. They spoke by the command of Piero de' Medici, a young and rather unwise man, son of Lorenzo de' Medici, who had died and who had been one of the wisest men of his time and who had managed that city almost as its lord; and the son was doing the same. For their house had already maintained itself thus [i.e., as dominant in Florence] during the lives of two men of former times, who were Piero, the father of Lorenzo, and Cosimo de'

Medici, who was the head of that house and who had founded it; and he was worthy of being listed among the very great. And in his occupation—which was commerce—this was the greatest house which I believe has ever existed in the world. For their servants have had so much consideration by virtue of the name of the Medici that it would be almost incredible, judging from what I have seen of this in Flanders and in England.

I saw one of them, who was named Gerardo Canisiani, maintain King Edward IV on his throne almost singlehandedly when the king was engaged in a bitter war in his kingdom of England and provide him with more than 120,000 *écus* with little gain for his master [Lorenzo]; he eventually recovered his money, however. I have seen another one named Tommaso Portinari stand surety between King Edward and Duke Charles of Burgundy for fifty thousand *écus*, and another time in another place for eighty thousand *écus*. I do not praise merchants for behaving in this manner, but I highly commend princes for acting properly toward the merchants and keeping their word to them; for they do not know at what moment they might need them, and sometimes a little money does a great deal.

It seems that this [Medici] line was already in decline, as is the case with kingdoms and empires, and the power of his predecessors was injurious to Piero de' Medici, although the domination of Cosimo, who was the first one, had been gentle and kind and such as was necessary in a free town. Lorenzo, the father of the Piero of whom we are now speaking, because of the quarrel mentioned in another part of this book between him and the Pazzi family as well as others, as a result of which several persons were hanged (and I was there at the time), took twenty men to guard him, by command and permission of the Signoria, which gave orders according to his pleasure. However, he wielded this great power with moderation, for, as I said, he was one of the wisest men of his age. But the son thought that this [power] was his by right, and he made himself feared by means of this guard; he perpetrated violence at night and fights, and he helped himself abundantly to their public monies. So had the father, but so shrewdly that they were almost happy about it.

The second time Piero sent to Lyon a person named Piero Capponi and others. And he gave as his excuse, as he already had, that King Louis [XI] had commanded those in Florence to make a league with King Ferrante in the days of Duke John of Anjou and to let fall his [France's] alliance [with Florence].[206] They added that since it was by the king's command that they had entered into this alliance, which was

206. See the genealogical chart in Appendix B for John, son of René of Anjou. John plays a prominent part in Book 1 of the *Memoirs*.

still valid for several years, they could not give up the alliance with the house of Aragon. But if the king were to come as far as their territories they would be of service to him. And they did not believe that he might come there any more than the Venetians did. In both of the embassies there was always someone who was an enemy of Piero de' Medici, and this time it was especially Piero Capponi, who underhandedly informed us of what should be done in order to have the city of Florence turn itself against Piero. And he made his allegations more bitter than was the case, and he also advised that all the Florentines should be banished from the kingdom [of France]; and so it was done. I say this in order that you may better understand what happened later; for the king as well as the seneschal and the [receiver-]general remained very hostile to Piero, and they had many transactions with his enemies in that city and especially with these Capponi and with two of Piero's first cousins who bore his own name [Lorenzino and Giovanni de' Medici].

7

I have explained what took place at sea at Rapallo. Don Frederick withdrew to Pisa and Leghorn and did not reassemble afterwards the infantrymen whom he had set ashore. And the Florentines were most annoyed with him since they were and always have been more partial to the house of France than to the house of Aragon. As for the [French] army which was in Romagna, although it was the weaker, it nevertheless progressed successfully and little by little Don Ferrandino, duke of Calabria, began to retreat. And the king decided to march forward, as he was urged to do by Lord Lodovico and the others whom I have named. At his arrival Lord Lodovico said to him: "Sire, do not fear this enterprise. In Italy there are three powers which we consider important. One of them is yours, and that is Milan. The other is quiet, and that is Venice. Therefore you have only Naples to contend with, and several of your predecessors have beaten us when we were all united. If you will trust me, I shall help to make you mightier than Charlemagne ever was, and we shall easily drive the Turk out of the empire of Constantinople after you have obtained the kingdom of Naples." And he was right about the Turk who now reigns, provided that everything had been well organized on our side.

Thus the king began to manage his affairs according to the will and leadership of Lord Lodovico, and this provoked envy on the part of some of our people—among them a certain chamberlain and someone else (without reason, for we could not do without him—but this [opposition to Lodovico] was made in order to please my lord of Orleans, who pretended to have rights to that duchy[207]) and particularly on the part of the [receiver-]general, for he already considered himself one of the great and there was some jealousy between the seneschal and himself. And Lodovico told the king what moved the [receiver-]general to speak against him, in order to have the king remain [where he was]; and he said that he would deceive all of them. It would have been more proper if he [Briçonnet] had been silent about this, but he had never had any reputation in state matters and was not an expert in them, and he was loose with his words although very devoted to his master.

In any case it was decided to send several men as ambassadors to Venice, and I was one of them. I postponed my departure for several days because the king was ill with smallpox and in danger of death, since he ran a fever; but it lasted only six or seven days [September 13–21, 1494]. And I started on my journey [September 26 or 27] while others went elsewhere. I left the king at Asti, and I was firmly convinced that he would not proceed farther. It took me six days to arrive at Venice with mules and an escort, for the road was the most beautiful in the world; and I was most hesitant to speak, for fear that the king might change his mind; but Our Lord had arranged things otherwise. He proceeded directly to Pavia by way of Casale, where he visited the marchioness [of Monferrato], who was good to us and a good lady, though a great enemy of Lord Lodovico (and he also hated her very much). As soon as the king arrived at Pavia, a few suspicions began to arise, for they wanted him to lodge in the town and not in the castle, but the castle was where he wanted to lodge and lodge there he did. His guard was reinforced that night, as I was told by some of those who were close to the king. Lord Lodovico was shocked at this and spoke to the king about it, asking whether he suspected him. The behavior on both sides was such that friendship could hardly last. But on our side we talked more than they did—not the king, but those who were closest to him.

In this castle of Pavia was the duke of Milan, who has been mentioned before and whose name was Gian Galeazzo, and his wife, who was the

207. The duke of Orleans' rights to the duchy of Milan were based on the marriage of his grandfather Louis, also duke of Orleans, to Valentina Visconti, daughter of Gian Galeazzo Visconti (duke of Milan, 1378–1402). Valentina brought as her dowry to her French husband not only the county of Asti (see n. 203, p. 455) but also the right of succession to the duchy of Milan, for Gian Galeazzo Visconti's first son was not born until 1388, two years after Valentina's marriage contract was drawn up. Thus, according to the Orleanist pretenders to Milan, after Valentina's only siblings had died childless (Giovanni-Maria [duke of Milan, 1402–1412] and Filippo-Maria [duke of Milan, 1412–1447]), the duchy of Milan should have passed to Valentina's descendants. But Filippo-Maria Visconti had had one illegitimate child, Bianca, who married Francesco Sforza. Sforza, in spite of his relatively low social origin and the questionability of his wife's rights to Milan, was able to gain effective control of Milan by 1450, as Commynes has mentioned on p. 451.

daughter of King Alfonso. She was very pitiful because her husband was there, ill, kept in this castle as if under guard, along with his son [Francesco] who is still living now and a daughter or two. The child was about five years old at the time. No one saw the duke, but the child was seen freely. I passed by there three days before the king,[208] but there was no way of seeing the duke and it was said that he was ill. However, the king spoke to him, for he was his first cousin, and the king told me about their conversation, which dealt only with general matters because he did not wish to displease Lord Lodovico in any way. However, he told me that he would willingly have warned him. At that very moment the duchess fell upon her knees before Lord Lodovico and begged him to have pity on her father and brother. He replied that this could not be done and that she might do better to ask favors for her husband and for herself, she who was still a beautiful lady and young.

From there the king proceeded to Piacenza, where Lodovico received word that his nephew the duke of Milan was dying. He took leave of the king to go there; and the king begged him to return, and he promised to do so. Before he arrived in Pavia the duke had died [October 22]. Immediately he went posthaste to Milan; and I saw this news in letters from the Venetian ambassador who was with him, and who wrote about this to Venice and notified them that he [Lodovico] wanted to make himself duke. And to tell you the truth, it was displeasing to both the doge and the Signoria of Venice. And they asked me whether the king would take the part of the child; and although this was a reasonable thing I expressed doubt about it to them in view of the need which the king had of Lodovico.

8

In the end he had himself accepted as their lord; and that was the reason why he had us come across the mountains, according to several persons; and they also charged him with the death of his nephew, whose relatives and friends in Italy were taking measures to take the government out of his hands. And they might have done it easily if the king had not come, for they were already in Romagna, as you have heard. But the count of Caiazzo and my lord of Aubigny made them retreat; for the lord of Aubigny had reinforcements of one hundred and fifty or two hundred French men-at-arms and a number of Swiss. And Don Ferrandino retreated toward their friends. They were a half day's march or so before our men. And they proceeded toward Forli, whose ruler

208. *Sic*. Commynes arrived in Venice on October 2, having traveled by way of Pavia, while the king arrived in Pavia only on October 14.

[Caterina Sforza] was an illegitimate daughter of [the house of] Milan, and the widow of Count Girolamo [Riario], who was a nephew of Pope Sixtus, or so it was said. And the lady had taken their side. But our men took a small place of hers by assault; it was battered only half a day, after which she turned to our side and with a good will to do so.

And from all sides the people of Italy began to take heart and to wish for change, for they were seeing things which they had never seen in their time. For they did not understand the management of artillery, whereas in France it had never been understood so well. And Don Ferrandino, as he was approaching his kingdom, proceeded to Cesena, a strong city which belongs to the pope on the march of Ancona. But the people robbed their pack animals and their bags when they found them isolated. For in all of Italy they desired nothing so much as to revolt, if on the king's side the affairs had been well managed and in orderly fashion and without plundering (but everything was done otherwise, and so I was very unhappy about it because of the honor and good reputation which the French nation could have acquired in this expedition), for the people adored the French like saints and believed that we were perfectly loyal and good. But this opinion did not prevail for very long among them, owing to our disorder and plundering, as well as to the speeches which the enemy made to the people in every quarter, in which they charged us with taking women by force, as well as money and other goods, wherever we could find them. They could not have charged us with anything worse in Italy, for they are more jealous and avaricious than others. About the matter of the women they were lying; but about the rest there was some truth.

9

Now I had left the king at Piacenza, as I said before, and there he had a solemn service celebrated for his first cousin the duke of Milan. And I believe that he hardly knew what else to do since the new duke of Milan had left him. And those who must have known about it told me that the army wanted very much to turn back because of the uncertainty [of the situation], and because they felt that they were insufficiently provided for. And those who at first had praised the expedition now condemned it, such as the grand equerry, lord of Urfé. Although he was not there but was ill in Genoa, he wrote letters which raised great doubts and in which he claimed to have received warnings. But as I said elsewhere, God showed that He was conducting the enterprise; and the king suddenly received news that the duke of Milan would return and that the Florentines were expressing certain feelings [in our favor] because of the enmity which I told you they had against Piero de' Medici, who acted as if he were their lord. And some of his closest relatives and many other persons of distinction (such as all the Capponi, the Soderini, and the Nerli, and almost the whole city) were envious of him.

For this reason the king departed and proceeded toward the territories of the Florentines in order to have them declare themselves for him or to take some of their towns, which were weak, so that he might take quarters there for the winter, which was already upon them. Several small places shifted [to the French side], and also the city of Lucca, which was an enemy of the Florentines; and they did everything to please and serve the king. The duke of Milan's advice had always been directed toward two ends: that we should not proceed any farther that season, and also that he hoped to obtain Pisa, which is an important and large city, as well as Sarzana and Pietrasanta. These last two had belonged to the Genoese not very long before, and they had been taken from them by the Florentines at the time of Lorenzo de' Medici.

The king passed by Pontremoli, which belonged to the duke of Milan, and he proceeded to besiege Sarzana, a very strong castle and the best that the Florentines had, but it was not well provided because of their great dissensions. And furthermore, to tell you the truth, the Florentines fought unwillingly against the house of France, of whom they have always been loyal servants and partisans because of the commercial business which they have to conduct in France, and because of their ties with the Guelphs.[209] And if the place had been well supplied, the king's army would have broken up; for the country is barren and it is located among mountains and no provisions were to be found there; and furthermore, the snows were heavy. The king remained only three days before the place [during the first week of November, 1494], and the duke of Milan arrived there before its surrender. He passed by Pontremoli, where some of his men from the town and garrison had a heated argument with some of our Germans, who were led by a person named Buset; and some of the Germans were killed. And although I was not present when these things happened, the king, the duke, and others told me about them. And this quarrel led to great drawbacks since that time, as you will hear later on.

209. Guelph factions in Italian cities generally arose in the twelfth and thirteenth centuries. Their antagonists were called Ghibellines and favored German (i.e., imperial) intervention in Italian affairs. By the time of the French invasion of Italy in 1494 Guelph-Ghibelline antagonisms represented little more than ideological chessmen which lent a grandiose air to infinitely complex and varied local struggles for power. Nevertheless, insofar as it represented a kind of inertial if moribund force, the traditional Guelphism of Florence probably did have something to do with the favorable climate of opinion which the French encountered in that city.

Deals were made in Florence and up to fifteen or sixteen persons were delegated to be sent to the king, since it was said in the city that they did not want to remain in danger of being hated by the king and the duke of Milan, who always had his embassy in Florence. And Piero de' Medici consented to this visit; and moreover, as matters stood, he would not have been able to help it. For they would have been destroyed, considering the few provisions they had and how inexperienced they were in warfare. When the ambassadors arrived, they offered to receive the king in Florence and in other places. And nothing mattered to most of them except that we should go there, in order to give occasion to banish Piero de' Medici; and they felt that they were on good terms with those who were managing the king's affairs at the time, whom I have named often enough.

On the other hand Piero managed his affairs by means of one of his servants named Lorenzo Spinelli, who directed his bank at Lyon. His estate was that of a man of means and he had lived for a rather long time in France, but he could have had no knowledge of the affairs of our court. Even those who have been raised there could understand what was going on only with great difficulty, so rapid were the changes there. He made deals with those who hated the ones in authority; and they were my lord of Bresse, who has since become duke of Savoy, and the lord of Miolans, who was the king's chamberlain and governor of Dauphiné. And he [Piero de' Medici] came to the king soon after the others [delegated officially as ambassadors], and some persons from the city were with him, in order to reply about the things requested of them. And he considered himself lost in the city, according to what he told me, unless he did everything the king wanted; and he hoped to gain the king's good graces and to do something more than the rest had done.

At Piero's arrival my lord of Piennes, a native of Flanders and the king's chamberlain, as well as [receiver-]general Briçonnet, who has often been mentioned, were sent to meet him. They spoke to him about obtaining the obedience of the place of Sarzana, and he did it immediately. In addition they requested that he procure for the king Pisa, Leghorn, Pietrasanta, and Librefatto [now called Ripafratta]. He agreed to everything without consulting his companions, who understood well that the king would have to stop in Pisa to refresh himself; but it was not their intention that he should keep these places, for this amounted to putting their state and their power into our hands. Those who dealt with Piero told me about it, making fun of him and expressing shock at how he granted such great things, things which they had never expected.

And to summarize, the king entered Pisa [November 9, 1494] and the above-named persons returned to Florence. And Piero had the king's lodgings prepared in his own house, which is the most beautiful house of a townsman or merchant that I have ever seen and the best furnished of any man in the world of comparable estate.

Now a few words are in order concerning the duke of Milan, who would have liked to have the king out of Italy already. He had made his profit from him, or still wanted to do so in order to obtain the places which he had conquered. And he pressed the king strongly in order to have Sarzana and Pietrasanta, which he claimed belonged to the Genoese; and at this time he lent the king thirty thousand ducats. He told me and told several others afterwards that he was promised that they would be handed over to him. And when he was refused, he left the king, marvelously displeased, saying that his affairs forced him to return home. And the king never saw him again. But he left Galeazzo di Sanseverino with the king, and expected him or Count Carlo di Belgioioso, who has been mentioned before, to be present at all councils.

While the king was in Pisa, Galeazzo at his master's instigation invited several of the principal citizens of the town [of Pisa] to his lodgings, and advised them to rebel against the Florentines and to request the king to give them their freedom, hoping that by this means the city of Pisa would fall into the hands of the duke of Milan, as formerly had been the case in the days of Duke Gian Galeazzo [Visconti], the first of that name in the house of Milan. He was a great and bad tyrant, but honorable nevertheless. His body lies in [the church of] the Carthusians at Pavia near the park [i.e., Certosa]; [his sepulcher is] taller than the main altar. The Carthusians showed it to me, or at least his bones (and one climbs up there by a ladder), and they smelled [like one would expect], given the order of nature. And a native of Borgo San Siro called him a saint in my presence, and I whispered in his ear and asked him why he called him a saint when he could see, painted around him, the arms of several cities which he had usurped, although he had no right to do so. (He and his horse were carved of stone, and were placed above the altar, and his body lay under the horse's feet.[210] He answered me softly: "In this region we call saints all those who do something good for us." And he had built this beautiful Carthusian church, which is made entirely of fine marble and is indeed the most beautiful that I have ever seen.

And so to continue, Galeazzo [di Sanseverino] wanted to make himself great. And I believe that it was also the intention of the duke of

---

210. This monument is not the one covering Gian Galeazzo Visconti's bones today. See Mandrot, II, 157, n. 1, for Commynes' possible confusion of Gian Galeazzo's tomb with someone else's in the Certosa at Pavia.

Milan, whose illegitimate daughter he had married; and he seemed to want to favor him as if he had been his son, for his own children were not yet of age. The Pisans were very cruelly treated by the Florentines, who regarded them as slaves, for they had conquered them some one hundred years before [1406], and it was the same year that the Venetians conquered Padua [1405], which was their first beginning [of conquest] on dry land [in Italy]. These two cities [Pisa and Padua] were almost in the same situation, for they had been ancient enemies of those who possessed them for many years before they were conquered and they were almost equal in strength. For this reason the Pisans held a council-meeting. And, seeing themselves advised by such a powerful man [as Galeazzo di Sanseverino], and being desirous of obtaining their liberty, they came in great numbers, both men and women, as the king was on his way to Mass, and they cried: "Liberty! Liberty!" And they begged him with tears in their eyes that he might give it to them. A *maître des requêtes* or one who was acting in that capacity came to the king. He was a counselor in the Parlement of Dauphiné and was named

---

The passage in the Memoirs *where Commynes calls the Certosa "the most beautiful [church] that I have ever seen" (page 465) is one of his rare expressions of aesthetic feeling. Commynes commissioned several illuminated manuscripts to be painted by major artists, including Jean Colombe and possibly also Jean Fouquet. This, together with the visual acuity demonstrated at so many points in the* Memoirs, *makes the absence of more aesthetic expression puzzling. Only richness in design or materials or size or number seems to have summoned his sense of beauty (see, e.g., page 465 and 471, pages 489–92, where Commynes speaks of the Grand Canal, San Marco and the doge's palace in Venice, and page 589 where he speaks of the castle of Amboise and of Charles VIII's art collecting). The bottom row of windows in the façade of the Certosa, of which this is one, was completed when Commynes visited Pavia in 1494; the rest of the façade was finished in 1497. While many of the details are inspired by ancient models, such as the portrait heads in the medallions arranged along the two sides of the window, the luxuriant flora-and-fauna motifs which encrust the stone, the contrasting marble hues, and the shadow-forming variability of the façade's indentations give this church a glittering opulence well calculated to summon Commynes' sense of value.*

Rabot. Either because he had promised to do so or because he did not understand what they were requesting, he told the king that it was pitiful, and that he should grant their request, and that never had people been so cruelly treated. And the king, who did not understand what that word implied and who could not by rights give them liberty (for the city was not his, and he was received there only for friendship's sake and because of his great need), and who was only beginning to be acquainted with the pitiful situation in Italy and with the treatment which the princes and the communes inflict upon their subjects, replied that he was content; and the counselor of whom I spoke told them so. And the people immediately began to cry: "Bravo!" And they proceeded to the end of their bridge on the river Arno, which is a fine bridge, and they threw down a large lion which stood upon a large marble pillar; they called it the Marzocco (and it represented the Signoria of Florence), and they put it in the river. And on this pillar they had a statue erected of the king of France, with his sword in hand, crushing the Marzocco, which is a lion, under his horse's foot. And afterwards, when the king of the Romans entered the town [in 1496], they gave the [statue of the] king the same treatment as they had given the lion. It is the nature of the people of Italy thus to gratify the strongest; but these people were and are so badly treated that they should be excused.

10

The king left from there—and he had not stayed there long [November 9–10, 1494]—and proceeded toward Florence. And there it was remonstrated to him that he had done harm to the Florentines and that it was contrary to his promise to have given the Pisans their liberty. Those whom he had appointed to respond concerning this matter made excuses for it, saying that it had not been his intention and was not his intention. And they entered into another agreement about which I shall speak, but only after I have said something about the end of Piero de' Medici, and also about the king's entrance into the city of Florence and how he left a garrison in the city of Pisa and other places which had been lent to him.[211]

Although he had had the places which I mentioned given to the king—

211. Charles VIII entered Florence on November 17, 1494, and began negotiating the agreement mentioned here. As Commynes indicates, he now makes one of his frequent shifts backward in time, beginning the next paragraph by recalling events in Florence which preceded Charles VIII's arrival in Florence and indeed preceded Charles VIII's arrival in Pisa on November 9. In the first paragraph of chapter 11 he returns to the time at which he has arrived here, with the king about to enter Florence and to establish himself in Piero de' Medici's house on November 17.

and some of them had been delivered with the consent of the city—Piero did not expect the king to retain them; and he thought that as soon as he left Pisa, where his business required a stay of only three or four days, he would return it to them. I well believe that if he had wanted to stay there the whole winter, they would have consented to it, although Pisa is more important to them than Florence itself, except for the buildings and furniture. Upon his arrival in Florence [on November 8] Piero realized that everyone gave him a cold welcome and not without cause; for he had deprived them of all their force and power and all that they had conquered in a hundred years, and it seemed that their hearts sensed the calamities which have befallen them since. And for this reason, which I believe was the principal one although they never said so, as well as for the hatred which they bore him which I have talked about, and because they expected to return to [a state of] liberty, of which they considered themselves deprived, and without recalling the kindnesses of his predecessors Cosimo and Lorenzo de' Medici, they decided to drive him out of the town.

Piero de' Medici, who did not know this although he surely suspected something, proceeded toward the palace to speak of the arrival of the king, who was still three miles away.[212] He had his usual guard with him, and he came and knocked at the door of the palace, where he was refused entrance by one of the Nerli family, which included several brothers (I knew him well, and their father too), all very rich men; and he said that he might enter alone if he wished, but otherwise not. And the man who gave this refusal was armed. Immediately Piero returned to his house, had himself and all his servants armed, and sent word to a person named Paolo Orsini who was in the paid service of the Florentines, for Piero on his mother's side was related to the Orsini and both his father and he had always kept some members of that house in their paid service. And he decided either to resist or to leave the town. But he soon heard everywhere cries of "Liberty! Liberty!" and saw the people in arms. And so, well advised, he left the town with the help of Paolo Orsini. It was a pitiful departure for him, for in terms of power and possessions he and his predecessors, beginning with Cosimo who had been the head [of the house], had been the equals of great princes. But on that day he began to tempt fortune and he lost both honor and possessions.

I was in Venice, and I learned the news from the Florentine ambassador who was there. I was very unhappy about the news because I had liked the father. And if Piero had been willing to believe me, he

---

212. *Sic.* On November 9, when the events now about to be recounted took place, the king was at Pisa.

would not have experienced such a misadventure; for at the moment when I arrived in Venice, I had written to him and had offered to negotiate an agreement, for I had the power to do so given to me orally by the seneschal of Beaucaire and the [receiver-]general. And the king would have been satisfied with [the right of] passage [through Florentine territory], or if worse came to worst, with having Leghorn delivered into his hands. Then he would have done everything that Piero might have asked. But he replied to me as if in mockery by means of the Piero whom I mentioned earlier [Capponi]. The next day the ambassador [from Florence] brought letters to the Signoria [of Venice] from the councillors [of Florence], informing them that Piero had been banished because he wished to make himself ruler of the town by means of the house of Aragon and the Orsini; and it contained a number of other charges which were not true. But such are the events of this world that the one who flees and is the loser is not only harassed by those who pursue him but [even] his friends become his enemies, as was the case with this ambassador named Paolo Antonio Soderini, who was one of the wisest men in Italy. The day before he had spoken to me about Piero as if he had been his natural lord, and at this moment he declared himself his enemy by the command of his Signoria [of Florence]. But on his own he made no declaration. The next day he learned that Piero was coming to Venice and that the king had entered Florence in great triumph; and they ordered him to take leave of the said Signoria [of Venice] and to return, and to sail with that wind (and I saw the letter, for he showed it to me). And he left.

Two days later Piero arrived in a doublet or in the dress of a valet; and they received him with great apprehension in Venice because they were so afraid of displeasing the king. However, they could not by rights refuse him, and they were rather anxious to find out from me what the king said about it; and he remained outside the town for two days. I wanted to help him, and I had not received any letter against him from the king; and I said that I believed his flight had taken place for fear of the people and not with the knowledge of the king. And so he came there [on November 18, 1494]; and I went to see him the day after he had spoken to the Signoria, who had him well lodged and permitted him along with fifteen or twenty of his attendants to bear arms —that is, swords—in the city. And they treated him most honorably, although Cosimo [de' Medici], of whom I have spoken, had formerly prevented them from obtaining Milan; but all this notwithstanding they treated him with reverence because of the honor of his house.

When I saw him, it seemed to me indeed that he was not a man who was about to rise up again. He told me at length about his fate, and I comforted him as best I could. Among other things he told me how he had lost everything; and among his other misfortunes a commercial agent of his in the town, to whom he had sent for cloth worth only one hundred ducats for his brother and himself and Paolo [Orsini], refused his request. Soon afterwards he had news by means of my lord [Philip] of Bresse, who has since become duke of Savoy. And the king wrote him to come to him; but the king had already left Florence, as I shall explain.

11

At this time I had to speak briefly about Piero de' Medici because it was an important affair. For that power [of the Medici] had lasted for sixty years, so great that it could not have been more so. And the next day [*sic*: November 17] the king entered the city, and Piero had his house prepared for him. The lord of Balzac was already there to get the lodgings ready; and when he saw that Piero de' Medici had fled, he began to pillage everything he found in the house, saying that their bank in Lyon owed him a large sum of money. And among other things he took a whole unicorn's horn, which was worth six or seven thousand ducats, in addition to two large pieces of another and many other goods. Others followed his example.[213] In another house in the town he had stored all his valuable possessions; the people plundered everything. The Signoria obtained part of the richest jewelry and some twenty thousand ducats in cash which he had in his bank in the town, as well as several beautiful agate pots and so many beautifully carved cameos that it was marvelous (and I had seen them before), and some three thousand gold and silver medals weighing about forty pounds; and I believe that there were not so many beautiful medals in [all of] Italy. What he lost on that day in terms of furniture in the city was worth more than 100,000 *écus*.

Now the king was in the city of Florence, as was said, and a treaty was made between them and I believe that they made it willingly. They gave the king 120,000 ducats, fifty thousand of which they paid in cash; and for the rest they arranged a term of two rather short payments. And they lent the king all their places, of which I have spoken, and they changed their arms, which consisted of the red fleur-de-lis, and they took the kind that the king wears; and he took them under his protection and his guard, and he promised them and swore at the altar of Saint

213. *Sic.* The pillage of the Medici took place after Charles VIII's departure on November 28.

John that he would restore the places to them four months after he was inside Naples or earlier if he should return to France. But matters took another turn, as will be explained later.

He stayed only a short time in Florence, and proceeded toward Siena, where he was well received, and from there to Viterbo [on December 10], where the enemy had intended to take up a position and to fortify themselves in order to fight, if they saw their advantage there (and the ambassadors of King Alfonso and of the pope, who were in Venice, told me so), for Don Ferrandino had retreated toward Rome. And to tell you the truth, I had expected King Alfonso to come there in person, since he was reputed to be very courageous, and to leave his son inside the kingdom; and it seemed to me that the place was favorable for them; for he would have had his kingdom as well as the pope's territories and the Orsini's places behind him. So I was utterly astounded to receive letters from the king informing me that he was in the town of Viterbo. One of the commanders had given him the castle; and all this had been done by means of the cardinal of Saint Peter in Chains [Giuliano della Rovere, the future Pope Julius II], who was the governor, and by means of the Colonna. Then it seemed to me that God wanted to conduct this expedition to the end, and I regretted that I had written to the king and advised him to make an advantageous arrangement, for he was being offered enough of them.

Acquapendente and Montefiascone as well as all the neighboring places were given up to him before Viterbo was, as I was notified by letters from the king and from the Signoria [of Venice], who were informed of what was happening day by day by their ambassadors; and they showed me several of these letters or had one of their secretaries tell me about them.

From there the king proceeded to Nepi and then to the territories of the Orsini, which were all surrendered to him by Lord Carlo Orsini, the illegitimate son of Lord Virginio Orsini; and he said that he had orders to do this from his father, who was in the paid service of King Alfonso, and maintained that as long as Don Ferrandino was in Rome and in the territories of the church, he would stay in his company, but no longer. That is the way the lords and commanders live in Italy; they invariably negotiate with the enemies and they are very much afraid of being on the weaker side. The king was received inside Bracciano, principal stronghold of Lord Virginio, which was beautiful and strong and well supplied with provisions. And I have heard the king speak very highly of that place and the reception he was given [there, December 19–31, 1494], for his army was in need for lack of provisions, so much so that it could not have been worse off. And if one were to consider well how many times this army was almost disbanded since it arrived at Vienne in Dauphiné, and how it was revived and by what exploits, it would seem indeed that God was its leader.

12

From Bracciano the king sent the cardinal of Saint Peter in Chains to Ostia, of which he was bishop. It is a very important place and was held by the Colonna, who had taken it from the pope, for the pope's men had taken it from the cardinal not long before.[214] The place was very weak; but for a long time afterwards it kept Rome in great subjection, with the [help of the] cardinal, a great friend of the Colonna, who were our partisans by the intermediary of Cardinal Ascanio [Sforza], the duke of Milan [Lodovico]'s brother and vice-chancellor [of the Roman church], and because of their hatred of the Orsini, with whom they are and have always been at odds. And all the territories of the church suffer from these divisions, which are similar, as we would say, to the [feuds in Navarre between the] Luxes and the Grammonts, or in Holland [between] the Hoeks and the Cabillaus.

And if it were not for this dissension, the territories of the church would be the most pleasant residence in the whole world for the subjects, for they do not pay direct taxes or scarcely any other assessments, and they would always be well governed, because the popes are always wise and well advised. But very often great and cruel murders and pillaging take place because of this dissension. During the past four years we have seen numerous examples of both; for since that time the Colonna have been against us to their great disadvantage, since they used to have income of twenty thousand ducats and more in the kingdom [of Naples] from fine domains such as the county of Tagliacozzo and others, which had previously been held by the Orsini, and whatever other advantages they were pleased to request in terms of men-at-arms and pensions. But they acted as they did out of pure disloyalty and without any motive. And it should be understood that from time immemorial they were partisans of the house of Aragon and other enemies of the king of France, because they were Ghibellines, and the Orsini were partisans of France, as were the Florentines, because they were Guelphs.

214. Here is another of Commynes' chronologically backward sentences. After the pope's men took Ostia from Cardinal Giuliano della Rovere, Fabrizio Colonna took the place on September 18, 1494, in the name of the Colonna, the cardinal, and the king of France. On December 25, 1494, the cardinal left Bracciano with a force of 350 infantry and entered Ostia personally.

Along with the cardinal of Saint Peter in Chains, Perron di Baschi, the king's major-domo, was sent to Ostia. Three days before he had brought his master twenty thousand ducats by sea (which was the money lent by the duke of Milan) and he landed at Piombino; the prince of Salerno had remained with the naval forces, which were small, along with a person from Provence named the lord of Serenon; fortune led them to Corsica, and their ships were badly damaged. And they took so long to be repaired that they were of no use; this fleet cost a great deal. And they joined the king at Naples.

With the cardinal in Ostia were about five hundred men-at-arms and two thousand Swiss, as well as the count of Ligny, the king's first cousin on the side of his mother, the lord of Alègre, and others. And there they expected to pass the Tiber, so as to proceed to enclose Don Ferrandino, who was inside Rome, with the certain favor and help of the Colonna, the heads of whose house were at the time Prospero and Fabrizio Colonna and Cardinal [Giovanni] Colonna, to whom the king paid, by the intermediary of Perron di Baschi, [the wages of] two thousand infantrymen, whom they had raised according to their pleasure; and they were assembling these troops at Genzano which belongs to them.

It should be understood that here several occurrences took place at the same time, and it is necessary to say something about each one. Before the king had obtained Viterbo, he sent to Rome the lord of La Trémoïlle, his chamberlain, and the president [in the Parlement of Paris, Jean] de Ganay, who had his seal, and the [receiver-]general [of finances in Languedoil, Denis de] Bidant, expecting to negotiate with the pope, who was always bargaining, as is the custom in Italy. While they were there, the pope placed Don Ferrandino and all his forces in the city at night and our men were seized, but not for long. The pope dismissed them the same day, but he kept as prisoners Cardinal Ascanio, vice-chancellor and brother of the duke of Milan, and Prospero Colonna; some said it was by their consent. And about all these happenings I immediately received letters from the king and the Signoria [of Venice] did too, being even more amply informed by their men. And all this took place before the king had entered Viterbo, for he never stayed more than two days in a given place; and things were turning out better than he might have expected. Indeed the Lord of lords had a hand in this, and everyone realized it.

The army which was in Ostia served no purpose because of the bad weather. It should also be understood that the soldiers whom my lord of Aubigny had led had retreated, and so had he, and he was no longer in charge of them. Also dismissed were the Italians who had been with him in Romagna, led by Lord Rodolfo [Gonzaga] of Mantua, Lord

Galeotto [Pico] della Mirandola, and Fracassa, brother of Lord Galeaz-zo di Sanseverino, who were well paid; and they consisted of about five hundred armed [men] who were paid by the king. And as you have heard, upon his departure from Viterbo the king went to Nepi which was held by Lord [Cardinal] Ascanio. And nothing is more certain than the fact that at the time when our men were in Ostia more than twenty arm spans of Rome's town wall fell down on the side from which we were to enter.

When he saw this young king so suddenly arrive with such good fortune, the pope consented to have him enter [on December 31, 1494,] (and anyway, he would not have been able to prevent it), and he requested a safe-conduct which he obtained for Don Ferrandino, duke of Calabria and the only son of King Alfonso, who withdrew to Naples at night. And Cardinal Ascanio accompanied him up to the gate [of San Lorenzo]. And the king entered Rome under arms, like one who has authority to do as he pleases everywhere. Several cardinals came to meet him, as well as the governors and senators of the town; and he lodged in the Palazzo di San Marco which is the headquarters of the Colonna, who were his friends and servants at the time, and the pope retired to the Castel Sant'Angelo.

13

Would it have been possible to believe that King Alfonso, who was so proud and who had been nourished upon war, and his son, and all these Orsini, who had so many partisans in Rome, would not have dared remain in the city, since they saw and they knew that the duke of Milan was faltering, as well as the Venetians, and that an alliance was being transacted which would have been concluded if there had been the least resistance at Viterbo or at Rome—as I was well assured—provided that they might have stopped the king for a few days? Indeed it was necessary that God showed how all these things were beyond man's sense and understanding; and it is worth noting that, just as the walls of the town had fallen, so some fifteen arm-spans of the outer walls of the Castel Sant'Angelo also fell, as I was told by several persons, and among others by two cardinals [Giuliano della Rovere and Ascanio Sforza] who were there, and who took great pains to persuade the king to take that for a miracle and to have the pope taken by force, as I shall explain later.

But I must speak a bit about King Alfonso. As soon as the duke of Calabria (named Don Ferrandino, who has been mentioned several times) had returned to Naples, his father King Alfonso judged himself unworthy of being king, because of the many wrongs which he had committed, and with great cruelty, against the persons of several princes and barons whom he had seized by violating the safe-conduct which he and his father had given them.[215] They were at least twenty-four in number, and he had them killed immediately after the death of his father (who had kept them for some time since the war which they had waged against him), as well as two others whom his father had taken by means of his assurance of safety; one of them was the prince of Rossano, duke of Sessa. This duke [*sic*] of Rossano had married Don Ferrandino's sister, and by her he had a son who had married the daughter of Don Ferrandino so that he would be safer; for the prince had wanted to betray him greatly, and he would have well deserved every sort of punishment if the king had not taken him in spite of his assurance of security when he came to him according to his summons. And he put him in prison, and later his son, as soon as he was fifteen or sixteen years old. And the father had remained there for thirty-four years at the time when Alfonso became king; and then he had all these prisoners taken to Ischia, a small island near Naples of which you will hear [more], and there he had all of them slain. He had kept a few of them in the castle of Naples, such as Rossano's son and the count of Popolo. And I made detailed inquiries as to how they were put to death; for several persons believed them to be alive when the king entered Naples, and I was told by a man who was one of their principal servants that he had them killed by a Moor from Africa (who left for Barbary immediately afterwards by his command, so that no news of this would spread), without sparing these old princes who had remained in prison for thirty-four years.

No man was more cruel than he was nor more vicious nor more greedy. The father was more dangerous, for no one could ever recognize his wrath; as he gave people a warm welcome, he would seize them and betray them, such as Count Iacopo [Piccinino], whom he seized and had put to death when he came to him as an ambassador from Duke Francesco of Milan, whose illegitimate daughter he had married. (But it was done with the duke's consent, for both of them feared him on account of his courage and for the followers whom he had in Italy among the Bracceschi; and he was the son of Nicola Piccinino.) And so, as was said, he seized all the others; and there was never any grace or mercy in him, as persons close to him have told me, and he had no compassion for the people.

As for money matters, he managed all the commerce of the kingdom, going so far as to distribute pigs to be looked after by the people, who

215. This violation has already been mentioned by Commynes on p. 441 above.

had to fatten them so that they would sell more advantageously; and if they died, the people had to pay for them. In the regions like Apulia where olive oil is produced, they bought it for almost any price they pleased; and they did the same with wheat, before it was ripe, and they sold it at as high a rate as they could. And if the price of the merchandise fell, they forced the people to take it back. And during the time that they wanted to sell, no one could sell except them. If a lord or baron was a good housekeeper or expected to save some money, they asked him to make them a loan and he was forced to give it. They took away from them their breeds of horses, of which they had several, and they kept them for themselves, and they took care of having them trained, and in such great numbers, whether horses, mares, or colts, that they were estimated at several thousands; and they sent them to graze in various places in the pastures of the lords and others to the great detriment of these people.

Both of them took several women by force. In ecclesiastical matters they showed no respect or obedience. They sold bishoprics, such as that of Taranto which the father sold for thirteen thousand ducats to a Jew, [who bought it in order] to give it to his son who, he claimed, was a Christian. He gave abbeys to a falconer, and [in fact] to several of them, [who took them] for their children, saying [to the falconers: "In return for this abbey] you are to take care of so-and-so many birds and you will mew them at your expense, and you will keep so-and-so many men at your expense." The son never observed Lent, nor did he pretend to do so. For many years he neither confessed nor received God. To conclude, it is not possible to do worse than both of them have done. Some people have said that young King Ferrandino would have been the worse, although he was humble and gracious when he died, but then, too, he was in need.

14

Now it might seem to the readers that I say all these things owing to some particular hatred which I might have had against them. But by my faith, I do not. I say this in order to continue with my memoirs, from which one can see that from the very beginning of the under-taking of this expedition, it was an impossible affair for the people who managed it if it had not proceeded from God alone, who wanted to make His instrument of this good young king, so poorly provided and conducted, in order to chastise such wise,[216] rich, and experienced kings.

216. See p. 33, n. 78, for Commynes' peculiar use of "wise" ("saige") here and at many other points in the *Memoirs*.

There were so many wise persons who were involved in the defense of the kingdom, and they had so many allies and supporters, and they saw this calamity coming upon them from such a distance, but they never were able to provide against it nor to resist it anywhere. For, aside from the castle of Naples, there was no other place which stopped the king for one single day; and, as Pope Alexander [VI] who reigns today has said, the French went there with spurs of wood and chalk in the hands of commissarial agents to mark up their lodgings, without further trouble. And he said "spurs of wood" because when young men ride about the town nowadays, their page puts a little wooden spike in their shoe, which is [flat like] a slipper, and so they ride on mules, shaking their legs.

Our men put on their armor only a few times as they made this expedition; and the king took only four months and nineteen days from Asti until he entered Naples. An ambassador would have taken a good part of this time [to get there]. Therefore I conclude this subject, as I say, after having heard it said by several good monks who lead a holy life and by many other kinds of people (for the voice of the people is the voice of God): Our Lord wanted to punish them visibly and to have everyone know it and to set them up as an example to all kings and princes so that they may conduct themselves properly and live according to His commandments. For the lords of the house of Aragon, of whom I am speaking, lost honor, kingdom, great riches, and movable possessions of all sorts; and they have been so dispersed that one hardly knows what became of them. And they lost their bodies, three in one year or a little more; but I hope that their souls have not been lost. For King Ferrante, who was Alfonso [I]'s illegitimate son—and Alfonso was a wise king and honorable and perfectly good[217]—endured great sorrow in his heart to see this army advancing upon him; and he could do nothing about it. He realized that he and his son had led bad lives and that they were greatly hated; for he was a very wise king. And, as some of the persons closest to him have assured me, there was a book which had been found when a chapel was torn down and on it was written: "[To] the king, with his secret council." And people say that it contained all the misfortunes which befell him. Only three persons saw it, and then he threw it into the fire.[218]

217. See Appendix C for an explanation of the house of Aragon's rights of inheritance to the southern Italian kingdoms of Naples and Sicily.

218. See Mandrot, II, 182, n. 2, for details about the "discovery" of this book, supposedly written by Saint Cataldus of Taranto, who lived in the fourth century. Mandrot explains why the words on the book's cover must be taken as an address, which explains in turn why the manuscript reading, "la voye," should be amended and translated to read "le roy" ("the king").

Another one of his sorrows was that neither his son Alfonso, nor Ferrandino, son of his son, wanted to believe in the [king's] coming, and they spoke most menacingly of the king and with great contempt, saying that they would go to meet him as far as the mountains; and they were very close to doing that. And in spite of his command they refused to be silent. And he said that he prayed to God that they should never see a king of France in Italy, and that he had seen only a poor man from the house of Anjou, who had caused him an infinite amount of suffering; it was Duke John, son of King René. He worked hard by means of an ambassador named Camillo Pandone to have the king stay [where he was] before he left [France], and offered to become his tributary to the amount of fifty thousand ducats per year, and to hold the kingdom from him in fealty and homage. When he realized that he could neither succeed in obtaining any sort of peace nor appease the state of Milan, he contracted an illness from which he died; and in his afflictions he made confession and, as I hope, expressed repentance for his sins.

Alfonso the son, who had been so terrible and cruel and had had so much experience in warfare, renounced his crown; before the king left Rome, he was taken with such fear that every night he never ceased to cry out that he heard the French and that the trees and stones shouted: "France!" And he never had the courage to leave Naples. But upon his son's return from Rome he put him in possession of the kingdom, had him crowned [January 25, 1495], and had him ride on horseback through the town of Naples, accompanied by the highest-ranking persons who lived there, such as Don Frederick his brother and the cardinal of Genoa. The new king rode between them and was attended by the ambassadors who were there, and he had all the required solemnities performed.

As for himself, he fled and went off to Sicily with the queen his stepmother ([Joanna,] the sister of Ferdinand of Castile who is still living and to whom the kingdom of Sicily belongs), to a place which she owned. This was important news throughout the world, and especially in Venice where I was. Some said that he had gone to join the Turk; others said that he did it for the advantage of his son, who was not hated in the kingdom. But it was always my opinion that it was from pure cowardice, for never was a cruel man bold; and so it can be seen in all histories, and it was in such a manner that Nero and many others despaired.

And he was so very anxious to flee that on the day he left he told his stepmother, as some persons who were in his service told me that he did, that if she would not go, he would leave her. And she replied that he should wait another three days so that he would have been in his kingdom for a full year. And he said that if anyone prevented him from going he would throw himself out of the window, and added: "Do you not hear how everybody is shouting 'France'?" And so they embarked on the galleys. He took with him all sorts of wines, which he loved more than anything else, and all sorts of grains for gardening, without giving any orders concerning his furniture or possessions, for most of them remained in the castle of Naples. He brought a few pieces of jewelry and a little money; they went to Sicily to the place I mentioned and then to Messina and Palermo. He brought with him several monks and vowed that he would have nothing more to do with the world; and among others he particularly cherished those from Monte Oliveto, whose habit is white (as they told me at Venice, where the body of Saint Helena lies in their monastery), and he proceeded to live the most holy life in the world and to serve God at all hours of the day and the night with the monks, as they do in their convents, and to spend his time in long fasts, abstinences, and almsgiving. And then a terrible disease came upon him: excoriation and gravel. And they told me that they had never seen any man so afflicted. Yet he endured everything with great patience and decided to go and spend the rest of his life in a monastery at Valencia and to take the habit of a monk. But he suffered such an attack of illness that he lived only a short time, and then died. And judging from his great repentance, it is to be hoped that his soul is glorious in paradise.

His son did not outlive him very long, and he died of fevers and flux. And I believe that they are better off than they were in this world. It seems to me that in less than two years' time [*sic*] there were five kings who wore the crown in Naples—the three whom I have named, King Charles VIII of France, and Don Frederick, Alfonso's brother, who reigns at present.

15

To make everything clearer, we must explain how the king, Don Ferrandino, as soon as he was crowned, became a new man; and it seemed to him that all the hatred and offenses had been wiped out by his father's flight. He assembled as many soldiers as he could, both horsemen and infantrymen, and proceeded to San Germano at the borders of the kingdom, which is a strong place and easy to defend and through which the French have passed two other times, and there he set up his camp and put a garrison in the town. The place is defended by means of a small river, which is sometimes fordable and sometimes not.

It is also protected by the mountain and the castle which is built on it. And so Ferrandino's friends began to take heart again.

The king was still in Rome, where he stayed for about twenty days at least [December 31, 1494—January 28, 1495]. Many affairs were being transacted. With him were about eighteen cardinals and others who lived in a state of neutrality; also present were the above-mentioned Ascanio, vice-chancellor and brother of the duke of Milan, and [the cardinal of] Saint Peter in Chains, great enemies of the pope and enemies of each other, the [bishop of] Gurk, [the cardinal of] Saint-Denis, [Federigo di] Sanseverino, [Giambattista] Sabelli, [Cardinal Giovanni] Colonna, and others. All of them wanted to have a new election and to take legal action against the pope, who was in the Castel [Sant' Angelo]. Twice the artillery was ready to fire, as some of the greatest persons have told me, but the king in his goodness always opposed it. The place is not defensible, for the mound [on which the castle is built] is man-made and it is small; and they strongly insisted that the walls had fallen by miracle. And they charged him with having bought this holy dignity and they spoke the truth. But Ascanio had been the principal merchant. He had conducted all the affair and had received a large sum of money as well as the pope's house when he was vice-chancellor, the furniture which was in it, his post as vice-chancellor, and several places in the papal territories. They had been close rivals for the papacy. I believe, however, that both of them would have consented to elect a new pope according to the king's pleasure, and even a French one. And I should not presume to say whether the king did well or not; however, I believe that he acted for the best in making an arrangement, for he was young and insufficiently attended to conduct such an important work as the reform of the church, although he would well have had the power to do so if he had understood how to go about it properly. I believe that all persons of knowledge and reason would have considered it to have been a good, great, and very holy task, but much hard work would have been necessary. The king's intentions were good, however, and they still are, provided that he were helped with this.

The king took another course and made a treaty [on January 15] with the pope, an accord which could not last because it was too violent in some points. The [character of the] accord served as a great pretext for making a league which will be spoken about later. By this accord there was to be peace between the pope and his cardinals, and some of them were to be paid according to the rights of their [i.e., which they possessed as holders of a cardinal's] hat, whether they were absent or present. He [the pope] was to lend the king four places: Terracina and

Civitavecchia he delivered and Viterbo was held by the king; Spoleto he did not give up, although he promised to do so. And they were to be returned to the pope upon the king's departure from Naples; and so it was done by the king, although the pope had deceived him. By this agreement he delivered to the king the Turk's brother [Jem], for whom he received forty-five thousand ducats a year from the Turk, and they held him [Jem] in great fear.[219] He promised not to appoint any legate in any locality or place under the jurisdiction of the church without the king's consent; and there were other articles relating to the consistory. And he gave his son [Cesare Borgia], the cardinal of Valencia, as a hostage, and he accompanied the king in the capacity of a legate. And the king rendered him filial obedience with all the humility that a king might manifest. And the pope created two cardinals for him: [Briçonnet], the [receiver-]general who was already bishop of Saint-Malo (and who has often been called the [receiver-]general), and a bishop of Le Mans [Philippe de Luxembourg], who was of the house of Saint-Pol and was in France.

16

After these things had been done, the king left Rome on seemingly very friendly terms with the pope. But eight cardinals left Rome unhappy with this arrangement; six of them belonged to the followers of the vice-chancellor and [the cardinal of] Saint Peter in Chains, although it was believed that it was only a feint on Ascanio's part, and that in his heart he was pleased with the pope. But his brother had not yet declared himself against us. The king proceeded to Genzano and from there to Velletri, from whence the cardinal of Valencia fled. The next day the king took Montefortino by assault (and those who were inside were killed). It belonged to Giacomo Conti, who had accepted money from the king and had then turned [against him], for the Conti are partisans of the Orsini. The king then proceeded to Valmontone, which belongs to the Colonna, and from there went to take quarters within four miles of Monte San Giovanni, a very strong place, which was battered for seven or eight hours and then taken by assault; all those who were inside were killed, or most of them. It belonged to the marquis of Pescara and it was church land; all the army was joined together there.

From there the king proceeded to San Germano (it was about sixteen

219. See p. 416, n. 174. Alessandro Benedetti supports and elaborates upon Commynes' idea of the usefulness of Jem's imprisonment when he says in his *Diaria de bello Carolino*, ed. D. Schullian (New York, 1967), p. 71, that it was "generally believed" that the pope's custody of Jem and the Turk's fear of his release had "thus far . . . kept [the Turks] outside Italy."

miles farther or so), where the newly crowned King Ferrandino was encamped with all the troops which he had been able to muster, as I said elsewhere. This was the last resort, and this was the place in which either to fight or never to do so, for it was the entrance to his kingdom and the place was favorable because of the stream as well as the mountain. He sent ever so many soldiers to guard and defend the pass of Cancello, which was a mountain pass six miles beyond San Germano.

Before the king arrived at San Germano, King Ferrandino left in great disorder and abandoned the town and the pass. My lord of Guise [Louis d'Armagnac] was in charge of the vanguard that day, and the king was at the tail end of the vanguard. My lord of Rieux had gone to the pass of Cancello against the Aragonese, who also abandoned it. And the king entered San Germano. King Ferrandino proceeded directly to Capua, where his men-at-arms were refused entrance, but they admitted him with a few men. He did not stay there and begged them to hold out for him, assuring them that he would return the next day; and he proceeded to Naples, fearing what actually happened: rebellion. All his soldiers or most of them were supposed to wait for him in Capua, but when he returned the next day he found that everyone had left. Lord Virginio Orsini and his cousin the count of Pitigliano went to Nola, where they and their men were taken by our men. They insisted on maintaining that they had a safe-conduct and that they were being wronged; and it was true, but it [the safe-conduct] was not yet in their hands. They did not pay anything, however, but they endured great losses and were wronged.

From San Germano the king proceeded to Mignano and Teano, and all the gates were opened. He lodged at Calvi, within two miles of Capua. And the people of Capua came there to negotiate surrender and the king entered the town with all his army. And from Capua he proceeded on the following day to Aversa, which is midway between Capua and Naples, five miles from one and the other; and there the Neapolitans came and made a settlement by which their ancient privileges were assured. The king sent there before him Marshal de Gié, the seneschal of Beaucaire, the president [of Parlement, Jean de] Ganay, who kept the seal, and several secretaries.

When King Ferrandino saw these things—the people and the noblemen in arms rebelling against him (they pillaged his stable, which was very large, upon his arrival)—he embarked on a galley and sailed to Ischia, which is an island eighteen miles beyond Naples. The king [of France] was received in great solemnity inside the town and everyone came to greet him, and those who were most obligated to the house of Aragon came first, such as all those of the house of Caraffa, who received from the house of Aragon revenues of forty thousand ducats in inheritances as well as in benefits. For the kings there can certainly give their own domains;[220] and indeed they give away the domains of others. And I do not believe that there are three people in the whole kingdom whose possessions are not held from the crown or from other people.

Never had people shown so much affection to the king or to a nation as they did to the king [of France]. It seemed to them that they were free from all tyranny and that they were conquering themselves, for in Calabria, where my lord of Aubigny and Perron di Baschi were sent without any men-at-arms, everyone passed over [to the king's side]. All the [places in] Abruzzi capitulated of their own accord; the first town to do so was Aquila, which has always been a good [friend of the] French. All the places in Apulia surrendered except the castle of Brindisi, which is strong and well guarded, and Gallipoli, which was also guarded—otherwise the people would have passed over [to the French]. In Calabria he held three places: Amantea and Tropea, which were formerly [faithful to the] Angevin [dynasty], raised the king's banners; but since he gave them to my lord of Précy and refused to receive them as part of his domain, they raised the banners of Aragon.[221] The castle of Reggio Calabria also remained Aragonese. But all those that held out did so because we failed to send [armed men] there. Taranto gave itself up—both town and castle, and entirely on their own, for we did not go with enough men to Apulia to guard a single castle. The king obtained Otranto, Monopoli, Trani, Manfredonia, Barletta, and everything except the places I mentioned. Those [the authorities] from the cities spent three days coming to meet our army, in order to surrender; and all of them sent people to Naples. And all the princes and lords of the kingdom came there to render homage except the marquis of Pescara; but his brothers and nephews came there.

The count of Arena and the marquis of Squillace fled to Sicily because the king gave their lands to my lord of Aubigny. The prince of Salerno was also there, returned from his fleet (which had not served

220. Alienation of crown lands had long been prohibited in France and this is presumably why the contrary custom in the kingdom of Naples struck Commynes. In the sentence following the one to which this note refers, Commynes is referring to the lack of alodial land in the kingdom of Naples.
221. The kingdom of Naples belonged in feudal law to Charles VIII by right of conquest as well as by right of feudal inheritance from the time when he entered Naples and King Alfonso fled. Consequently, he could either confiscate and redistribute any of the fiefs in the kingdom to any of his French followers, or he could claim any or all fiefs as part of his royal domain, taking them under his personal administration. The latter is what the towns of Amantea and Tropea had hoped for, but the former is what happened, and so they revolted.

any purpose), as well as his cousin the prince of Bisignano, and his brothers, the duke of Amalfi, the duke of Gravina, the old duke of Soria, who had sold his duchy a long time before to the cardinal [of] Saint Peter in Chains (and his brother [Giovanni della Rovere] the prefect [of Rome] still owns it), the count of Montuoro, the count of Fondi, the count of Tripalda, the count of Celano, who had been banished for a long time and had gone with the king, the young count of Troja, who had been educated in France and was from the house of Cossa, the count of Popolo, who was found a prisoner in Naples, the young prince of Rossano, who had been delivered and whom I mentioned before (he had been a prisoner for a long time with his father, who had been one for thirty-four years; and this young man accompanied Don Ferrandino), the marquis of Cotrone, all the Caldoras, [Gian-Tomaso Caraffa] the count of Maddaloni, [Gian-Francesco Caraffa] the count of Marigliano (they and their relatives had always governed the house of Aragon), and generally speaking all those of the kingdom with the exception of the three whom I mentioned to you.

17

When King Ferrandino fled from Naples, he left the marquis of Pescara and several Germans in the castle. And he went to his father in order to obtain aid in Sicily. Don Frederick kept at sea with some few galleys and came twice under safe-conduct to speak to the king [March 5 and 7, 1495]. He requested the king that some portion of the kingdom might be left to his nephew [Alfonso II], along with the title of king, and that his own [Frederick's] possessions and those of his wife might be retained. His own case was not very important, for he had received a small share [of the royal inheritance when King Ferrante I died]. The king offered him estates in France for him and his nephew, and I believe that he would have obtained a fine and large duchy; but they refused to accept it. In any case, they would not have kept any agreement that might have been arranged for them if they had remained in the kingdom, once they saw their advantage [in not keeping it].

The artillery was placed in front of the castle of Naples and fired. Only the Germans were in it; the marquis of Pescara had left. And if four cannons had been sent as far as Ischia [where Ferrandino had taken refuge], it would have been taken; it was from there that misfortune returned. We took all the places which were holding out, which were only four or five in number. But everyone spent time in good cheer, jousts, and festivals, and we became so full of our glory that it did not even seem to us that Italians were men.

And the king was crowned [May 12, 1495]; he was lodged in the [Castello di] Capoana [in Naples], and he sometimes went to Poggio Reale. He granted many favors to the subjects and abated some of their taxes; and I do believe that the people would not have rebelled on their own (although they are a fickle people), if a few of the noblemen had been satisfied; but they were not received by anyone, and they were treated rudely at the gates. The best treated were those of the house of Caraffa, who were true Aragonese. Even they suffered certain losses: thus no office or estate was left untouched. But [those favorable to] the Angevins were treated worse than [those favorable to the] Aragonese like the count of Marigliano. An order was sent out, and the president de Ganay and the seneschal, who had newly been made duke of Nola and grand chamberlain of the kingdom, were accused of taking money. By this order everyone was maintained in his possessions, but the Angevins were excluded from returning to theirs except through legal action. And as for those who had entered into them [i.e., their former estates] on their own, such as the count of Celano, force was used to throw them out. All offices and estates were given to the French, and [sometimes the same office was given] to two or three [different Frenchmen].[222] All the provisions which were in the castle of Naples when it was taken—and they were considerable—and which the king knew about, he gave to those who asked for them.

In the meantime the castle [i.e., the Castel Nuovo in Naples] was surrendered [on March 7] by the transactions of the Germans [i.e., the Swiss in Charles's pay], who as a result obtained a world of goods which were inside; the Castel dell'Ovo [a second castle in Naples] was also taken after being fired upon [on March 22]. And from this conclusion it may be seen that those who conducted this great work did not do it at all on their own; it was truly the work of God, as is evident to everyone. But these great faults which I mentioned were the work of men blinded by glory, who did not recognize from where this advantage and honor came to them; and they proceeded in accordance with their nature and experience. And their fortune changed as promptly

---

222. When King Alfonso I of Aragon conquered Naples in 1443 (see Appendix C), he confiscated the fiefs of the more ardent supporters of the Angevins and invested his own followers with them. The descendants of these Angevin partisans naturally expected to be reinstated in their fiefs and to see the Aragonese holders sent into exile in their turn when Charles VIII conquered Naples. But Charles had also to satisfy the avarice of his newly victorious French companions. If Commynes is correct, he satisfied his fellow warriors—sometimes haphazardly, giving the same office to several people, it seems—rather than the exiled barons and their followers. Commynes also suggests that the failure to molest those favorable to the Aragonese may have been the result of bribing Ganay and de Vesc. See Calmette, III, 100, n. 9, and 101, n. 4, for discussion of the accuracy of this passage.

and visibly as the day rises in Halland[223] or in Norway, where the summer days are longer than elsewhere, and so much so that when day ends at night, at the same time or shortly after, such as a quarter hour later, one can see the next day rise again. And similarly every wise man saw this good and glorious undertaking change, and in as short a span of time, an undertaking from which so many good things and honors for all Christendom might have resulted if it had been recognized as proceeding from the One from Whom it came. For the Turk would have been as easy to disturb as King Alfonso was, for he is still alive and he is a man of no value in the world; and the king [of France] had in his hands his brother [Jem], who lived only a few days after the cardinal of Valencia had fled (and it was said that he was handed over [to the French already] poisoned); and he was the man whom the Turk feared more than anyone else in the world.[224]

And so many thousands of Christians were ready to rebel that no one could imagine it. For from Otranto to Vlorë [in Albania] is only sixty miles, and from Vlorë to Constantinople is about eighteen days' walking distance by land, as those who often make the trip have told me; and there are no fortified places between the two—or at most two or three; the rest is demolished. And all these countries are Albanian, Slavonic, and Greek, and they are densely populated; they heard this news of the king by their friends who were in Venice and Apulia, with whom they also correspond, and they waited only for this Messiah in order to rebel.

An archbishop of Durazzo, who is Albanian, was sent there by order of the king; and he spoke to so many people who were ready to turn [to our side] that it was incredible. They included children and nephews of many lords and persons of high estate in those marches, such as [George Kastrioti, called] Skanderbeg, a son of the emperor of Constantinople himself [Andreas Paleologus], and some nephews of Lord Constantine, the present governor of Monferrato, who are nephews or cousins of the king of Serbia. More than five thousand janizaries would have turned [to our side]; and in addition Shkodër and Kroja would have been taken by means of intrigues on the part of Lord Constantine (who was hidden for several days in Venice with me), because Mace-

223. Halland is in southern Sweden which in Commynes' time was a Danish possession. The Polignac manuscript and all early editions read "Holland." Dupont and Calmette suggest the change followed in the text here as more consistent with the atmospheric conditions to which Commynes refers.

224. See p. 482 above for the agreement between pope and king to take Cesare Borgia and Jem as hostages with the French army. Pope Alexander VI was accused by the historian Guicciardini, among others, of poisoning Jem with a "white powder."

donia and Thessaly, which were Alexander [the Great]'s patrimony, belong to him as his patrimony, and Vlorë is part of it. Shkodër and Kroja are near there; and in his time his father or his uncle handed them over to the Venetians, who lost Kroja; and Shkodër they gave up to the Turk when they made peace.

Lord Constantine was within three leagues [of Venice], and the enterprise would have been put into execution if it had not been for the archbishop of Durazzo, who remained in Venice several days after Lord Constantine. And every day I urged him to leave, for he seemed to me to be a man who was light with his words; he said that he would do something that would be talked about. Unfortunately, on the [very] day that the Venetians learned of the death of the Turk's brother, whom the pope had delivered into the hands of the king, they decided to have the Turk informed of this by one of their secretaries; and they gave orders that no ship should pass in the night between the two castles which form the entrance to the gulf, and they had a patrol set up there, for they were afraid only of small ships, such as *grippi* [brigantine-like vessels] (of which there were several in the port) from Albania and from their islands in Greece; for the one who brought this news [to the Turk] would receive a good present.

And so that very night the poor archbishop decided to leave, in order to join in the enterprise of Lord Constantine, who was waiting for him; and he carried many swords, round shields, and javelins to give to those with whom he was intriguing, for they have none. As he passed between the two castles, he was taken [January 7, 1495], and he and his servants were put in one of the castles; and the ship passed on with clearance. He was found to be in possession of several letters which uncovered the affair. And Lord Constantine told me that the Venetians sent word to the Turk's men in the neighboring places and to the Turk himself; and if it had not been for the *grippo* which passed on and whose captain, an Albanian, warned him, he [Constantine] would have been taken; and he fled to Apulia by sea.

18

Now it is time that I should say something about the Venetians and why I went to them, for the king was in Naples where he had the upper hand in his affairs.

I left from Asti [on September 26 or 27, 1494,] in order to thank them for the good answers which they had given to two of the king's ambassadors and to maintain them in friendly relations with him, if it were possible for me to do so; for in view of their strength, their sense, and their management, they could easily make trouble for him, such as no one else in Italy could.

The duke of Milan, who helped to send me on, wrote his ambassador who resides there (for there is always one there) that he should keep me company and guide me. His ambassador receives one hundred ducats a month from the Signoria, as well as finely furnished lodgings and three barges which do not cost him anything to take him around the town. The one from Venice has the same advantage in Milan, except for the barges, because people ride on horseback there whereas in Venice they travel by water.

On my way I passed by their cities, such as Brescia, Verona, Vicenza, Padua, and other places. Everywhere I was treated most honorably in deference to the one who was sending me; and a great number of people came to meet me, with their *podestà* or their captain; for both of them did not come at once, but the second came up to the gate from the inside. They led me to the inn and ordered the host to treat me well, and with most honorable words they had my expenses defrayed. But if one were to count carefully what must be given to the trumpeters and drummers, one hardly gains anything from this defrayal; but the treatment is honorable.

The day that I entered Venice [October 2, 1494] people came to meet me from as far as Fusina, which is five miles from Venice; and there one leaves the boat in which one came from Padua along a river [the Brenta] and gets into neat little barges covered with tapestry, and with beautiful thick rugs inside to sit on. And the sea reaches up to there, and there is no closer land by which one may arrive in Venice; but the sea is very calm there unless there is a storm; and because it is so calm a great number and all kinds of fish are taken there.

And I marveled greatly to see the placement of this city and to see so many church towers and monasteries, and such large buildings, and all in the water; and the people have no other form of locomotion except by these barges, of which I believe thirty thousand might be found; but they are very small. In the neighborhood of the city within a radius of less than half a French league there are some seventy monasteries (and all of them are on islands; they are for men as well as women and they are extremely beautiful and rich in buildings as well as in what decorates them, and they have very beautiful gardens), not including those which are within the town, which comprise the four mendicant orders, some seventy-two parishes, and many confraternities; and it is a very strange thing to see such beautiful and large churches constructed in the sea.

In the place called Fusina twenty-five gentlemen, elegantly and richly dressed with beautiful scarlet silk material, came to meet me; and there they told me that I was welcome, and they led me to a church of Saint Andrew near the city, where I found again as many other gentlemen, and with them the ambassadors of the dukes of Milan and of Ferrara. And there too they made another speech to me and ushered me to some other boats which they call *piatti*, which are much larger than the others. There were two of them, covered with crimson satin, and carpeted with tapestries. There was room for forty people to sit in each one. They had me sit between these two ambassadors (to be seated in the middle is the place of honor in Italy), and they took me along the main street, which they call the Grand Canal, and which is quite wide. Galleys pass along it, and I have seen ships weighing four hundred tons and more near the houses there. I believe that it is the most beautiful street in the whole world and the one with the most beautiful buildings. It goes all the way through the town.

The houses are very large and high, and the old ones are made of fine stone and are all painted. The others have been made in the last hundred years and all have a façade of white marble which comes to them from Istria, one hundred miles from there, and they also have many large slabs of porphyry and serpentine in the front. On the inside most of them have at least two rooms which have gilded ceilings, rich mantlepieces of cut marble, gilded bedsteads, and painted and gilded screens, and very fine furniture inside. It is the most sumptuous city which I have ever seen and the one that treats ambassadors and foreigners with most honor and the one that is governed most wisely and the one in which the service of God is celebrated most solemnly. And although they may well have other faults, I do believe that God helps them for the reverence which they bring to the service of the church.

In this company of fifty gentlemen they led me as far as San Giorgio [Maggiore], an abbey of black [i.e. Benedictine] reformed friars where I was lodged. The next day they came to fetch me and to take me to the Signoria. And I presented my letters to the doge, who presides at all their councils; he is honored as a king for life and all the letters are addressed to him, but he cannot act entirely on his own. However, this one [Agostino Barbarigo (1486–1501)] has much authority and more than any prince of theirs ever had. Moreover, he has been the doge for twelve years already, and I found him to be a worthy man and a wise one, very knowledgeable about Italian affairs, and a gentle and amiable person.

On that day I said nothing more; they had me look at three or four rooms with richly gilded ceilings, beds, and screens. The palace is beautiful and rich for its contents; it is all of well-cut marble; all the façade and the edges of the stones are gilded for about the width of a thumb, perhaps. And in the palace are four beautiful and richly gilded rooms and very spacious living quarters. But the courtyard is small. From his room the doge can hear Mass at the high altar of the chapel of San Marco [today referred to as San Marco Cathedral] which, though it is called only a chapel, is the most beautiful and richest chapel in the world; it is made entirely of mosaics. Furthermore, they boast of having rediscovered the art and they keep workers busy making mosaics, as I have seen.

In this chapel is their treasure, about which people talk [so much]; it consists of objects designed to ornament the church. There are twelve or fourteen large diamonds; I have never seen any others so large. There are two of them of which one weighs seven hundred carats and the other eight hundred, but they are not flawless. There are twelve parts for cuirasses made of gold with their front and sides well furnished with very fine gems,[225] and twelve golden crowns, which were formerly worn by twelve women whom they called queens at certain festivals during the year: they would proceed through the islands and the churches. [But once upon a time] they were carried away, along with most of the women of the city, by thieves who came from nearby Istria or Friuli, who had hidden behind these islands; but the husbands went

225. Commynes' language is very obscure in this phrase, so obscure that most previous editors and translators either have emended the phrase in such a way as to gloss over its difficulties or have passed over it in silence: "Il y a douze haulz de pièces de cuirasse d'or, le devant et les borts bien garniz de pierreries très bonnes...." Gerhard Heidel, whose *La Langue et le style de Philippe de Commynes* (Leipzig and Paris, 1934) provides an extremely useful alphabetized dictionary of unusual phrases in the *Memoirs*, believes that "haulz" should be translated as "autres" and "cuirasse" as "carat." That is, roughly: "There are twelve other pieces of weighty gold...." Even if "haulz" is emended to read "autres," however, this does not explain the "de" following "haulz," nor is the "de" between "cuirasse" and "or" well accounted for grammatically in this translation. Secondly, it seems strange that Commynes should use "cuirasse" to mean "carat" (Heidel defends this by referring to the Arabic word "qirat" from which both "cuirasse" and "carat" might be derived) when he used the word "carats" ("caratz") to mean "carats" in the preceding sentence.

Is it not more reasonable to suppose that Commynes is referring to some kind of gem-studded armor in this phrase? "Haulz" would then refer to the upper part of the breastplate or "cuirasse." "Haulz de pieces de cuirasse" was perhaps a technical phrase for a certain part of a suit of armor. Emile Littré in his *Dictionnaire de la langue française*, V (Paris, 1942), 1852, under the fourth meaning of the word "pièce" mentions "haute pièce": "a metallic piece which for jousting was added to the front part of the cuirass [that is, to the plastron] and to the nose-piece of the helmet." This passage in Littré has been adopted as our authority for translating Commynes' strange phrase as we have in the text. But we translate it so without any strong feeling of conviction. In view of the fact that Commynes has said at the beginning of this paragraph that these objects were "designed to ornament the church," he may rather be referring to a bejeweled reliquary or gold bust of some sort: "There are twelve busts of gold [plate] with their front and edges well ornamented with very fine gems."

after them and recovered them and put these objects in San Marco, and they founded a chapel [Santa Maria Formosa] where the Signoria goes every year on the day [February 1] when they had this victory. There are very great riches with which to ornament the church, along with many other gold objects that are in it in pots of hyacinth, amethyst, agate, and a rather small one of fine emerald; but it is not so great a treasure as to deserve the reputation it has. They do not have gold and silver in cash in their treasury. And the doge told me in the presence of the Signoria that it is a capital offense among them to say that it is necessary to accumulate a treasure; and I think they are right, in view of the danger of division among them.

Afterwards they had me visit their arsenal, which is the place where they keep their galleys and make all the things necessary for the fleet, which is more beautiful than anything in the rest of the world today; and it was formerly and still is the best managed fleet for its purpose.

Indeed I stayed there eight months [October 2, 1494–May 31, 1495] with all my expenses defrayed, as were [those of] all the other ambassadors who were there. And I assure you that I have known them to be so wise and so inclined to increase their power that if something is not done about it soon, all their neighbors will curse this hour. For at the time when the king was there and since then they understood better than [anyone] ever [has] the manner of defending and guarding themselves; they are still at war with him and they have even dared to enlarge their territories, such as when they took seven or eight cities in Apulia as security. I do not know when they will return them.[226] When the king came to Italy they could not believe that the places could thus be taken or taken in such a short time, for such is not their custom. But they and others in Italy have fortified since then and are fortifying many places.

They do not believe in increasing their possessions in haste, as the Romans did, for their people do not have such virtues; and then none of them make war on land, as the Romans used to do, except their *provveditori* and paymasters, who accompany their [mercenary] captain and counsel him and provide for their [mercenary] army.[227] But all the naval war is conducted by their gentlemen as leaders and captains

226. *Sic.* Four places—Otranto, Brindisi, Pulignano, and Monopoli—were taken as security for a loan to King Ferrandino in 1496 of 200,000 ducats. They were held until 1509.

227. The cautious Venetians, to forestall the corruption notorious among Italian mercenary armies, decreed that whenever a foreign captain was hired to defend Venetian interests, two *provveditori* or commissarial agents from Venice would be appointed to accompany the army. Their task was thus not only to channel any requests for military supplies back to the Venetian Signoria, but also to survey the use of those supplies already sent.

of galleys and vessels, and by others among their subjects. But although they do not go personally to serve in the armies on land, they obtain as a result the advantage that they have no man of sufficient heart or of sufficient virtue to be able to rule, as they had in Rome; and therefore they do not have civil strife in the city, and this is the greatest wealth that I can see that they have. And they have marvelously well provided for that and in many ways, for they have no tribunes of the people such as the Romans have [*sic*], which was part of the cause for their dissension; for the people have no influence and are not consulted in any matter and all the office-holders are gentlemen except for their secretaries: these people are not noblemen. Moreover, most of their people are foreigners. And they are well acquainted through Titus Livius with the mistakes that the Romans made; for they have his history and also his bones in their palace at Padua. And for these reasons and many others which I have recognized in them, I say once more that they are on their way to becoming very great.

19

Now I should explain the purpose of my mission, which was to give thanks for the favorable replies which they had made to two of the king's servants who had come to them, upon the assurance of whom he proceeded further in this enterprise; for this was before he left Asti. And I also reminded them of the long and ancient alliances which had existed between the kings of France and them; and I further offered them Brindisi and Otranto on condition that when they would be given something better in Greece they would be bound to return them. They spoke to me of the king and his affairs in the kindest possible terms, for they did not believe that he would go very far. And concerning the offer that I made to them they said that they were his friends and servants and that they did not wish him to buy their love. Anyway, the king did not hold these places, and he wanted them to become involved in the war, which they did not want to do.[228]

And then there were embassies from Naples, entreating them every day and offering them whatever they might want; and King Alfonso, who reigned at the time, admitted that he had failed them; he showed them the peril in which they would be if the king should have the upper hand in his enterprise. The Turk immediately sent them an ambassador whom I saw several times and who, at the request of one of the pope's

228. A résumé of Commynes' speech to the doge is translated into French from the Italian originals preserved in the archives of the Venetian Senate in Kervyn de Lettenhove, II, 11 ff., along with the Senate's reply to Commynes on October 9, 1494 (see p. 84 for full citation of Kervyn's work).

men, threatened them if they did not declare themselves against the king. They gave a good answer to everyone, but at the beginning of this they were not afraid of us and they only laughed at us. And in addition the duke of Milan had them told by his ambassador that they should not worry and that he knew well enough how to send the king back without letting him hold anything in Italy; he sent the same message to Piero de' Medici, who told me so.

But when they and the duke of Milan saw that the king had the Florentines' places in his hands, and especially Pisa, they began to be afraid, and they discussed means of preventing him from proceeding farther. But their councils are long and in the meantime the king proceeded forward and envoys came and went from the ones to the others. The king of Spain also began to be afraid for these islands of Sicily and Sardinia. The king of the Romans began to be jealous; and he was made to fear for the imperial crown and was told that the king wanted to take it and that he had asked the pope about it, which was not true.

And because of these fears these two kings sent large embassies to Venice while I was there, as I said before. The king of the Romans sent four ambassadors there [on February 15, 1495], for he is their neighbor [geographically]. The bishop of Trent was the principal one, and the others were two knights and a doctor, who were treated most honorably and were given well furnished lodgings like I was, ten ducats per day for their expenses, and whatever their horses cost, which had remained in Treviso. Then a very honorable knight from Spain came [on January 5, 1495], well attended and well dressed, and he also was highly honored and [his expenses] were defrayed. In addition to the ambassador who was representing him there, the duke of Milan also sent the bishop of Como and Francesco Bernardino Visconti [on March 4, 1495].

They began to communicate with each other secretly and at night, first by means of their secretaries, and they did not yet dare declare themselves publicly against the king, especially the duke of Milan and the Venetians, who did not yet know whether the league which was being discussed would materialize. Those from Milan came to see me and brought me letters from their master, and told me that the reason for their coming was that the Venetians had sent two ambassadors to Milan, whereas it was their custom to have only one there, and that was what they had in the end; but this was a lie, for all these people were assembled in order to make a league against the king. However, that many fiddles cannot be set in tune in a short time.

Afterwards they [the Milanese ambassadors] asked me whether I knew why this embassy from Spain and the ambassadors of the king of the Romans had come, so that they could tell their master about it. Now I had already been notified from several places by servants of ambassadors as well as by other means, that the ambassador from Spain had passed through Milan in disguise and that the Germans were all being led by the duke [of Milan]. And I also knew that the ambassador from Naples constantly distributed packets of letters which came from Naples; for all this took place before the king had left Florence.[229] I spent a certain amount to be informed of this, as I could well afford to do, and I already knew the first drafts of their articles as they were projected but not agreed upon, for the Venetians take a very long time to come to such conclusions. And for these reasons, and because I saw the league so close [to realization], I did not want to pretend to be ignorant any longer, and I answered the ambassador from Milan that since they were talking to me in such strange terms, I wanted to show them that the king did not want to lose the duke of Milan's friendship if he could help it. And I as their servant wanted to acquit myself of this and to excuse the bad reports that might have been made to the duke their master. I said that I believed him to be misinformed, that he should think twice before losing the [king's] gratitude for such service and for what he had done for the king, that our kings of France have never been ungrateful, and that whatever words might have been said, the love between the two of them, which was so well suited to each of the parties, should not be broken. And I begged them to tell me their grievances, in order that I might let the king know about them before they took other steps. They all swore to me and took solemn oaths that they had no intention of doing this. They were lying, however, and they had come with the intention of negotiating this league.

The next day[230] I went to the Signoria to speak to them about this league and to say what seemed to me would be most useful. Among other things I said to them that according to the alliance which they had with the king and which they had had with the late King Louis his father, they could not support each other's enemies and [so] they could not form this league which people were talking about without going against their promises. They had me retire, and when I came back, the

229. *Sic.* Charles VIII left Florence on November 29, 1494, while the first of the intriguing diplomats mentioned by Commynes two paragraphs earlier arrived on January 5, 1495. Commynes, evidently embarrassed by his failure to prevent or at least forewarn the king earlier about the formation of the anti-French league (N.B. the penultimate sentence of this chapter), juggles his dates in order to appear more prescient and "wise" than he probably was.

230. Calmette, III, 120, n. 3, believes this day to be March 10, 1495, basing his assertion on indirect evidence which seems to me insufficient. Marino Sanudo, the well-informed contemporary Venetian chronicler, places Commynes' visit to the Signoria sometime in the first week of March (see Mandrot, II, 220, n. 1).

doge told me that I should not believe everything I was told in the town, for everyone there was free and could say whatever he pleased. However, they had never thought of making a league against the king, nor had they ever heard of one; on the contrary, they wished to arrange a league between the king and the other two kings and all of Italy, and it would be against the Turk and each member would bear his share of the expense. And if there was anyone in Italy who should not want to pay what would be decided, the king and they would compel him by force to do so. And they wanted to make an arrangement according to which the king would receive a certain amount of money in cash which they would advance and they would keep certain places in Apulia as security (as they are doing at this moment); and the kingdom would be recognized as his by the consent of the pope, and he would be paid a certain sum of money each year, and the king would hold three places there. Would that it had been God's pleasure to have had the king be willing to accept this at the time.

I told them that I did not dare enter into this agreement, begging them not to conclude this league hastily, and that I would inform the king of everything. I requested them, as I had the others, to tell me their grievances and not to keep them secret, as those of Milan had done. They complained about the places which the king held from the pope, and even more about those which he held from the Florentines, and especially about Pisa, saying that the king had sent written word to several places and to them that he wanted nothing in Italy except the kingdom, and that he wanted to proceed against the Turk, but at this moment he gave the impression of wanting to take everything he could in Italy and of not asking anything of the Turk.[231] And they claimed further that my lord of Orleans, who had remained in Asti, was frightening the duke of Milan and that his servants spoke very menacingly; however, they would not do anything new until I received an answer from the king or until the time to have received it was past. And they showed more respect than the duke of Milan['s men did]. I informed the king of everything and received meager response. And from then on they assembled every day, since they knew that their undertaking had been discovered.

231. This interpretation of Charles's intentions was evidently widespread, at least at Venice, for Marino Sanudo uses almost exactly the same terms as Commynes does here in explaining the formation of the Holy League: "They [the Venetians], having seen that the king was not content to have taken the kingdom [of Naples], that he wanted something else in Italy, and that he no longer spoke of moving against the infidels, pushed matters ahead and liberated Italy from this great danger." See his *La Spedizione di Carlo VIII in Italia* (Venice, 1873), p. 470 (quoted in Benedetti, *op. cit.*, p. 28, n. 48; translation mine).

At that time the king was still in Florence;[232] and if he had found resistance in Viterbo, as they had expected, they [the Venetians] would have sent forces, and to Rome also if King Ferrandino had remained inside. They had never thought that he was going to abandon Rome, and when they saw that it was abandoned they began to be afraid. Meanwhile the embassies of the two kings pressed them hard to come to some conclusion, for otherwise they wanted to leave, having already been there four months. Every day they went to the Signoria. I was doing the best I could, for I saw well enough that if the league were to be concluded, this conquest and great glory would all go up in smoke. They had further hope that resistance would be offered at San Germano and that all the kingdom would come there, as it did.

20

When [the Venetians] saw that all these places had been abandoned and that the king was in Naples, they sent for me [on March 5, 1495,] and told me this news, and they gave the impression of being joyful about it. However, they said that the castle was well garrisoned, and I could well see that they had hopes that it would hold out. And they consented to have the ambassador from Naples raise soldiers in Venice to send there [Naples] and to Brindisi. They were just concluding their league when their ambassadors wrote them that the castle had been surrendered. They sent for me once again one morning and I found them assembled in great numbers, about fifty or sixty, in the chamber of the doge who was ill with colic. And he told me this news with a cheerful face, but no one among the company knew how to pretend as well as he did. Some were seated on the footboards of the benches and had their heads leaning against their hands; others acted differently, but all of them showed that their hearts were very sad. And I believe that when the news reached Rome about the battle which they had lost at Cannae against Hannibal, the senators who had remained were no more astounded or terror-stricken. For not one of them even tried to look at me or said a word to me except him. And I looked at them with great astonishment. The doge asked me whether the king would keep the promise which he had always made them and would observe what I had told them. I strongly assured them that he would, and I opened up ways of remaining in good peace, and I emphatically offered to help in it, hoping to make them lose their suspicions; and I took my leave.

Their league was as yet neither made nor broken; and the Germans

232. See n. 229. Calmette's attempts to explain away Commynes' juggling of the dates in III, 122, n. 5, are unconvincing.

who were not satisfied wanted to leave. The duke of Milan once again had himself coaxed about some article or other. However, he sent word to his representatives that they should ratify everything; and indeed they concluded this league quickly [on March 31, 1495]. And while this was being debated I kept notifying the king over and over of everything, pressing him to bring the matter to a conclusion, either to remain in the kingdom and to provide himself better with infantrymen and money, or to be on his way soon in order to retire, leaving the principal places well guarded, before all of them were assembled. I also notified my lord of Orleans, who was at Asti with only the men from his household since his company [of soldiers] was with the king; and I told him to put soldiers inside, assuring him that they were about to charge down upon him. And I wrote to my lord of Bourbon, who had remained in France as the king's lieutenant, to send soldiers to Asti in haste in order to guard it; for if that place were lost, no help could reach the king from France. And I also advised the marchioness of Monferrato, who was very good to us and who was an enemy of the duke of Milan, so that she would help my lord of Orleans with men if he were in need of them. For if Asti were lost, the marquisates of Monferrato and Saluzzo were lost.

The league was concluded one night, very late. The next morning the Signoria sent for me earlier than they usually did. As soon as I had arrived and was seated, the doge told me that in honor of the Holy Trinity they had concluded a league with our Holy Father the pope, the kings of the Romans and of Castile, and themselves, and the duke of Milan, for three purposes: firstly, to defend Christendom against the Turk, secondly, to defend Italy, and thirdly, to preserve their estates; and they asked me to inform the king of this. And they were assembled in great numbers, one hundred or more, and they held their heads high and their expressions were happy. Their countenances were not at all like those which they had on the day when they told me about the taking of the castle of Naples. He also told me that they had written their ambassadors who were attending the king that they should return, and that they should take leave. One of them was named Antonio Loredano and the other Domenico Trevisano.

My heart was heavy and I had great fears for the person of the king and for all his company; and I thought that the matter was more advanced than it was, and so did they. I was also afraid that they might have had some Germans in readiness; and if that had been true, the king would never have gotten out of Italy. I had decided within myself not to talk too much in my anger; however, they smoked me out a little bit. I replied to them that already on the preceding night I had written about it to the king, and [had written about it] several times, and that he too had written to me about it, since he had been informed of it from Rome and from Milan. The doge had a rather strange expression when I said that I had written about it the night before, because there are no people in the world so suspicious, or who keep their councils so secret; out of suspicion alone they often imprison people. It was for this reason that I said what I did. And furthermore, I told them that I had also written about it to my lords of Orleans and of Bourbon, so that they might reinforce Asti; and I said so in the hope that it might make for some delay before they proceeded against Asti, for if they had been as ready as they boasted and thought that they were, they would have taken it without anyone being able to help it, for it was poorly garrisoned [at that time], and [remained so] for a long time afterwards.

Thereupon they told me that they had nothing against the king but were only trying to protect themselves against him, and that they did not want him to abuse people with such words as to imply that he only wanted to have the kingdom and then wanted to proceed against the Turk, since he acted quite the opposite and wanted to destroy the duke of Milan and the Florentines and to hold the lands of the church. To which I replied that the kings of France had augmented [the stature of] the church and had increased and defended it, and that the king would do the same rather than take anything away from them, but that all these reasons were not those that stirred them, and that they wanted to involve Italy in trouble and to make their profit from it, and that I thought that they would indeed do it. They took that a little bit amiss, as I was told; but it is obvious from what they hold in Apulia as security from King Ferrandino, in order to help him against us, that I was speaking the truth.

And I wanted to rise to take leave. They had me sit down again, and the doge asked me if I wished to make any peace overtures, because I had mentioned something about it the previous day. But that was on condition that they should be willing to wait another fifteen days before concluding the league, so that I might send word to the king and receive his answer.[233]

After these events about which I spoke, I retired to my lodgings. They sent for the ambassadors, one after the other. And when their council was adjourned I met the ambassador from Naples, who was

233. Commynes' version of the doge's announcement of the Holy League to him and its effects on him differ entirely from those of the Venetian chroniclers, who report that he was so angry or stunned by the news that he almost lost consciousness! See the accounts of Sanudo, Malipiero, Bembo, and Benedetti, reported in Benedetti, *op. cit.*, pp. 77 and 212–13, n. 70.

wearing beautiful new clothes and a happy expression; and he had cause for this because this was important news for him.

After dinner all the ambassadors of the league met together on their barges, as is their pleasure in Venice; everyone has some, according to the number of men in his retinue, and at the expense of the Signoria; and there may have been forty barges, all of which had pennants with the arms of their masters. And all this company came and passed in front of my windows, and there were many musicians. And those from Milan, or at least one of them who had kept me company for several months, acted very much as if he did not know me any more. And I passed three days without going through the town, and the same was true of my attendants, although no ungracious words were ever spoken in the town to me or to anyone of my men. At night they had a wonderful celebration with fireworks on the steeples; many lanterns were lighted on the houses of these ambassadors and artillery was fired. I went in a closed barge along the streets to see the festival at about ten o'clock at night, and especially in front of the houses of the ambassadors where banquets and fine feasts were taking place.

This was not yet the day of the publication or of the great celebration; for the pope had sent word that he wished it to be postponed for another few days in order to have it done on Palm Sunday, which they call Olive Sunday. And he wanted all the princes in whose lands it would be published and the ambassadors who might be there to carry an olive branch in their hand and to proclaim it a sign of peace and alliance. And he wanted it to be published on the same day in Spain and Germany. And in Venice they set up a well-made wooden walk above the ground, as they do on the day of Corpus Christi, and it reached from the palace up to the end of the Piazza San Marco. And after Mass, which was sung by the pope's ambassador, who gave absolution from punishment and sin to whomever would be present at the publication, the Signoria and the ambassadors, all well dressed, marched in procession along this walk. Many wore crimson velvet robes which the Signoria had given, at least the Germans [did]; and all their servants had new robes, but they were rather short. At the return of the procession a great number of mystery [plays] and [allegorical] personages were presented: first Italy, and afterwards all the kings and princes, and the queen of Spain. And at the return they had the league proclaimed at a porphyry stone, where such publications are made. And there was an ambassador from the Turk who was present, hidden at a window; he had been dismissed but they wanted him to see this festival. And at night, by the intermediary of a Greek, he came to speak to me and he was at least four hours in my room. And he was very anxious for his master to be our friend.

I was twice invited to this festival, but I asked to be excused. And I remained in the town about a month afterwards and was as well treated as before. I was then recalled by the king and took my leave with their permission [on May 31, 1495]. I was conducted in perfect security and at their expense as far as Ferrara. The duke of Ferrara came to meet me, gave me a fine reception for two days, and defrayed my expenses. I received the same treatment from Giovanni Bentivoglio at Bologna. And from there the Florentines came to attend me and I proceeded to Florence in order to wait for the king, of whom I shall now speak once more.[234]

234. The need to make one's account serve as self-justification, which seems among other things to define memoir-writing as a genre, is clear throughout this chapter and perhaps accounts for the glossing-over in this paragraph in particular of several important aspects of Commynes' first embassy to Venice. For example, although Commynes says that he was being "as well treated as before," he was in fact being very carefully watched, and after his departure at least one of those involved in the spying which he carried on in Venice was arrested (cf. Calmette, III, 132, n. 5). Moreover, Commynes fails to tell us that during the last month of his stay in Venice a second French ambassador—Jean Bourdin, royal secretary, inferior in rank to Commynes, to be sure—was sent by Charles VIII on a special mission to Venice in late April, 1495, and joined Commynes in negotiating with the Venetians henceforth. (Commynes does mention Bourdin in passing on p. 508 below.)

Commynes' description of his "master's" usual appearance accords well with this hardly flattering likeness, although the idea that this is a portrait of Charles VIII has sometimes been contested. The king is a "small person," "rather fearful," but with "a kind face and good coloring," Commynes says (see page 526). At other points in his narrative the memorialist asserts that Charles is "willful," yet easily swayed by his officers and favorites. The king's hands, held one above the other against his body, suggest timidity, while the largeness of his eyes seems to express credulity. Charles possesses his father's long, straight, protruding nose, but his lips and mouth are represented as much larger and coarser. The king's coiffure, reducing the area of his visage to little more than that occupied by eyes, nose, and mouth, makes him seem perhaps unwontedly stupid. Whether or not this portrait is correctly thought to represent His Majesty King Charles VIII, however, it offers an extremely strong impression of pre-Renaissance portraiture, of man surrounded and almost smothered by "things"—his clothes, his coiffure, his emotions, his physique—rather than dominating them with an idea of, or an aspiration toward an ideal vision of, himself.

BOOK EIGHT

The French Retreat from Italy and
Charles VIII's Last Years, 1495-1498

1

In order to better continue with my memoirs and to better inform
you, I must go back and speak of the king, who from the time he
entered Naples to the moment when he left it thought only of killing
time, while others thought of taking things and making a profit; but
his age was his excuse. No one could excuse the others for their faults,
[however,] because the king believed them in everything. And if they
had known enough to tell him that he should furnish ample provisions
for three or four castles, he would still be holding the kingdom, or at
least Naples, the provisions for which he had given away, as I said, and
the castle of Gaeta. If he had retained the castle of Naples, the town
would never have rebelled. After the formation of the league he gathered all the men-at-arms around him and appointed five hundred French
men-at-arms and twenty-five hundred Swiss and a few French infantrymen to guard the kingdom [of Naples], and with the rest decided to
return to France by the same way he had come. The league prepared
itself to prevent him from doing so.

The king of Spain had sent and was sending some caravels to Sicily,
but there were few men on board them. Before the king had left, however, they had already garrisoned Reggio Calabria, which is near Sicily,
and I had written the king several times that they would land there, for
the ambassador from Naples had told me so, believing that they were
there already. And if the king had sent men there immediately, he would
have taken the castle, for the people of the town were holding out for
him. People from Sicily also came to Amantea and Tropea, for want of
having sent soldiers there; and at Otranto in Apulia where they had
[formerly] raised the banners of the king, they raised the banner of
Aragon because of the league and because they were situated near
Brindisi and Gallipoli and because they could not raise any troops; and
Don Frederick who was in Brindisi garrisoned it. And throughout the
kingdom people began to change their minds and fortune began to
change, when two months before it had been the contrary. This was
because of the league and the king's departure and the forces that were

left, which were poorer with respect to leadership than with respect to numbers.

My lord of Montpensier remained there as a leader; he was from the house of Bourbon and he was a good and valiant knight, but he was not very wise. He did not get up before noon. In Calabria he left my lord of Aubigny, of Scottish nationality, a good, wise, and honorable knight who was grand constable of the kingdom; and the king gave him the county of Arena, as I said, and the marquisate of Squillace. At first he left the seneschal of Beaucaire, named Étienne de Vesc, as captain of Gaeta. He was made duke of Nola and grand chamberlain and [was given] other lordships; and all the money of the kingdom passed through his hands. And that man had more burdens than he was able or would have known how to bear. He was very anxious to retain the kingdom. He [the king] left my lord Domjulien, a Lorrain, as duke of Monte Sant'Angelo, where he did a fine job of conducting himself well. In Manfredonia he left Gabriel de Montfaucon, a man whom the king held in great esteem; and to all of them he gave large domains. Montfaucon conducted himself very badly and gave up the place at the end of four days for lack of provisions, although he had found it well provided for, and it was in a region which was abundant with wheat.[235] Many people sold everything they found in the castles, and this man, so it is alleged, was one of them. At Trani he left Guillaume de Villeneuve; his valets sold him to Don Frederick, who kept him for a long time in a galley. In Taranto he left Georges de Sully, who conducted himself very well there and died there of the plague; and he kept that city for the king until famine forced it to turn [to the other side]. The bailiff of Vitry remained in Aquila, where he conducted himself well; and Gracien de Guerre, who conducted himself very well, remained in the Abruzzi.

All the places remained badly provided with money. They were assigned [sources of income] from the kingdom where every penny was exhausted.[236] The king left the princes of Salerno and Bisignano

235. The word "bledz" ("wheat") was used to denote any kind of edible grain and even some kinds of vegetables in the fifteenth and sixteenth centuries. In order to differentiate Commynes' word "bledz" from Commynes' word "grains" ("grain"), however, we have always translated "bledz" as "wheat" in this edition, allowing the reader to guess whether Commynes is speaking generically or specifically in each passage where the word occurs.

236. It is impossible to be certain whether Commynes means the kingdom of France or Naples here, though it would seem more likely that he means the former in view of his comments about the relative availability of funds in the two areas in Book 7. Note how Commynes refers sometimes to France and sometimes to Naples, without ever making himself explicit, whenever he uses the word "kingdom" in the paragraph preceding this one.

with good positions (and they served him well as long as they could) and he also gave the Colonna everything they could ask for; and he left them more than thirty places for themselves and their relatives. If they had been willing to keep them for him, as they should have done and as they had sworn to do, they would have been very useful to him and [would have achieved] honor and profit, for I believe they had not been so powerful for the past one hundred years; but before his departure they began to make bargains. And furthermore they were his servants on account of Milan, because naturally they were of the Ghibelline party; but that should not have made them break their word, considering that they were so handsomely treated.[237]

The king did even more for them, for he took under guard as semi-prisoners Lord Virginio Orsini and the count of Pitigliano, as well as some of the Orsini, who were their enemies. And this was wrong, for although they had been taken, the king well knew and understood that there was a safe-conduct; and he showed [that he knew] it, for he only wanted to take them as far as Asti and then to send them back; he was doing it at the request of the Colonna. And before he arrived there, the Colonna had turned against him, the first to do so, without alleging any cause.

2

After the king had given orders as to how he intended his business to be managed he set out [on May 20, 1495] with all the men he had, which I estimated at nine hundred men-at-arms at least, including his household, twenty-five hundred Swiss, and I believe about seven thousand mercenaries in all. And there may have been fifteen hundred guardsmen following the train of the court as servants. The count of Pitigliano, who counted them better than I did, said that there were nine thousand in all; and he told me after our battle [of Fornovo], of which I shall speak. The king proceeded to Rome, [arriving on June 1,] from which the pope had wanted to leave before [the French arrived] and to go to Padua which was in the power of the Venetians; and his lodgings were prepared there.

After that they had taken heart [again] and had sent some of their soldiers there [Rome], and the duke of Milan sent people there; and although they were there in time, the pope did not dare wait, although

237. That is, the Colonna, as Ghibellines, would "naturally" support the duke of Milan, for the duchy of Milan was an imperial fief and therefore the duke was traditionally thought of as aligned with the Ghibelline faction (see nn. 193 and 209 on pp. 445 and 463). Therefore, when the duke of Milan turned against the French, the Ghibelline Colonna family might be expected to do the same.

the king had done him all possible honor and service and had sent him ambassadors to beg him to wait; but he retired to Orvieto [on May 27] and [proceeded] from there to Perugia. He left some cardinals in Rome and they received the king, who did not stay there at all; and no displeasure was done to anyone. And he wrote to me that I should come to him at Siena, where I found him [on June 13]. He kindly gave me a good welcome and asked me laughingly whether the Venetians would send someone to meet him; for all his company consisted of young men and they did not believe that there was anyone else who bore arms.

I told him what the Signoria had told me at my departure, in the presence of one of his secretaries named Bourdin, that they and the duke of Milan would put forty thousand men in the field, not in order to assail him but in order to defend themselves; and that on the day when I took leave of them at Padua, they had me told privately, by means of one of their *provveditori* who was advancing against us, that their men would not pass a river near Parma (and I believe that it is called Oglio), which is in their territory, unless he [Charles VIII] assailed the duke of Milan. And we agreed on certain signals, the *provveditore* and I, in order to be able to communicate with each other in case of need, so that we could arrange things well. And I did not want to break off any [negotiations] because I did not know what might befall my master. And when these words were spoken, a person named Aloys Marcello was present; he was governor of Monte Vecchio for that year, which is like [the office of royal] treasurer; and they had sent him to escort me. There were also the marquis of Mantua's men, who were bringing money to him; but they did not hear the words of these men or others. I brought the king a written account of the number of their horsemen, infantrymen, and stradiots,[238] and of those who were in charge of them. Few persons from the king's entourage believed what I was saying.

When the king was in Siena I pressed him to leave after he had been there for two days and his horses had rested, for his enemies had not yet assembled themselves. And I did not fear anything except that the Germans might come, for the king of the Romans was assembling them, [though] slowly; he wanted very much to obtain ready money [for their payment].

In spite of anything I said, the king took brief counsel on two matters: first, whether we should return their places to the Florentines and take thirty thousand ducats which they still owed from their gift and seventy thousand ducats which they offered to lend the king for his service on his passage, along with three hundred men-at-arms under

238. Commynes describes the stradiots on p. 520 below.

the command of Francesco Secco, a valiant knight whom the king trusted, and two thousand infantrymen. It was my opinion and that of others that the king should do it, and retain only Leghorn until he should be in Asti. He would have paid his men well, and he still would have had money left to take men away from his enemies and then to go after them. It did not happen, however, and my lord of Ligny, who was a young man and the king's first cousin, prevented it; and he did not know exactly for what reason unless it was out of pity for the Pisans. The other point was one that my lord of Ligny promoted by means of a person named Gaucher de Dinteville and by means of a party of people from Siena, who wanted my lord of Ligny as their lord; for the town is always in division and it is governed more foolishly than any city in Italy.

I was asked about this first. I said that it seemed to me that the king should be on his way and not waste time with these foolish offers which could last hardly a week; and moreover, since it was an imperial town, we would have the empire against us. Everyone agreed with this opinion; however, it was done otherwise. And the people from Siena took Ligny as their captain and promised him a certain sum of money each year, of which he did not receive anything; thus the king spent six or seven days [*sic*: June 13–17]. And they showed him the ladies; and the king left at least three hundred men there and became the weaker by that number. And from there he proceeded to Pisa [June 20] by way of Poggibonsi and Castelfiorentino. And those who were left in Siena were driven out before a month was up.

3

I forgot to say that after I had arrived in Florence on my way to meet the king, I went to visit a preaching friar named Brother Girolamo [Savonarola], who lived in a reformed convent [San Marco in Florence], a man of holy life, as they said, who had lived in that place for fifteen years; and with me was one of the king's major-domos named Jean François, a wise man. And the cause [of my visit] was that he had always preached very much in favor of the king; and his words had prevented the Florentines from turning against us, for never had any preacher enjoyed so much credit in a city. He had always assured them of the king's coming, whatever may have been said or written to the contrary, saying that he had been sent by God to chastise the tyrants of Italy and that no one could resist him or defend himself against him. He had also said that he would come to Pisa and that he would enter it, and that the state of Florence would change on this day (and so it happened, for on that day Piero de' Medici was banished). And he had predicted many other things before they came to pass, such as the death of Lorenzo de' Medici; and he said publicly that he saw it by revelation. He preached that the state of the church would be reformed by means of the sword; this has not yet happened but it was close to happening, and they still maintain that it will.

Many blamed him for saying that God had revealed this to him; others believed it. As far as I am concerned, I hold him to be a good man. And so I asked him whether the king could pass [out of Italy] without danger to his person, in view of the large assembly [of soldiers] that the Venetians were making, about which he was better able to speak than I, who came from there. He replied to me that he would meet with some difficulties on the way, but that honor would remain with him, even if he had only one hundred men in his company; and that God, who had led him when he came, would lead him again on his return. But since he had not acquitted himself well of the reformation of the church, as he should have, and since he had suffered his men thus to plunder and rob the people, both those of his party (and they had opened their doors freely to him) and the enemies, God had pronounced a sentence against him. And he would soon feel the crack of a whip, but I should tell him that if he wished to have pity on the people and to resolve in himself to prevent his men from doing wrong and to punish them when they did it, as his office required him to do, then God would revoke his sentence or diminish it; and he should not consider himself excused by saying, "I am not doing any harm." And he told me that he himself would go to meet him and would tell him so; and so he did [at Poggibonsi on June 18], and he spoke of the restitution of the Florentines' places.

The death of my lord the dauphin came to my mind, for I do not see anything else that the king took to heart; but I say this so that one can better understand that all this enterprise was a true mystery of God.[239]

4

As I said, the king had entered Pisa, and the Pisans, both men and women, begged their hosts that for the love of God they would intercede with the king so that they would not be put once again under the

239. The use of the past tense in the first clause of this sentence seems to indicate that Commynes had, when talking with Savonarola, a premonition of the death of the dauphin Charles-Orland (born October, 1492; died December, 1495, as reported by Commynes in chapter 20 of this book). Commynes, who had suffered through the regency which ruled during Charles VIII's youth, would be especially liable to fear the instability which nearly always attended an uncertain royal succession.

tyranny of the Florentines, who indeed treated them very badly. But such is the situation of many other cities in Italy, which are subject to others; and anyway Pisa and Florence had been enemies for three hundred years before Florence had conquered it. And these words and tears moved our men to pity, and they forgot the promises and oaths which the king had made at the altar of Saint John in Florence; and all sorts of people became involved in it, including the archers and the Swiss, and they threatened those whom they suspected of wanting the king to keep his promise, such as the cardinal of Saint-Malo (I heard an archer threaten him; elsewhere I have referred to him as the [receiver-] general of Languedoc). There were also some who said vulgar words to Marshal de Gié. President de Ganay went more than three days without daring to sleep in his quarters. And more than anyone else the count of Ligny was helping this along; and the Pisans came before the king, weeping bitterly, and they were a pitiful sight to everyone who could with reason help them.

After dinner one day forty or fifty gentlemen of his household assembled, wearing their [battle-]axes around their necks, and they came to see him in a room where he was playing checkers with my lord of Piennes and one or two *valets-de-chambre*; there were no others.[240]

---

240. The king's household troops were many and various in the late fifteenth century and neither modern scholars nor Commynes sort them out satisfactorily. G. Daniel, *Histoire de la milice française* (Paris, 1774), 11, 72 ff., offers the most precise, although still incomplete information which I have found. According to Daniel, in 1474 Louis XI founded a special company for his personal protection consisting of one hundred lance-teams, each of which consisted of three rather than six men: a man-at-arms and two archers. These men were chosen for the most part, says Daniel, from among "the gentlemen of his household, or pensioners." The official name of this corps was "the company of one hundred lance-teams of gentlemen of the king's household, ordained for the guard of his body" ("la compagnie de cent lances des gentilhommes de la maison du Roi, ordonnez pour la garde de son corps"). In 1475 Louis XI separated the archers from the men-at-arms, calling the former "the small guard of his body" ("la petite garde de son corps"). In January, 1498, a second company was set up by Charles VIII, called "the company of special gentlemen" ("la compagnie des gentilhommes extraordinaires"), after which time the first company of men-at-arms became known as "the company of one hundred ordinary gentlemen" ("la compagnie des cent gentilhommes ordinaires"). Presumably the second company, like the first, consisted of merely one hundred men-at-arms, without archers or other assistants. Daniel states, *ibid.*, 74, that the pay of these men was twenty *écus* per month in the time of Louis XI, Charles VIII, and Francis I. Thus, he says, they were also called "gentlemen of twenty *écus*" "as we learn from Philippes de Comines [*sic*]." Roger Doucet's *Les Institutions de la France au XVIe siècle*, II (Paris, 1948), 628, adds the information that these two companies of men carried battle-axes. It is an error to conclude, as Charles Oman does in his *History of the Art of War in the Sixteenth Century* (New York, 1937), p. 40, that royal "pensioners" and "gentlemen of twenty *écus*" were the same. For Commynes refers to the pensioners in chapter 8 of Book I when speaking of events of 1465, some nine years before Louis XI created the "gentlemen of twenty *écus*"

And one of the sons of Salazar the elder made a speech in favor of the Pisans, charging some of those whom I have named or all of them, saying that they were betraying him. The king sent them out most firmly; but the matter was not taken up afterwards.

The king lost at least six or seven days' time in Pisa [*sic*: June 20–23]; and then he changed the garrison and put in the citadel a person named [Robert de Balzac, lord of] Entragues, a bad man, who was the servant of the duke of Orleans; and it was the lord of Ligny who had recommended him. And some foot-soldiers from Berry were left there. Entragues did so much that he even had Pietrasanta in his hands (and I believe that he gave money for it), and another place nearby called Motrone. He obtained another one called Librefatto near Lucca. The castle of Sarzana, which was very strong, was put by means of the count of Ligny into the hands of an illegitimate son of my lord of Roussy, one of the count's servants; another place called Sarzanella was put into the hands of another one of his servants. And the king left many soldiers in these places (although he had never been in such great need of them), and he refused the aid of the Florentines and the offer of which I spoke, so that they were reduced to desperation.

And he had known before he left Siena how the duke of Orleans had taken the city of Novara from the duke of Milan [June 13, 1495]; and so the king could be certain that the Venetians would declare themselves [against him], since I had told him at their request that if he

---

(see p. 124 where we have poorly translated "les gens de sa maison pensionnaires" as "gentlemen-at-arms from his household"). And on p. 531 below Commynes, speaking of the battle of Fornovo in 1495, distinguishes "gentlemen of twenty *écus*," "others from the king's household," and "gentlemen-pensioners." If we envision these three kinds of troops mentioned by Commynes as three concentric circles, the largest, outermost circle is that containing the king's household troops. Some of these troops receive a special salary or pension and thus form a second smaller circle which may be labeled that of the gentlemen-pensioners (see Commynes' other mentions of this body of troops in chapter 3 of Book 6, pp. 389–91). Then in 1474 some of these gentlemen-pensioners were chosen to form what became known later as the "ordinary company" of "gentlemen of twenty *écus*," thus creating a third still smaller circle inside the second. This third circle was doubled in size in 1498 with the creation of the "special company." In view of the date 1498 for this creation it is strange that Paolo Giovio reports that when Charles VIII entered Rome in December, 1494, he was preceded by his elite guard of "two hundred [*sic*] men-at-arms, all French, chosen for birth and valour; these men carried on their shoulders iron maces as big as axes. . . ." (John S. C. Bridge quotes this passage in *A History of France from the Death of Louis XI*, II [Oxford, 1924], 113–14. The original Latin text appears in Giovio's *Historia sui temporis* [Florence, 1550], p. 33, ll. 50–53). It is even more strange that we could have translated in Volume One Commynes' words, "ung gentil homme de la maison du roy appellé Jacques de Grassé, lequel estoit de vingt escuz," as "a gentleman of the king's household named Jacques de Grassay . . . was among those who [belonged to a company in the standing army whose members] receive twenty *écus* a month" (see p. 268).

waged war against the duke of Milan, they would give the duke all sorts of help because of the newly created league; and they had their men ready in great numbers.

And one should bear in mind that when the league was formed the duke of Milan intended to take Asti;[241] and he did not expect to find anyone there; but my letters, of which I spoke, had well served to help the advance of the men whom the duke of Bourbon was sending there. But the first to come there were about forty lance-teams from the company of Marshal de Gié which had remained in France—and these people came at the right moment—and five hundred infantrymen who were sent there by the marquis of Saluzzo.

This stopped the soldiers of the duke of Milan, who were led by Galeazzo di Sanseverino [and arrived before Asti on April 6, 1495]; and they took lodgings at Castello d'Annone, a castle which the duke of Milan owns within a half league of Asti. Little by little about three hundred and fifty men-at-arms [of the French reinforcements] arrived there, as well as gentlemen from Dauphiné and some twenty-five hundred Swiss and some free archers from Dauphiné. There were in all about seventy-five hundred mercenaries, but they took a long time to arrive, and they were of no use toward the purpose for which they had been sent, which was to come to help the king; for instead of helping the king it was necessary to help them. And written word had been sent to my lord of Orleans and to the commanders that they should not undertake anything against the duke of Milan, but that they should concentrate only on guarding Asti and on coming as far as the river Ticino to meet the king and help him in his passage; for there was no other river to stop him. And one should understand that the duke of Orleans had not gone farther than Asti, and that the king had left him there. However, in spite of what the king had written him, he became most avid in the bargaining through which they gave up to him this city of Novara, which is within ten leagues of Milan; and he was received there with great joy by the Guelphs as well as the Ghibellines; and the marchioness of Monferrato helped considerably to bring this about.

The castle held out for two or three days [June 13–14]; but if, on the

241. Asti belonged to the duke of Orleans, as explained in n. 203 on p. 455. Here Commynes begins another of his jumps backwards in time. Having carried his account of the king's progress northward to late June, Commynes remembers that the fall of Novara to the duke of Orleans in mid-June introduced a whole new set of military considerations, and so in the last three paragraphs of this chapter he traces events in north Italy from March 31, 1495, when the Holy League was formed, to June 13, 1495, when Novara fell. See Bridge, *op. cit.*, II, 228–30, for the causes and significance of the quick victory gained at Novara.

other hand, he had gone or had sent men before Milan (where there was enough bargaining going on), he would have been received with greater joy than he ever was at his castle of Blois, as some of the highest-ranking persons of the duchy have told me. And he could have done this without danger during the first three days because the duke of Milan's men were still at Castello d'Annone near Asti when Novara was taken, and they came only four days later; but perhaps he did not believe the news which he received about it.

5

From Siena the king had come to Pisa, as you have seen, and you have heard what he did there; and from Pisa he came to Lucca [June 23], where he was well received by the townspeople; and he stayed there for two days; and then he came to Pietrasanta, which was held by Entragues. Neither he nor those upon whom he relied feared his enemies in any way. And between Lucca and this place he found some extraordinary passages through the mountains which were easy for infantrymen to defend. But they [the Italian infantry] were not together yet. Near Pietrasanta is the pass of the Serravezza with the Rotaio on one side and on the other very deep salt marshes; and one must pass along an embankment which is like those alongside pools; and that was the passage which extended from Pisa to Pontremoli, which I feared the most and about which I had heard the most, for a cart thrown across the path and two strong pieces of artillery would have prevented us from passing, and no one could have found a remedy for it with our small number of men.

From Pietrasanta the king proceeded to Sarzana, where the cardinal of Saint Peter in Chains urged him to foment revolt in Genoa and to send people there. And the matter was referred to the council (and I was there in the company of many persons of quality and commanders), where it was concluded by all that we should not agree to this; for if the king won the battle [which was about to take place between the French and the Holy League], Genoa would come and present itself on its own; and if he lost, he would have no use for it. And this was the first time that I had heard it mentioned that anyone believed that a battle would take place. And a report of this deliberation was made to the king; but all this notwithstanding, he sent there my lord of Bresse, who has since become duke of Savoy, the lord of Beaumont [John] of Polignac, my brother-in-law,[242] the lord of Aubijoux of the house of

242. Jean de Polignac's wife, Jeanne de Chambes, was the sister of Hélène de

Amboise with his twenty men-at-arms from the standing army, and fifteen hundred crossbowmen who came all fresh from France by sea. And I was amazed at how it was possible that such a young king did not have a few good servants who would have dared tell him in what peril he was putting himself. As far as I was concerned, it seemed to me that he believed nothing I said.

We had a small fleet which came from Naples, and in it was my lord of Miolans, governor of Dauphiné, as well as a certain Etienne de Nèves of Montpellier; and in all there were about eight galleys. And they came to La Spezia and to Rapallo, where they were defeated at the time of which I am speaking at the very place where our men had defeated King Alfonso's men at the beginning of the journey, and by the very people who had been on our side at the other battle, that is, Luigi Fieschi and Giovanni Adorno. And everything was taken to Genoa. It would have been better if everyone had been with us, for even so we would have been few. My lord of Bresse and the cardinal went to lodge in the suburbs of Genoa, believing that their partisans would rise up in their favor in the town; but the duke of Milan had provided for this, as well as the Adorni who governed and Giovan Luigi Fieschi who is a wise knight. And they were in great danger of being defeated as the fleet had been, considering the smallness of their number; and they would not have held out, had it not been for the fact that the party that was governing in Genoa did not dare leave the city, for fear that the Fregosi might rise and close the gates upon them. Our men had great difficulty in getting to Asti; they were not in a battle which the king fought [i.e., Fornovo] where they would have been very useful.

From Sarzana the king came to Pontremoli [June 29], for he was obliged to pass by there; it is the entrance to the mountains. The town and the castle were rather strong and in rugged country; and if there had been a sufficient number of people, it would not have been taken. But it seemed that what Brother Girolamo had told me was true: that God led him by the hand until he was safe; for it seemed that his enemies were blinded and stupefied, since they were not defending this pass.[243]

There were three or four hundred foot-soldiers inside. The king had sent his vanguard there, and it was led by Marshal de Gié; and with him was Gian Giacomo Trivulzio, whom he had taken over from the service of King Ferrandino when he fled from Naples, a gentleman from Milan

---

Chambes, Commynes' wife. The sole manuscript for Books 7 and 8, the Polignac manuscript (see p. 81), belonged to Jean de Polignac's daughter Anne.

243. As Mandrot points out, II, 251, n. 1, this blindness and stupefaction is explained, as far as Venetian forces go, by the Senate's stipulation that none of their army be risked beyond the northern side of the Apennines.

with noble family connections, a fine commander and a man of high estate, and a great enemy of the duke of Milan, who had exiled him to Naples; and by his means the place was straightway given up without a shot and the people left.

But a great disadvantage came about there, for the Swiss recalled how, the last time that the duke of Milan came there, a quarrel had taken place between those of the town and some Germans, as I already said, and at least forty of them were killed. And in spite of the surrender they killed in revenge all the men, pillaged the town, set it on fire, and burned provisions and everything else, including more than ten of their own men who were drunk; and the marshal could not help it. And they besieged the castle in order to take those who were inside, who were the servants of Gian Giacomo Trivulzio, and he had put them there when the others had left; and the king had to send word to them to make them leave. And the destruction of the place was a great pity, not only because of the shamefulness of it but because of [the waste of] the considerable provisions in it, which we already greatly lacked, although the people were not against us in any way except for those in the vicinity of this place [who were angry] because of the harm we were doing them.

But if the king had been willing to lend an ear to the overtures that Gian Giacomo was making, many places and gentlemen would have turned [to his side]; for he wanted the king to order hoisted everywhere the banner of the small son [Francesco II Sforza] whom Lodovico held in his hands, who was the son of the late duke who had died in Pavia, about whom you heard before, and whose name was Gian Galeazzo. But the king did not want [to do this] for love of my lord of Orleans, who laid claim to the duchy and still does. And the king proceeded beyond Pontremoli and went to take lodgings in a little valley where there were not even ten houses. I do not know its name. And he remained there for five days [July 2–5], although I could not tell why, and they experienced great famine, and within thirty miles of our vanguard, which had gone ahead; there were very high and very rugged mountains in the vicinity, and never had anyone carried large pieces of artillery over there, such as cannons and large culverins, which were passed there this time. Duke Galeazzo carried four falcons [small cannon] which probably weighed five hundred pounds at least, and the people of the region made much of that.[244]

244. "Duke Galeazzo" is Galeazzo-Maria Sforza, presumably, who was duke of Milan from 1466 to 1476. (See p. 416 above where Galeazzo-Maria Sforza is referred to as "Duke Galeazzo" in a list of the sovereigns who lived during Louis XI's time.) The Sauvage edition of 1552, which was based on a manuscript now lost, attaches

Book Eight

6

At this time of which I am speaking, we should speak of the duke of Orleans. After he had taken the castle of Novara, he wasted time there for a few days and then proceeded toward Vigevano. Two little towns which are nearby sent word to him in order to put him inside, but he did the wise thing in not accepting their offers. But those of Pavia sent word to him twice; in this case he should have listened. He found himself in a battle before Vigevano where all the army of the duke of Milan was stationed, and it was led by the sons of Sanseverino whom I have named so many times. The town is not worth as much as Candes-Saint-Martin, which is worthless; I was there shortly after the duke of Milan had been there and [shortly after] all the commanders who had been there [were there]. And they showed me the places where both of them had a battle. But they [the Milanese] were [stationed] right next to the city and inside it; and if the duke [of Orleans] had marched one hundred steps, they would have [been forced to] pass over the river Ticino. They had built a large bridge of boats over it, and they were on the edge; and I saw a bulwark of earth being dismantled which they had made on the bank of the river in order to defend the passage. And they had wanted to abandon the town and the castle, which would have been a great loss for them. And that is the place in the world where the duke of Milan stays most willingly, and it is the most beautiful spot for hunting and hawking of all sorts that I know anywhere.[245]

It seemed, perhaps, to my lord of Orleans that they were in a strong place and that he had done enough, and he retired to a place called Trecate; and the lord of the place, who held it from the duke of Milan, spoke to me a few days later. Some of the leading persons of Milan sent

---

the phrase "at this time of which I am speaking," ("durant ce jour que je diz") to this sentence rather than to the first sentence of chapter 6, and Calmette, II, 157, follows the Sauvage edition on this point. Such a construction makes good sense, perhaps better sense than the construction in the Polignac manuscript, for Commynes would in this case be commenting upon how the Italians living in the neighborhood were still talking about the duke of Milan's exploit in carrying the small cannon called falcons across the Apennines some twenty years later in 1495 "at this time of which I am speaking." If the phrase is attached to the beginning of chapter 6, as we have done in our translation, following the Polignac manuscript and Mandrot's edition, it makes good sense, too, for in this case Commynes would be calling attention to the contemporaneousness of the passing of the mountains and the battle of Vigevano.

245. Neither the date nor other circumstances of the battle of Vigevano are given by previous editors of the *Memoirs*. But see Francesco Guicciardini, *La Storia d'Italia*, ed. A. Gherardi (Florence, 1919), I, 122–24 (Book II, Chapter 6) for more details. It must have taken place between June 15 and July 1, to judge from Bridge's comments on subsequent events, *op. cit.*, II, 271.

word to the duke of Orleans at Trecate in order to put him in it, and they offered their children as hostages; and they would have done it easily, for some men who enjoyed great authority there and who knew this (although they [the duke of Orleans and his men] did not know it) told me so, saying that the duke of Milan would not have been able to find enough soldiers to allow himself to be besieged in his castle of Milan, and that the nobility and the people wanted the destruction of the house of Sforza. The duke of Orleans and his men also told me about these dealings which I have described but they did not have much faith in these people, and they lacked a man who understood them better than they did; and furthermore, his captains were not all of one mind.

Some two thousand Germans who were sent by the king of the Romans joined the duke of Milan's army, as well as some one thousand German horsemen led by Friedrich von Kappeller, a native of the county of Ferrette, and this made Galeazzo and the others take heart; and they went to Trecate to provoke the duke of Orleans to battle. He was advised not to fight, although his army was in better condition than the other. And perhaps the captains did not want to risk their army, fearing that if they lost it, this would mean the destruction of the king, of whom they had no news since the roads were guarded. And all this company retired to Novara, using very bad discipline in regard to their provisions, both as to preserving those which they had, and as to stocking wheat in the town. They could have obtained enough of it in the vicinity of the city without money, and afterwards they suffered greatly for lack of it. And their enemies took up quarters within a half league of their encampment.

7

I interrupted my account of the king at the time when he was in the valley on this side of Pontremoli, where he had stayed for five days in a state of great famine, although there was no necessity of doing so. Our Germans performed an honorable feat; it was the same people who had made that great error at Pontremoli (and they were afraid that the king might hate them forever on account of this), and they came of their own accord to offer to convey the artillery along this extraordinary path in the mountains. (I can call them mountains, because they are very high and steep, and there is no traveled path there; and I have seen all the principal ones of Italy and Spain, which would have been much easier to pass across.) And they made this offer on condition that the king should forgive them, which he did. And there were fourteen pieces of large and powerful artillery. As we left this valley, we began to climb up by a very steep path, and I saw some mules pass there with very great difficulty. These Germans coupled themselves two by two with strong cords, and they worked in groups of one hundred and two hundred at a time; and when they were tired, others came [to relieve them]. And as if this were not enough, the horses of the artillery were there too; and all the people from the king's household who had a [baggage-]train each lent one horse, in order to try and hasten the passage. But if it had not been for the Germans, the horses would never have passed along it.

And to be truthful, not only did they convey the artillery along, but if they had not been there, the [whole] company would never have got over. Of course, they were well assisted, for they were in as great need and had as great desire to get over as the others; and they made their full share of blunders, but the good made up for the bad. The worst was not to climb up, for immediately afterwards one would find a valley (for the path is such as nature made it, and nothing has been fixed up), and the horses and men, too, had to be put [in a position] to hold back against the reverse slope, and this was much more difficult by far than the hauling up, and at every moment carpenters or farriers were needed, or some piece or other fell which we had trouble getting back up. Many were of the opinion that all the large artillery should be broken in order to get across sooner; but the king would not consent to it for anything.

Marshal de Gié, who was thirty miles away from us, pressed the king to hurry; and we took three days to join him. And he had the enemy encamped before him in a beautiful field, within at least a half league from where he was; and they would have had an easy victory over him and then later over us, if they had made an assault. He was lodged at Fornovo (which means "a new hole"),[246] which is a fine village at the foot of the mountain and which is the entrance to the plain, in order to prevent them from coming to assail us on the mountain. But we had a better guard than he, for God had put another thought into the hearts of our enemies. For their avarice was so great that they wanted to wait for us in the plain so that nothing would escape [them]; for it seemed to them that from the mountains we might have been able to flee toward Pisa [and to fortify ourselves] in the places belonging to the Florentines. But they were mistaken, because we were too far [from the Florentine forts], and furthermore, since we would have waited until we had come to grips with them, they would have been able to pursue as fast as we could have fled, and they knew the paths better than we did.

246. The Italian word *foro* may mean "hole" or "forum." The latter is the correct meaning of Fornovo: "New Forum" (the town was Roman in origin).

Up to this point no combat had yet occurred in our area; but Marshal de Gié sent word to the king that he had passed the mountains and had sent out forty horsemen toward the enemy army to scout, and that they had been badly repulsed by the stradiots. And they killed a gentleman named Le Beuf; they cut off his head, attached it to the banner of a lance, and brought it to their *provveditore*, in order to obtain a ducat from him.

Stradiots are soldiers like jennetaries[247] and they are dressed, whether on foot or on horseback, in the manner of the Turks except for the head, on which they do not wear the cloth which they call a turban; and they are hardy people and they sleep in the open all year around, as do their horses. They were all Greek, and they all came from the places which the Venetians own in Greece—some from Nauplia in Argolis in the Morea and others from Albania around Durazzo; and their horses are strong and are all Turkish horses. The Venetians make good use of them and they trust them. I had seen them all arrive in Venice and appearing for the muster in an island where the abbey of Saint Nicholas is located, and there must have been about fifteen hundred of them. They are valiant men, and they cause infinite worry to an army.

The stradiots pursued [our men], as I said, up to the marshal's lodgings where the Germans were quartered, and they killed three or four and took away their heads, for such was their custom. For when the Venetians were at war with the Turk named Mohammed the Ottoman, the father of the present Turk, he did not want his men to take any prisoners; and he gave them a ducat for each head and the Venetians did the same. And I believe indeed that they wanted to frighten the company, as they did. But the stradiots were also very frightened by the artillery, for a falcon fired a shot and killed one of their horses and this made them immediately retire, for they were not used to this. And as they were retiring, they took prisoner one of our German captains, who had mounted his horse to see whether they were retiring and had received a blow across his body from their lances, for he was unarmed. He is a wise man, and he was brought before the marquis of Mantua, who was the commander-in-chief of the Venetians; also present were his uncle, Lord Rodolfo of Mantua, and the count of Caiazzo, who was commander by appointment of the duke of Milan, and he knew the captain well. And one should understand that all their army was in the fields, at least that part that was assembled, for all the troops had not

247. "Jennetaries" ("genetaires") are light-armed soldiers who ride jennets, small Arabian horses common in Spain in Commynes' time and later. The Spanish, according to Mandrot, II, 257, n. 3, called Turkish and Moorish knights "jennetaries."

arrived yet; and they had been assembled there for eight days. And the king might well have retired to France without danger, if it had not been for these long stays of which you have heard, which served no purpose; but Our Lord had ordered otherwise.

8

The marshal, who was afraid of being assailed, went up into the mountains. He had about one hundred and sixty men-at-arms, as he told me at the time, and eight hundred Germans, and no more; and he could not expect help from us, because we arrived there only one-and-a-half days later, on account of this artillery; and the king lodged in the houses of two petty marquises on the way.

Once the vanguard had climbed the mountain in order to wait for those whom they saw in the fields, who were rather far, they were not without worry.[248] God, however, who always wanted to save [our] company, dulled the sense of the enemy once more. And our German was questioned by the count of Caiazzo as to who was leading this vanguard; he [the German] named the person to him. He inquired further about the number of our men, although he knew all this better than we did, since he had been fighting on our side during the whole campaign. The German represented the company as a strong one, and said that it consisted of three hundred men-at-arms and fifteen hundred Swiss. And the count replied to him that he was lying and that in the whole army there were only three thousand Swiss and that therefore we would not have sent half of them there. And he was sent as a prisoner to the marquis of Mantua's pavilion; and they spoke among themselves of assailing the marshal. And the marquis believed the number quoted by the German, saying that they [the Holy League] did not have infantrymen as good as our Germans, and also that all their [the Holy League's] soldiers had not arrived, and that to fight without them was to wrong them greatly; and if they were repulsed, the [Venetian]

248. The Polignac manuscript, most previous editions, and most translations give the reading "in order to reach" ("pour atteindre") and not "in order to wait for" ("pour attendre"). But the last thing Marshal de Gié wanted to do was to reach the Italian army gathered in the fields below him. His best means of defense was to wait for the Italians to venture into the hills above the valley where he was stationed, for there the Italians' superior numbers would count for less. "Those whom they saw in the fields" must refer to the fields below holding the Italian army, and not to any fields above in the mountains holding the French army, for Commynes has just used the phrase "in the fields" ("aux champs") with reference to the Italian army in the last paragraph of chapter 7. The French army, as he tells us in the first paragraph of chapter 8, was too far away to be seen. We have accordingly emended the text here. (Mandrot has printed "attendre" ["wait for"] without comment, II, 259.)

Signoria might be angry at this, and that it would be better to wait for them in the plain, and anyway, they [the French] could not avoid passing in front of them. And the two *provveditori* agreed with him, and they would not have dared argue against their opinion.

Others said that if their vanguard were broken, the king would be taken. However, everyone easily agreed to wait for the company in the plain, and it seemed to them indeed that no one could escape them. And I learned this from the very persons whom I have named, and we had a talk about this afterwards, Marshal de Gié and I, when we met together with them. And so they retired to their camp, resting assured that by the next day or so the king would have passed the mountain and that he would be lodged in the village called Fornovo. And in the meantime all the rest of their men arrived; and we could not avoid passing right in front of them because the place was so narrow.

When we came down the mountain, we saw the plain of Lombardy, which is among the most beautiful and the finest in the world and among the most populated. And although it is said to be a plain, it is hard to ride through because it is as full of ditches as Flanders, or even more so; but it is much better and more fertile in good wheat as well as in good wines and fruit; and they never let their land lie fallow. And it was a great comfort to us to see it, because of the great hunger and suffering which we had endured along the way since our departure from Lucca. But the artillery gave us considerable trouble to get it down because the path was so steep and difficult. And from the top we saw the enemy camp in which there were a large number of tents and pavilions and it seemed to be very large, and indeed it was; and the Venetians made good what they had told the king through me, when they said that they and the duke of Milan would put forty thousand men in the field; for if they were not that many there, they were not far from it, including at least thirty-five thousand mercenaries; but out of every five, four were from [Venice, the republic of] Saint Mark. And there were about twenty-six hundred men-at-arms in armor, each of whom had a crossbowman on horseback or another man in equipment with him, making a total of four horses for one man-at-arms.[249]

---

249. Italian lance-teams, in contrast to the French, consisted of four men rather than six (see p. 112, n. 23). Commynes' estimate of the size of the Italian army—10,400 men in the lance-teams, 5,000 stradiots or light-horsemen, and some 25,000 infantrymen—is compared by Bridge, *op. cit.*, II, 285–87, with those of other contemporary writers, whose estimates vary from 30,000 to 60,000 men, as compared with Commynes' 40,000. Bridge makes no explicit estimate himself, although he appears to favor the lower figure of 30,000, as does Delaborde, *op. cit.*, p. 634 (see n. 195, p. 447, for full citation of this work).

They had five thousand men who were either stradiots or light-horse-men; the rest of them were infantrymen, and they were lodged in a strong place which was well set up and well supplied with artillery.

9

The king descended from the mountain about noon, and went to lodge in the village of Fornovo; and it was the fifth day of July on a Sunday in the year 1495 when he took these lodgings; and there were great quantities of flour and wines and food for the horses. The people gave us a warm welcome everywhere (and moreover, no man of good standing did them any harm), and they brought provisions such as bread, which was small and very dark—and they sold it at a high price, and [they added] three parts of water to the wine—and some fruit, and gave pleasure to the army.

I had some things bought, but I had them try them out in front of me; for we strongly suspected that they had left this food there in order to poison the army and at first we did not touch it. And two Swiss killed themselves from drinking too much. They caught cold and died in a cave, and this made the people even more suspicious. But before it was midnight, the horses started first, and then the people, and then every-one was much relieved. And on this occasion one must give honor to the Italians, for we did not find that they had used any poison; and if they had wanted to do it, we could hardly have been able to protect ourselves against it during this journey.

We arrived, as you have heard, on a Sunday at noon, and many a man of high rank ate a piece of bread at the place where the king stayed and drank; and I believe that there was hardly any other food to be had at the time, because we did not yet dare eat the food of the locality.

Immediately after dinner some stradiots came and charged into the camp and gave us a great alarm, for our men did not know them yet. And the whole army sallied out to the fields in exceptionally good order and in three divisions: vanguard, main corps, and rear guard, and there was not a stone's throw from one division to the other, and they could easily have come to each other's help. It was nothing and we retired to our lodgings; and soon another alarm or two was sounded before it was night. We had a small number of tents and pavilions, and our encampment extended close to theirs; and therefore only twenty stradiots were sufficient to give us an alarm, and they never left [the vicinity of] our outermost lodgings, for there was a wood, and they came under its cover.

And we were in a valley between two small hills and in this valley flowed a river which was fordable except when it flooded, which happens easily and often in this region, although it does not last long; they call these rivers torrents. The valley was full of gravel and large stones and [thus it was] difficult for the horses. The valley was about a quarter of a league wide and on one of the small hills which was at the right our enemies were quartered, and we were forced to pass in front of them with the river between us; and their camp was about half a league away. And there was indeed another way to go up the hill on the left, for we were encamped on their side; but it would have seemed as if we were drawing back.[250]

About two days earlier it had been suggested to me that I should go and speak to them (for fear was beginning to take hold of the wisest), and that I should take someone with me to make a good count and to obtain some knowledge of their affairs. I did not undertake this willingly, and in any case I could not go there without a safe-conduct. But I replied that I had worked out an understanding with the *provveditori* at my departure from Venice on the night when I arrived in Padua,[251] and that I thought that they would probably speak to me at a point halfway between the two camps. And anyway, if I offered to go [all the way] to them, I would encourage them too much; and [besides] they had told me this too late.

On that Sunday of which I am speaking I wrote to the two *provveditori* (one was named Luca Pisani, and the other Marco Trevisano); and I begged them that one of them might come to speak to me on the strength of a safe-conduct, as had been offered to me at my departure from Padua, as was said before. They replied that they would have done so willingly if it had not been for the war which had been started against the duke of Milan, but that in spite of this, one of them or both, according to whatever they would decide, would be in some locality midway [between the two camps].[252] And I received this answer that

250. See the map of the terrain surrounding Fornovo at the head of this volume. Commynes seems to contradict himself in this sentence by saying first that the Taro River was between the armies and then that the French were encamped on the same side of the valley (which is divided in two by the river) as the army of the Holy League was. The river, however, takes a meandering path, passing very close to the hills on the left just north of Fornovo and then moving to almost the exact center of the valley some three miles northeast of Fornovo. Fornovo is on the right bank, and thus the French and Italian armies were encamped on the same side, the right bank. But those in the French army hoped to pass in the face of the enemy to the *other* side of the river, moving northward down the valley and keeping the river between the two armies.

251. See p. 508 above.

252. Mandrot, II, 264, n. 3, basing himself on Sanudo, *op. cit.*, reports the contents

Sunday night. None of the persons in authority attached any importance to it. I was afraid to undertake too much, and I thought that it might be taken for cowardice if I insisted too much, and so I let the matter stand for that night, although I would willingly have helped to get the king and his company out of there if I had been able to do so without danger.

About midnight the cardinal of Saint-Malo, who had just spoken to the king (and my pavilion was near his), told me that the king would leave the next morning and would pass along their side, and would have a few cannonshots fired in their camp as an act of bravado, and would then proceed ahead without stopping there. And I well believe that this was his own suggestion, one of a man who knew little about discussing such a matter and who was not familiar with the case. It would have been fitting if the king had gathered around him wiser men and commanders, and if he had taken advice; but I have seen a meeting called only three times during this expedition, and then the measures taken were the opposite of what was decided there. I told the cardinal that if we came so close as to shoot in their camp, it would be impossible that people would not sally forth to skirmish, and it would never be possible to retire to one side or the other without coming to a battle; and furthermore it would be contrary to what I had started [with the *provveditori*].

And I was most displeased that things were going this way; but at the beginning of the reign of this king my affairs had been such that I did not dare intervene strongly, so as not to make enemies of those to whom he gave authority, which was so great, when he decided to give it, that it was truly excessive. That night we had two other great alarms, all because we had not secured ourselves against these stradiots, as we should have and as we are accustomed to do against light cavalry, for twenty of our men-at-arms with their archers always stopped two hundred of them; but this was still a novelty. And that night there was great rain, lightning, and thunder, so strong that one could not imagine more; it seemed that heaven and earth were splitting, or that it signified a great misfortune to come. We were also at the foot of these large mountains and in a hot region and in summer; and although it was a natural thing, it was still terrifying to be in this peril and to see so many people before us, and not to be able to pass any other way than by fighting, and to see ourselves so small a company; for we had no more than nine thousand men, partly good and partly bad, and I include two

_____

of Commynes' letter to the *provveditori*, which was sent on to Venice, and also reports the greeting which Commynes' overture received in the enemy camp.

thousand followers and servants of the high-ranking people of the army. I do not include pages and stablemen, and such persons.[253]

10

On Monday morning at about seven o'clock on the sixth day of July in the year 1495 the king mounted on horseback and had me called several times. I came to him and found him all armed and mounted on the most beautiful horse which I have ever seen in my time; it was called Savoie. Many persons said that it was a horse from Bresse; Duke Charles of Savoy had given it to him. It was black and had only one eye, of medium size and a good size for the one who was riding it. And it seemed that this young man was entirely different from that suggested by his nature, his appearance, or his character. For he is rather fearful when he speaks even today (besides, he had been raised in great fear); and he is a small person and this horse made him appear tall; and he had a kind face and good coloring and his words were bold and wise. And it seemed indeed—and I remember that Brother Girolamo told me the truth [when he said]—that God was leading him by the hand and that he would have difficulties on the way but that honor would remain with him. And the king told me that if these people wanted to have a parley, then I should speak; and since the cardinal was present, he designated him and Marshal de Gié (which was hardly possible, because on that morning he was still leading the vanguard: this was because of a dissension which had taken place between the counts of Narbonne and Guise, who had occasionally led some units; and each one said that it behooved him to lead the vanguard). I replied to him: "Sire, I shall be happy to do it; but I have never seen two such large companies so close to each other depart without fighting."

All this army had come forth on this bank [of the river], and they were in order of battle and close to each other, as they were on the previous day; but to me the forces seemed to be very small compared to those which I had seen under Duke Charles of Burgundy and under the king his father [Louis XI]. And on the bank we drew aside, the cardinal and I, and dictated a letter to the two above-mentioned *provveditori* (which was written by [Florimond] Robertet, one of the king's secretaries, whom he trusted), in which the cardinal said that it behooved him, in view of his office and estate, to bring about peace, and that the same was true of me, since I was an ambassador recently ar-

---

253. Bridge, *op. cit.*, II, 285–86, and Delaborde, *op. cit.*, p. 634, both argue on the basis of other contemporary estimates that the French numbered closer to 10,000 than to 9,000 fighting men.

rived from Venice and had already begun to be a mediator; he explained
to them that the king wanted only to be on his way and that he did not
want to harm anyone, and that therefore, if they wanted to come to
talk, as had been undertaken the day before, we would be pleased and
we would do everything [to achieve this].

Skirmishers had already appeared on both sides; and as we proceeded
step by step on our way, passing in front of them with the river between
us, as I said[254] (there must have been a quarter of a league between us
and them; and they were drawn up in order in their camp, for it is their
custom to choose an encampment large enough so that all of them can
be assembled in it in order of battle), they sent part of their stradiots
and crossbowmen on horseback and some men-at-arms, who came
along a rather covered path, entered the village [Fornovo] which we

254. See n. 250. The French must have already forded the river and have arrived
on the left bank at the time to which Commynes is referring in this paragraph. The
reason why the Italians allowed the French to ford the river rather than attacking
them before they crossed or as they crossed it is probably the nature of the terrain,
as the map at the head of this volume shows. Having crossed the river at the village
of Bernini (there is a convenient fording place at this point, according to Mandrot,
II, 269, n. 3), the French army found itself at the point where the Taro River passes
most closely to the hills on the left side of the valley. Thus the French were wedged
in between hill and river and could not maneuver to good effect, while the Italian
skirmishers were able to come up along the "covered path" (see text above) along
the right bank near Fornovo, pass the river, and move up into the hills on the left
bank where Charles VIII had placed the baggage train, out of the way of the troops
yet moving parallel to the troops as they proceeded down the valley. As Commynes
tells us in the next paragraph, the main body of the Italians was also able to cross
the river and to attack the French rear with little fear of effective counterattack,
both because the narrowness of space allowed little maneuvering and because the
French had placed their most capable troops not in the rear but in the vanguard.
To keep the vanguard engaged, a body of Italians under the command of the count
of Caiazzo passed down the valley on the right bank, crossed the river at a fording
place near the village of Oppiano, and attacked the French in front. Such is the
conjecture of Delaborde, *op. cit.*, p. 641, n. 1, and it is certainly one which makes
sense out of Commynes' elliptic description of the battle here and in chapter 11. This
is why Commynes concludes this paragraph by saying that "at the pass," that is, the
narrow area between river and hill on the left bank of the Taro near Bernini, the
French were assailed "all around"—by the count of Caiazzo in front, by stradiots
and crossbowmen in the hills on one side, by the impassable river (at the point
where they were) on the other side, and by the marquis of Mantua in the rear. It
is interesting to note that Delaborde, who offers one of the most detailed modern
accounts of the battle, considers Commynes' account the "clearest" of all contemporary sources (*op. cit.*, p. 646, n. 1). Both Delaborde and Bridge, *op. cit.*, II,
249 ff. (whose account and map of the battle rival Delaborde's in detail), make full
use of the other contemporary sources, which are conveniently listed in Mandrot, II,
269, n. 4. This interpretation of the strategy of the Italians at Fornovo accords well
with the praise of Commynes, who says later in this paragraph that the enemy
could not have ordered their battle formation better than they did. It conflicts with
the interpretation of other historians, however, such as Bridge, *op. cit.*, II, 257-58,
who criticizes the Italian leaders harshly.

were leaving, and passed there this little river in order to come and assail our baggage-train, which was large; and I believe that six thousand pack animals passed—mules, horses, and donkeys. And several days in advance they had ordered their battle formation so well that nothing better could be said about it, and in such a way that, relying on their great number, they assailed the king and his army all around, so that not a single man would have been able to escape if we had been routed at the pass where we were engaged. For the people whom I have mentioned charged upon our baggage.

From the left side came the marquis of Mantua and his uncle, Lord Rodolfo, Count Bernardino di Montone [called Fortebrazzi], and all the flower of their army, which included six hundred men-at-arms, as they told me since. They came and threw themselves upon the [left] bank directly at our rear, and they were all men-at-arms in armor with fine plumes and beautiful *bordonasses* [long lances with strong wooden handles], well accompanied by crossbowmen on horseback, stradiots, and infantrymen. The count of Caiazzo came to place himself facing Marshal de Gié and our vanguard, with about four hundred men-at-arms accompanied as above and with a great number of infantrymen. Near him was another company of about two hundred men-at-arms, under the command of the son of Giovanni di Bentivoglio of Bologna, a young man without experience (and they were in as great need of leaders as we were); and he was to charge on the vanguard after the count of Caiazzo. And in like manner there was a similar company following the marquis of Mantua to serve a similar purpose, which was led by a person named Antonio d'Urbino, illegitimate son of the late duke of Urbino. And two large companies remained in their camp. I learned this from them, for on the very next day I spoke to them and I saw it with my own eyes. And the Venetians did not want to hazard everything at once, nor to leave their camp unguarded; it would have been better for them, however, to have put all their forces in the field, since they were the ones to begin.

I shall leave this subject for awhile in order to say what became of the letter we had sent, the cardinal and I, by a trumpeter. It was received by the *provveditori*; and after they had read it our artillery, which had not yet fired, began to fire the first shot; and immediately [afterwards] their [artillery], which was not nearly as good as ours, fired [back]. The *provveditori* immediately sent back our trumpeter, and the marquis sent one of his, and they sent word that they would be happy to have a parley but that we should have the artillery cease fire and they would have theirs do the same.

At the time I was far from the king, who was coming and going, and he sent the two trumpeters back to report that he would have everything cease; and he sent the master of the artillery the following message: "Do not fire any more." And everything ceased on both sides for a while. Then suddenly theirs fired a shot, and ours started [firing] again more than before; and they moved up three pieces of artillery; and when our two trumpeters arrived, they took ours and sent him to the tent of the marquis [of Mantua] and decided to fight.[255] And as those who were present told me, the count of Caiazzo said that this was no time to talk and that we were already half vanquished. And one of the *provveditori* who told me about it agreed with this and the other did not; the marquis agreed with it and his uncle who was good and wise contradicted them with all his might; he liked us and it was with great regret that he was against us. In the end all of them came to agree.

11

Now it should be understood that the king had put all his strength in his vanguard, where there were about three hundred and fifty men-at-arms and three thousand Swiss who were the hope of the army. And the king had three hundred archers from his guard march on foot with them, which was a great loss for him, and some mounted crossbowmen from the two hundred which he had in his guard. There were few other foot-soldiers, but those who were available were put there. And marching on foot with the Germans were my lord Engilbert of Cleves, the duke of Cleves's brother, Lornay, and the bailiff of Dijon, leader of the Germans; and in front of them was the artillery. Here we were in great need of those whom we had left in the territories of the Florentines and those whom we had sent to Genoa, contrary to everybody's opinion. This vanguard had already advanced as far as their camp, and it was believed that they would start [to attack us] there, and that was why the vanguard was made so strong.[256] The other two parts of our army

255. In this sentence Commynes refers to one thing with the word "our" and to another thing with the word "ours." "Our two trumpeters" refers to the trumpeter representing the cardinal and Commynes and to the trumpeter representing the marquis of Mantua. "Ours" seems to refer only to the trumpeter representing the cardinal and Commynes, whom "they," the Italians, took prisoner. Calmette, III, 180, n. 6, asserts that three trumpeters are mentioned in this sentence—the third one, "ours," representing Commynes exclusively—but this seems implausible since Commynes twice asserts in this paragraph that there were two trumpeters, not three.

256. That is, the French vanguard had reached a point on the left bank of the Taro River opposite the village of Giarola on the right bank, outside which the Italian army was encamped, according to Bridge, *op. cit.*, II, 249. The French mistook the Italian strategy described in n. 254 entirely, believing that the Italians would try to bar their further progress down the valley rather than that they would

[main corps and rear guard] were not so close nor so well placed to help each other as they had been on the previous day. And since the marquis had already arrived at the bank and had passed the river to our side and was exactly behind our backs about a quarter of a league behind our rear guard (and they came with small steps, very close together, and so well that it was a beautiful sight to behold), the king was forced to turn his back on his vanguard, face his enemies, move toward his rear guard, and recede from the vanguard. I was with my lord the cardinal at the time, waiting for an answer, and I told him that I could see that there was no more time to waste there, and I went to the place where the king was (and I left the proximity of the Swiss); and on the way I lost a page who was my first cousin and a *valet de chambre* and a lackey, who were following me at a small distance; and I did not see them killed.

I had not taken a hundred steps when some noise began [in the area] from whence I came, or at least [from a place] a little bit behind [me]. It was the stradiots, who were among the baggage and at the king's quarters, where there were three or four houses, and they killed or wounded four or five men; the rest escaped. They killed at least one hundred stablemen and they put the baggage-train in great disorder. When I arrived where the king was, I found him knighting some people; and the enemy was already very close to him; and he was made to stop. And I heard Matthew the bastard of Bourbon, who had credit with the king as did a person named Philippe du Moulin, a mere gentleman but a man of quality, both of whom called to the king, saying: "Come, sir, come!" And they had him come to the front of his main corps before his battle-standard; and I did not see any man closer to the enemy except the bastard (and it happened in an instant, and I arrived less than a quarter of an hour before), and the enemies were within one hundred steps of the king, who was thus poorly guarded and attended. His predecessors did not go to battle in such a manner; they were better guarded. In short, the one whom God guards is well guarded, and Brother Girolamo's prophecy according to which God led him by the hand was indeed true.

His rear guard was on his right-hand side, a little bit to the rear, and those who were the closest to him on that side were Robinet de Framezelles, who was leading the duke of Orleans' men, about eighty lance-

---

attack the French rear. In fact, the French were lucky to be almost penned in geographically and to be attacked from the rear. For in this relatively narrow space the Italians' superior numbers and light cavalry availed little, while the qualities of fierce hand-to-hand fighting in a melee, which French men-at-arms traditionally cultivated, possessed their full effectiveness.

teams, and the lord of La Trémoïlle, who had about forty lance-teams. The one hundred Scottish archers were there too, and they put themselves in the battle-line like men-at-arms. I was on the left side, where the gentlemen of twenty *écus* were and the others from the king's household and the gentlemen-pensioners.[257] For the sake of brevity I shall not name the captains, but the count of Foix was the leader of this rear guard.

As I said, a quarter of an hour after I had arrived, while the king was near them, the enemies laid their lances in rest and came on at an easy gallop, charging upon two companies. Our two companies on the right and the Scottish archers charged upon the enemy at almost the same time, and so did the king. Those on the left side, where I was, charged upon them from the side, which was a great advantage. And no one in the world could have attacked more boldly than both sides did. Their stradiots, who were at their rear, saw the mules with the baggage flee toward our vanguard and realized that their companions were winning. All of them went in that direction without following their men-at-arms, who were not attended, for certainly if fifteen hundred light-horsemen had mingled among us, with their scimitars (which are terrible swords) in their fists, they would have routed us beyond repair, considering the small number of our forces. God gave us this help, and once these lance-blows were over all the Italians began to flee, and their infantrymen or most of them rushed toward the hill.

At the same moment as they were attacking us, the count of Caiazzo attacked the vanguard; but they did not mingle together so closely, for when the time came to lay lances in rest, they took fear and broke up in disorder by themselves. The Germans took fifteen or twenty of them by their bridles and killed them. The rest fled, poorly pursued, for the marshal was taking great pains to keep his company together since he saw a large company still rather close to him. They pursued some of them, however, and part of those fleeing men came along the path on which we had fought by the bank, their swords in hand since their lances had been thrown away.

Now you should know that those who assailed the king immediately began to flee, and they were pursued most diligently, for everyone went after them. Some took the path of the village from which we had left, and others took the shortest way to their camp. And everyone pursued them except the king. He remained with few people, [and so] he put himself in great peril by not having come along with us. One

257. See n. 240 on p. 511 for a commentary on the three kinds of elite troops mentioned in this sentence. The mounted Scottish archers formed still another part of the king's household troops.

of the first men to be killed was Lord Rodolfo of Mantua, the marquis'
uncle, who was supposed to send word to Antonio d'Urbino when it
was time for him to march; they thought that the thing would last [a
considerable time], as their Italian battles do. The said Antonio used
this as an excuse; but I think that he saw no signs to make him come.

We had a great retinue of valets and servants, who were all around
these Italian men-at-arms, and they killed most of those who died. And
almost all of them had in their hands hatchets used for cutting wood
with which they built our lodgings, and with them they broke the
visors of the helmets, and they hit them strongly on the head. And they
were not easy to kill, because they were so strongly armored; and I
have not seen one person killed who was not surrounded by three or
four men. In addition the long swords which our archers and servants
had were very effective. The king remained for a time at the place
where he had been assailed, and said that he did not want to pursue or
to proceed toward the vanguard, which seemed to have drawn back. He
had ordered seven or eight young gentlemen to remain near him. He had
escaped the first charge well, considering that he was in the front line,
for the bastard of Bourbon was taken less than twenty steps from him
and brought to the enemy camp.

12

Now the king was in the place which I mentioned, and in such small
company that he had no one to attend him except a *valet de chambre*
named Antoine des Aubus, a small man poorly armed; and the others
were rather dispersed, as the king told me that very evening in their
presence; and they should have been much ashamed of themselves to
have left him thus. However, they still came to him in time, for a small
band of men-at-arms who were among the defeated, proceeding along
the bank which they saw clear of people, came to assail the king and
this *valet de chambre*. The king had the best horse in the world for himself; and he moved around and defended himself. And some of his other
men, who were not very far from him, arrived at that moment and the
Italians began to flee. And the king followed the advice [that was given
to him] and proceeded to the vanguard, which had never moved, and
that was a lucky thing for the king. But [on the other hand] if it [the
vanguard] had advanced one hundred steps, all the army of the enemy
would have fled. Some said that it should do so and others that it
should not.

Our group, which was pursuing [those who fled], went almost as far
as the edge of their camp, moving toward Fornovo, and I did not see

any of our men receive a blow except Julien Bournel, whom I saw drop dead, felled by an Italian who was passing; he was poorly armed. And there we stopped, saying: "Let us go to the king!" And upon these words everyone stopped to let the horses catch their breath; and they were very tired, for they had run for a long time across difficult paths and stony land. A group of some thirty fleeing men-at-arms passed near us; and we asked nothing of them. And we were afraid.

As soon as the horses had caught their breath a bit, we started to go to the king although we did not know where he was, and we went along at a good trot. And we were hardly on our way when we saw him from afar, and we had the valets dismount and gather lances in the field, and there were many of them, especially *bordonasses*, which were not worth much and which were hollow and light and did not weigh as much as a javelin, but they were well painted, and we were better supplied with lances than in the morning. And we moved directly toward the king, and on the way we found a number of their infantrymen who were crossing the field. They were some of those who had hidden in the hills and whom the marquis had led against the king. Many were killed; others escaped and crossed the river; we did not waste much time there. Several times some people had shouted as they were fighting: "Remember Guinegatte!" It referred to a battle against the king of the Romans in the days of King Louis XI which was lost because of having spent time in pillaging the baggage.[258] But here nothing was taken or pillaged.

Their stradiots took from the pack animals anything they wanted, but they carried off only fifty-five of the best and most elegantly covered ones among them, such as those of the king and all his chamberlains and one of the king's *valets de chambre* named Gabriel, who was carrying on his person the relics which had belonged to the kings for a long time; and he led these pack animals because they carried the king's bed. A great number of other coffers were lost there and thrown away and robbed by our own men; but the enemy obtained only what I mentioned. In our company was a large following of men and women vagrants on foot who stripped the dead.

On one side and the other (I believe that what I say about it is close to the truth, since I was informed on both sides), we lost Julien Bournel, the captain of the king's gate [Colinet du Gal], and a gentleman of twenty *écus*; nine of the Scottish archers died, and we lost about twenty of the other horsemen of this vanguard, and around the pack animals, sixty or eighty stablemen. The enemy lost three hundred and fifty men-at-arms who died on the spot, and never was anyone taken prisoner,

258. See p. 394 ff. for Commynes' description of the battle of Guinegatte.

which perhaps had never happened before in a battle. Few stradiots died, for they spent their time pillaging; and in all about thirty-five hundred men died, as many of the highest-ranking people from their side have told me (others have told me that it was more); but several worthy people died there, and I saw a list of them with up to eighteen important persons, among whom were four or five by the name of Gonzaga, which is the name of the marquis [of Mantua]. And he lost there at least sixty men-at-arms who were gentlemen from his territories. And among all these men was not a single infantryman.[259]

And it is noteworthy that so many people were killed in hand-to-hand fighting, for I do not believe that the artillery on both sides killed ten men, and the combat did not last a quarter of an hour; for as soon as they had broken or thrown away their lances, everyone fled. The pursuit lasted about three quarters of an hour. Their battles in Italy are not usually so fast, for they fight squadron by squadron, and it sometimes lasts all day without one side or the other winning.

The flight was great on their side, and about three hundred men-at-arms and most of their stradiots fled. Some fled to Reggio Emilia, which is rather far from there; others went to Parma, which is about eight leagues away. And at the moment when the troops thus encountered each other that morning the count of Pitigliano and Lord Virginio Orsini fled from us, but the latter went only to the house of a gentleman; and they were there on the strength of their word of honor. But it is true that they were greatly wronged. The count proceeded directly to the enemy. He was a man who was well known to the men-at-arms, for he had always had a command from the Florentines as well as from King Ferrandino and he began to shout "Pitigliano, Pitigliano!" and went after those who were fleeing, for when he arrived there they were loading up the tents in their camp. And there were a great number of loaded mules. He went after the fleeing men more than three leagues, shouting that everything was theirs, and that they should come to get the loot, and he brought back most of them and reassured them; and if he had not been there, everyone would have fled. And it was of no small comfort to them that such a man had parted with us. And he

259. Bridge, *op. cit.*, II, 287, after weighing contemporary evidence, concludes that Commynes exaggerates the Italian losses a bit while minimizing the French. He concludes that "the Italians lost 3,000 men at the least and the French 200 at the most. . . ." But Commynes' exaggerations are as nothing compared to the reports shortly afterwards sent out from the Italian camp about their "victory" at Fornovo. The notion of victory was zealously fostered by the marquis of Mantua who vowed on the battlefield, he said, to commission a votive altarpiece to the Virgin should he win, a vow to which we owe Andrea Mantegna's great altarpiece, "La Madonna della Vittoria." See Mandrot, II, 304, n. 1, and Benedetti, *op. cit.*, p. 231, n. 37, for these Italian reports.

proposed to assail us that night, but they would hear none of it. He has told me since, and the marquis of Mantua has told me too, that it was he who proposed this; but to speak the truth, if it had not been for the count, they would all have fled that night.

As everyone was assembled near the king, a great number of men-at-arms could be seen drawing up in order of battle outside their camp, and only their heads and their lances were visible, and also some infantrymen, and they had always been there. But the distance was greater than was apparent, and it would have been necessary once more to pass the river, which had swelled and was still swelling, for all day there had been thunder and lightning, and it had rained heavily, and especially during the combat and the pursuit. The king brought before the council the question of whether he should march against them or not. With him were three Italian knights; one was Gian Giacomo Trivulzio, who is still alive and who conducted himself well that day; the second was named Francesco Secco, a very valiant knight in the pay of the Florentines, a man of seventy-two; the third was Camillo Vitelli. He and his three brothers were in the pay of the king and although he had not been sent for, he had come there from Citta di Castello to near Sarzana, which is a great distance, in order to take part in the battle. And when he saw that he could not reach the king with his company Camillo came there alone.

These two [sic] were of the opinion that we should march against those whom we could still see. The Frenchmen who were asked about this did not agree and said that we had accomplished enough and that it was getting late and that we should retire to our lodgings. Francesco Secco gave strong support to his opinion; he pointed out the people coming and going along a big road which led to Parma, which is the closest town to which they retreated, and said that they were fugitives or people who were returning after having fled. And from what we learned since, he was speaking the truth, and his words and countenance were those of a bold and wise knight; and if we had marched ahead, everyone would have fled (and all the leaders have admitted this to me, and one of them did so in front of the duke of Milan), and this would have been the greatest and most profitable victory which would have taken place in the last two hundred years. For if we had known how to make good use of it and to make our profit and to conduct ourselves wisely and to treat the people properly, eight days later the duke of Milan would have had nothing left, in the best of cases, except the castle of Milan, judging from the desire which his subjects had of turning [against him]. And it would have been the same with the Venetians and there would have been no need to worry about Naples, for the

Venetians would have been unable to assemble men except in Venice, Brescia, and Cremona, which is only a small town; they would have lost everything else [which they held on the mainland] in Italy. But God had done to us what Brother Girolamo had told me: honor had remained with us. For when we consider the little sense and order that was among us, we were not deserving of such advantages, for we would not have known how to make use of them then. But I believe that if at this time, which is the year 1497, such an advantage were to come to the king, he would know how to manage it better.

While we were discussing this, night was approaching and the company that was before us retired to their field, and we retired to our side. We went to take lodgings a quarter of a league from the place where the battle had been, and the king stayed in a farm or rural house which was poorly built, but there was an infinite amount of wheat in sheaves from which the whole army benefited. There were a few other small houses nearby which were of little use, for everyone lodged as best he could without taking formal quarters. I remember well how I slept in a vineyard, closely pressed upon the earth without any other shelter and without a coat; for the king had borrowed mine in the morning, and my pack animals were rather far, and it was too late to go and look for them. Those who had some food had a meal; but very few had any, unless it was a piece of bread taken out of the mouth of a valet. I saw the king in his room, where there were wounded men such as the seneschal of Lyon and others whom he had cared for and he was in a cheerful mood. And everyone estimated that he had had a good bargain; and we were not so proud as we were shortly before the battle when we saw the enemy near us. That night all of our Germans were on patrol, and the king gave them three hundred *écus*; and they watched well, and beat their drums well.

13

The next morning I decided to continue with our negotiations for an agreement, as I was always desirous that the king should pass safely; but I could hardly find a trumpeter who was willing to go to the enemy camp because nine of their trumpeters, who had not been recognized, had been killed in battle, and they had taken one of ours and they held one whom I have mentioned, whom the king had sent before the battle had started. One of them went, however, and he carried a safe-conduct from the king; and they brought me back one, in order to have a parley midway between the two camps, which seemed to me difficult to do.

But I did not want to break off anything or make difficulties. The king designated the cardinal of Saint-Malo and the lord of Gié, marshal of France, the lord of Piennes, his chamberlain, and myself in their company; the others designated the marquis of Mantua, commander-in-chief for the Signoria [of Venice], the count of Caiazzo (who has been named several times in these memoirs and who recently had been on our side, and was [now] commander of the duke of Milan's men), and Luca Pisani and Marco Trevisano, *provveditori* for the Signoria of Venice, and we walked close enough to them to see them (and only the four of them were on the bank), for the river, which had swelled considerably since the previous day, flowed between us and them; and there was no one else outside their camp, nor on our side was there anyone out in front except us and our patrol, which was stationed there. We sent them a herald to find out whether they wished to pass the river.

As I said, I found it very difficult to have us meet, and I believed indeed that each person would express his fears; and they showed this, since they answered that it had been agreed that the parley should take place midway between the two camps, and that they had come more than halfway, and that they would not pass the river, and that they were all leaders of the army, and that they did not want to put all of them in danger. Those on our side, for their part, expressed certain doubts too out of concern for their own persons, and they told me to go over there without telling me what I was to do there and what I was to say. I said that I would not go alone and that I wanted a witness; and a person named Robertet, the king's secretary, came with me, as well as one of my servants and a herald. And thus I passed the river; and it seemed to me that if I did not accomplish anything, at least I did my duty toward these people who had gathered together by my means.

And when I had arrived I showed them that they had not come midway [between the two camps], as they had said, and that they should at least come to the bank of the river. And it seemed to me that if they were so close they would not leave before holding a parley. They told me that the river was too broad and that it flowed too strongly, and that therefore they would not understand each other speak; and I was not able to do anything to persuade them to come farther. And they told me to make some overture. I had no commission, and I told them that I alone would not tell them anything else, but that if they wished to make any overtures, I would make a report of it to the king.

And while we were discussing this, one of our heralds came and told me that the above-mentioned lords were leaving and that I should make any overtures I pleased, which I did not want to do because they knew more about the king's will than I did, since they were closer to him than I was and they had whispered in his ear at our parting; but about this present business I knew as much as they did at the time.

The marquis of Mantua began talking to me in strong terms about the battle and asked me whether the king would have had him killed if he had been taken. I told him no, he [would have been] given a warm welcome, and that the king had reason to like him because he was allowing him to acquire great honor by assailing him. Then he recommended the prisoners to me, and especially his uncle Lord Rodolfo; and he believed him to be alive but I well knew that it was otherwise. I assured him that all the prisoners would be well treated and I recommended to him the bastard of Bourbon, whom he held. The prisoners were very easy to care for, since there were [practically] none, which perhaps had never happened before in any battle, as I said: And the marquis had lost many of his relatives there, as many as seven or eight—and from all his company at least one hundred and twenty men-at-arms. And after these exchanges, I took leave of them, saying that I would return before nightfall, and we made a truce until the night.[260]

When I arrived at the place where the king was, along with the secretary, they asked me for news. And the king called a council meeting in a humble room, and nothing was concluded, and everyone looked at his neighbor. The king whispered in the cardinal's ear; and he told me to return to see what they might want to say (now the initiative of the parley had come from me; therefore it was likely that they would want me to speak first); and the cardinal told me not to conclude anything. I was not afraid of concluding anything, since I was not told anything. I did not want to say anything [in the council meeting] nor to interrupt my enterprise, for I hoped not to spoil anything and at least to see something of the countenance of our enemies, who probably were more panic-stricken than we were, and perhaps might drop a few words which would reassure both parties; and I went on my way.

But night was already approaching when I arrived on the bank of the river. And there one of their trumpeters came to me and told me that the four persons of whom I spoke sent word to me that I should not come that night, since it was late, and that their patrol was composed of stradiots who did not know anyone, and that it might be dangerous for me; but the trumpeter wanted to stay [with us] that night, in order to guide me the next morning. I sent him back, saying that in the morning at about eight o'clock I would be on the bank of the river and that he should wait for me there; or if there were some change, I would send a

260. Calmette, III, 200, n. 8, and especially Mandrot, II, 289, n. 1, add a number of details from Italian sources about Commynes' words at this interview.

herald to them. For I did not want him to learn anything about our situation that night. And I did not know what decision the king would make; for I saw advice being whispered in people's ears, which made me suspicious. And I returned to tell the king these things.

Everyone supped on whatever he had and went to bed on the ground. Shortly after midnight I found myself in the king's chamber. His chamberlains were there, ready to mount on horseback, and they told me that the king had decided to proceed in all haste to Asti or to the territories of the marchioness of Monferrato. And they suggested that I remain behind to hold the parley; I asked to be excused, saying that I did not want to have myself killed wittingly, and that I would not be among the last on horseback.

The king woke up early, heard Mass, and mounted on horseback one hour before daybreak. A trumpet sounded *Faites bon guet* [Be on the watch], but nothing else signaled the decampment, and moreover I do not believe that there was any need for it. However, it was frightening to the army, at least to those who knew something, because we were turning our backs on the enemy and were taking the path of flight, which is a very frightening thing for an army; and the exit from our camp was a bad one, owing to low-lying roads and woods. And we did lose our way, for there were no guides. And I heard how people asked those who were leading the standards and the one who served as grand equerry for a guide; but everyone answered: "I have none."

Note [however] that a guide was not lacking, for God alone had guided the company on the journey coming; and according to what Brother Girolamo had told me, he still wanted to conduct us on the return trip. For it was not possible to believe that such a king would have ridden by night without a guide, since he could have found enough of them. Our Lord showed an even greater sign that he wanted to preserve us, for the enemy did not notice anything about our decampment until noon, and they were still waiting for the parley which I had initiated.

And the river swelled so much that it was four o'clock in the afternoon before any man dared venture to pass there in order to follow us; and then the count of Caiazzo passed there with two hundred Italian light-horsemen, who were in great danger because of the force of the water; and one or two men drowned there, as he told me since. And we proceeded by a bumpy path through the woods, and it was necessary to march in single file; and this lasted for six miles or so. And afterwards we found a beautiful large meadow where our vanguard, artillery, and baggage-train already were. The baggage-train was very large and looked like a big band [of troops] from a distance. And at first we were afraid of it because of the white and square standard of Gian Giacomo Trivulzio, which was similar to the one which the marquis of Mantua had carried during the battle. And the vanguard was afraid of our rear guard which they saw advancing from afar, off the path, so as to come by the shortest distance. And everyone got ready to fight. But this fear did not last long, for horsemen came from all sides and they recognized each other immediately.

And from there we went to eat at Borgo San Donnino [present-day name: Fidenza], where an alarm was given in order to drive the Germans out of there, for fear that they might pillage the town. And we went to sleep at Fiorenzuola. The second day we slept near Piacenza, and we passed the river Trebbia; but two hundred lance-teams, our Swiss, and all the artillery remained on the other side, with the exception of six pieces which the king kept with him. And this was done so that we would be quartered better and more spaciously, for the river is ordinarily low, and especially during that season; however, about ten o'clock at night the river swelled so much that no man would have been able to pass it on foot or on horseback, and no company could have come to the other's help. And this was cause for great fear because our enemies were near us, and we searched all night to find some help on one side and the other; but there was no help to be had until the river subsided of itself, which happened at about five o'clock in the morning. And at that moment cords were set up from one end to the other to help the infantrymen pass across, for they were in the water up to above their stomach.

Soon afterwards the horsemen and the artillery passed; but it was an unexpected and perilous adventure, considering the place where we were and the enemy nearby, that is, the garrison of Piacenza and the count of Caiazzo, who had entered the place;[261] for some people of the town were making transactions to put the king in it, but they wanted it to be under the title of [Francesco] a small surviving son of Gian Galeazzo, the duke [of Milan] who had died a short time before, as you have heard. And if the king had been willing to lend an ear to this transaction, many towns and many other persons would have taken part in it by means of Gian Giacomo Trivulzio and others, but the king did not want to cause such displeasure to his cousin the duke of Orleans, who was already in Novara as you have seen. And to speak the truth, he had at the same time no great desire to see his cousin so powerful, and he was satisfied to pass and let this dissension take whatever course it would.

261. *Sic.* Not the count of Caiazzo but his brother Gasparo di Sanseverino, called Fracassa, entered Piacenza.

The third day after the departure from the place where the battle had been fought [July 11, 1495], the king went to Castel San Giovanni for dinner and slept in a wood. The fourth day he had dinner at Voghera and slept at Pontecurone. The fifth day he slept near Tortona and passed the river called Scrivia, which Fracassa was defending; for the men who were under his command were at Tortona and they were for the duke of Milan; but when he was advised by those who were preparing the king's lodgings that the monarch wanted only to pass by, he retired into the town and sent word that he would supply as many provisions as desired; and so he did, for the whole army passed close to the gate of Tortona and Fracassa, who was in armor, came to meet the king; but he had only two persons with him, and he apologized profusely to the king for not having him lodge in the town, and he had an abundance of provisions put outside the town, and the whole army was well supplied with them. And at night he came as the king was going to bed. And it should be understood that he was of the house of Sanseverino, and that he was the brother of the count of Caiazzo and of Galeazzo, and that he had been in the king's pay in Romagna a short time before, as was said elsewhere.

And from there the king came to Nizza Monferrato [July 14] in the marquisate of Monferrato, which we were anxious to find so that we would be in a friendly region and a safe one, for these light-horsemen whom the count of Caiazzo was leading were invariably at our rear, and during the first days they caused us great trouble, and we had few horsemen who were willing to place themselves at the rear, for the closer we came to a place of security the less our men showed that they had any intention of fighting. That is what people say about the nature of us Frenchmen, and the Italians have written it in their histories, that on their arrival the French are more than men, but on their retreat they are less than women. And as to the first point I believe them, insofar as they are truly the fiercest men that can be encountered in the whole world (I am referring to the horsemen); but on the retreat from an enterprise all people in the world are less courageous than when they leave their homes.

14

So to go on with this subject, our rear was defended by three hundred Germans who were well provided with culverins; and mounted hackbuts were brought to them.[262] And indeed they forced the stradiots,

262. These hackbuts were evidently so large that they required a support of some kind on which to prop them when firing.

who were not very numerous, to retire. The large army which had fought against us at Fornovo was advancing as best it could; but since they had left one day after us and since their horses were armored, they were not able to catch up with us. And we never lost one man on the way, nor was the enemy army ever within twenty miles of us. And when they saw that they could not catch us (and perhaps, too, they had no great desire to do so), they proceeded toward Novara, where the duke of Milan's men and some of theirs were, as you have heard before; but if they had been able to reach us on our retreat, they might have had a better bargain than they had at Fornovo.

I mentioned in several places how God had shown everywhere that He had guided this enterprise; but it serves me well to say it once more here. For from the day of the battle to [the day when we arrived at] Nizza Monferrato, no lodgings were ever distributed; everyone took quarters as best he could. We were in great need of provisions; however, the people of the region brought us some, and they could easily have poisoned us if they had wanted to by means of their food and wine and also their waters, which were drunk dry in a moment, as were the wells (and I saw only small fountains). And they would not have failed if they had wished to try to do so, but one must believe that Our Lord took away their will to do this.[263] And I saw thirst so great that a host of infantrymen drank from the ditches of these small towns through which we passed. We took big long drinks and we drank dirty, stagnant water; and in order to drink, men got into the water up to their belts. For many people who were not soldiers and a very large number of pack animals were following us.

Furthermore, I never witnessed an argument about lodgings. The king would leave before daybreak, and I don't believe that he ever had a guide, and he rode on horseback until noon, when he had lunch; and everyone took a place and had to bring the food for the horses in his arms, and had to feed his own horse. And I know that I did it twice, and I went for two days without eating anything except very bad bread; and I was among those who were the least in need.

This army should be praised for one thing, and that is that I have never heard any man complain of any need he might have had, and it was the most painful journey I have ever seen in my life, although I have seen some rather rough ones with Duke Charles of Burgundy. We

263. According to Heinrich Kretschmayr, *Geschichte von Venedig*, II (Gotha, 1920), 99, the use of poison was openly spoken of by Italian state authorities and ambassadors. Some years later during the war of the League of Cambrai (i.e., 1508 ff.) regular reward lists for poisoning certain people were drawn up by Venetian authorities.

did not go any faster than these large pieces of artillery could go, and we often had to attend to their maintenance, and we were greatly wanting in horses; but every time they were needed, they were obtained from persons of quality in the army who gave them willingly, and never was a single cannonball or a pound of powder lost. And I do not believe that anyone ever saw artillery of that size pass by the places through which this one passed, nor with such speed. And if I spoke of the disorder which prevailed in the matter of our lodgings as well as in other matters, it was not because there were no experienced persons of quality in the army; but, as chance would have it, they were the ones who had the least authority. The king was young and willful, as was said elsewhere; and to conclude the subject, it seems that Our Lord wanted all the glory of the journey to be attributed to Him.

The seventh day after our departure from the place where the battle had been fought, we left Nizza Monferrato and camped all together in a field rather close to Alessandria; and a careful watch was made all night. And in the morning before daybreak we left and proceeded to Asti [July 19]; that is to say, the king and the men from his household did. The men-at-arms remained close by in the field. And we found the town of Asti well supplied with all sorts of provisions, which gave great comfort and aid to the whole company, which was in great need of them, because the army had endured great hunger and thirst, much trouble and heat, and very great lack of sleep; and the equipment was all damaged and broken.

After the king arrived in Asti and just before bedtime, I sent a gentleman named Philippe de la Couldre, who had formerly been in my service but who was now in the service of the duke of Orleans, to Novara where he was besieged by his enemies, as you have heard. The siege was not yet so close that people could not go and venture out, because they were not aiming at anything except to starve the town. And I sent word to him by that gentleman that several negotiations were being transacted with the duke of Milan by the king's will, and that I was arranging one of them with the help of the duke of Ferrara; and that for this reason it seemed to me that he should come to the king, and that he should strongly reassure those whom he would leave inside that he would return shortly and come to their rescue; and they consisted of seventy-five hundred mercenaries, and for their numbers they were the most beautiful company that one could imagine, both French and Swiss.

After the king had spent one day in Asti he was advised by the duke of Orleans as well as by others that the two [Italian] armies were assembled before Novara. And the duke of Orleans wanted to be helped because his provisions were becoming scarce. Poor discipline had been enforced there at the beginning, for there was enough food in the town and in the vicinity—particularly wheat; and if provisions had been gathered early and had been well parceled out, they [the Italians] would never have had the town, but our men would have come out of it with honor and their enemies with great shame, if they had been able to hold out for one more month.

15

After the king had stayed a few days in Asti he went to Turin [July 31]. And at his departure from Asti the king dispatched a major-domo named Perron di Baschi to form a fleet at Nice in order to give help to

---

Commynes commissioned an elaborate funerary chapel to be built for himself in the convent of the Augustinian monks at Paris about 1505. The tomb was ruined during the French Revolution, but the polychrome sculptural portraits of Commynes and his wife (d. 1531) have been preserved, along with other assorted fragments of the chapel. The "rather brutal character" of the "realism" of these portraits should be attributed to the traditions of the North Italian artists who under Guido Mazzoni's direction executed the chapel, according to Michèle Beaulieu. The other remaining portions of the chapel include representations of tritons, nymphs, and putti, as well as of traditional Christian symbols like the tree of Jesse, the Evangelistic lion and bull, and the unicorn. Such iconography is very unusual in France in the early sixteenth century and perhaps indicates that Commynes had acquired a taste for North Italian artistic conventions during his embassies there. His funerary statue shows a man in his late fifties with the fleshy parts of his face somewhat sagging as compared with his appearance in the chalk portrait reproduced on page 89. The description of Commynes by Matthew d'Arras, quoted on page 88, is borne out again here. He appears very tall, almost ungainly, with hands awkwardly clasped above his lion-headed prayer stool. The mouth here is clasped shut even more firmly than in the earlier portrait and the slight stoop in his shoulders, like the glance of his eyes beneath the strongly arched brows, suggests a certain apprehension. Commynes' appearance seems to reflect in some degree the religious fear and constant caution expressed and advocated at many points in the Memoirs.

the castles of Naples which were still holding out; which he did. And my lord of Arbent set up this fleet, of which he was leader and commander. He went as far as Ponza, where the enemies were in sight, but a change in the weather prevented them from approaching; and they were of little use because Arbent returned to Leghorn, where most of his men fled on land and left the ships empty. And the enemy army came to Porto Longone near Piombino [present-day name: Porto Azzurro], where it stayed for at least two months without leaving; and if the men from our fleet had not gone out of these ships, our army would easily have gone to help these castles, for Porto Longone is such that one cannot leave it except with [the aid of] one wind, which does not often occur in winter. Arbent was a valiant man, but he lacked experience in naval matters.[264]

When the king arrived in Turin, many negotiations were carried on between the king and the duke of Milan. And the duchess of Savoy was involved in this; she was a daughter of [the house of] Monferrato, a widow, and the mother of a little duke who was alive at the time [Charles II, duke of Savoy, born 1488, died 1496]. Others also had a hand in these transactions. I was involved in them too, and those of the [Holy] league—that is to say, the leaders who were encamped before Novara—very much wanted me to be involved, and they sent me a safe-conduct. But since envious people are [often found] among courtiers, the cardinal whom I have mentioned so often broke things up so that I would not manage them; he wanted the transactions of my lady of Savoy, which were managed by his host the treasurer of Savoy, a wise man and a good servant to his mistress, to be successful. This affair lasted a long time; and for this reason the bailiff of Dijon was sent as an ambassador to the Swiss, to raise as many as five thousand of them.[265]

A short time ago I explained how the army was assembled at Nice in order to help the castles of Naples, which was not possible for the above-mentioned reasons. Thereupon my lord of Montpensier and other persons of high rank who were in these castles, seeing this misfortune, decided to leave the castles with the help of the fleet, which was close to these castles at the time; and they left them supplied with a sufficient number of men to guard them, proportionate to the provisions which were so restricted that they could not have been more so; and twenty-

264. The naval maneuvers reported in this paragraph took place during October, 1495.

265. Mandrot, II, 301, n. 2, basing himself on Kervyn de Lettenhove's *Lettres et négotiations* ... (see p. 84 for full citation), offers excerpts from the letters of Commynes and of the Signoria of Venice which expand on Commynes' laconic remarks about his role in the negotiations here.

five hundred persons departed with them; and they left Ognoys and two other persons of rank as leaders.

And the lord of Montpensier, the prince of Salerno, the seneschal of Beaucaire, and others who were there went to Salerno [October 27].[266] And King Ferrandino insisted that they had broken the agreement and that he could have the hostages whom they had surrendered a few days before killed; and they were my lord of Alègre, and a person named [Robert] de la Marck from Ardenne, and a lord of La Chapelle from Anjou, a person named Rocaberti [who was a] Catalan, and a person named Genlis.

And it should be understood that about three months earlier [July 6] King Ferrandino had entered Naples by compact and because of the lack of order of our men, who were well informed of everything but could not help it. I might indeed say more about this matter, but I can speak of it only from having heard the principals talk about it, and I do not willingly say very much about things where I was not present. But while King Ferrandino was thus in the town of Naples, rumors and news came there that the king had died at the battle of Fornovo; and this was certified to our men who were in the castle by means of letters and lies which the duke of Milan was spreading which said this was so; and they believed it; and so did the Colonna, who turned immediately against us with the great desire which they had of always being on the stronger side; for they were greatly bound [by feudal ties and honors] to the king, as was said elsewhere.

And because of these lies and principally because our men saw themselves confined in great numbers in the castle with few provisions (they had lost all their horses and other possessions which they had in the town), they made an agreement on the sixth day of October in the year 1495. They had already been besieged for three months and fourteen days [*sic*]. And about twenty days later they left, as was said [*sic*]. And they promised that if they were not helped within a certain number

266. Once more Commynes narrates events backwards chronologically. The agreement which he mentions in the following sentence is explained two paragraphs later. It was made on October 4, not October 6, less than three months after the siege of the castles of Naples began. The agreement allowed two months, not twenty days, for the French defenders of the castles to leave. It was on December 5, after the expiration of the two months, that King Ferrandino brought the hostages mentioned in this paragraph from Ischia to Naples, for the defenders had not yet given up the castles. On December 8, after an appeal by one of the hostages, the Castel Nuovo surrendered. The less important Castel dell'Ovo held out longer, until February 17, 1496. (Wherever Commynes speaks, as he does in the paragraph following the one to which this note refers, of "the castle" rather than of "the castles" of Naples, he presumably is speaking of the Castel Nuovo.)

of days, they would go to Provence and would leave the castles without waging war against the kingdom any more either by sea or by land; and they gave up the above-mentioned hostages. However, according to King Ferrandino, they broke their agreement the moment they [the French leaders who went to Salerno] left without leave. Our men maintained the opposite; but the hostages were in great danger, and not without cause. And I believe that our men did the wise thing in leaving regardless of any agreement there may have been, but they would have done better to give up the castles on that day and to take back their hostages; for indeed they held out only twenty days afterwards [*sic*], owing to lack of food and because they had no hope of help. And the [surrender of the] castle of Naples meant the total loss of the kingdom.

16

While the king was in Turin, as I said, and in Chieri where he sometimes went for his pleasure, he was waiting for news of the Germans [i.e., Swiss] whom he had sent for, and he tried to see if he could win over the duke of Milan, for he was very desirous of doing so. And he was not too concerned about the problems of the duke of Orleans, who was beginning to be pressed by lack of provisions and was writing every day in order to be helped. Indeed, he was more narrowly enclosed than before. And the [duke of Milan's] army was increased by one thousand Germans on horseback, who were led by Friedrich von Kappeller of the county of Ferrette, a valiant knight who had acquired great experience in France as well as in Italy. And there were also eleven thousand Germans[267] from the territories of the king of the Romans, and lansquenets who were led by Georg von Ebenstein, a native of Austria and a valiant knight (he was the one who took Saint-Omer [from Charles VIII in February, 1489] for the king of the Romans). And when it was realized that the enemies were increasing and that no agreement could be reached that would be to the king's honor, he was advised to retire to Vercelli, in order to see how the duke of Orleans and his company could be saved, for, as was said elsewhere, they had small provision of food when they first entered Novara.

267. *Sic*. It seems likely that the manuscript should read "eleven hundred" rather than "eleven thousand," in view of Commynes' statement on p. 518 where he says that Maximilian sent "some two thousand Germans": eleven hundred Germans plus the contingent led by Georg von Ebenstein, mentioned later in this sentence, might have made a total of "some two thousand." Similarly, on p. 558 Commynes says that the enemy included "fifteen hundred Germans." On the other hand, Mandrot, II, 307, n. 2, quotes a document from the Venetian archives estimating that 8,000 Germans, together with 10,000 Venetians and 2,000 other Italian troops had arrived before Novara on September 1, 1495.

And it would have been better if he had acted according to what I had advised him when we first arrived in Asti, as can be seen [from what I said] above, which was to leave [Novara] and get rid of all useless people and come [and join his forces] to [those of] the king; for his presence [by the side of the king] would have made it possible to arrange for part of what he would have wanted [in the negotiations which the king was carrying on with the duke of Milan]; or at least those whom he would have left would not have suffered from such extreme hunger as they did, for he would have made a decision earlier, if he had seen that there was no other way out. But the archbishop of Rouen [Georges d'Amboise, the duke of Orleans' favorite and later his chief minister when he became king] who had been with him at the beginning in Novara and had [afterwards] come to the king in order to be of service to him and was present when these affairs were taking place, sent word constantly to the duke that he should not leave and that he would be helped; and he based his statement on what the cardinal of Saint-Malo, who had all the [king's] credit, was telling him. It was his great affection which made him speak [thus to the duke], but I was assured of the contrary, for no one wanted to fight any more unless the king went there, and he had no desire to do so. For it was a question only of this one town [Novara] which the duke of Orleans wanted to retain and the duke of Milan wanted to recover; it is ten leagues from Milan, and [thus whoever obtained] one [either Milan or Novara] would necessarily get everything. For in the duchy of Milan there are nine or ten large cities near one another within a small compass. So indeed the duke of Milan said that if we left him Novara and did not ask him for Genoa, he would do everything for the king.

Several times flour was brought to Novara, but half of it was lost on the way. And once some sixty men-at-arms were routed; they were led by a person named Châtillon, who was a young gentleman from the king's household. Some were taken, others entered, and others escaped with great difficulty. It is impossible to realize the distress this company in Novara found itself in, for each day people died of hunger and two-thirds of them were ill. We received ciphered letters, with various difficulties, which were pitiful. We always encouraged them, but it was all deception. Those who were managing the king's affairs were eager for a battle; but they did not consider that no one except them wanted it. For all the great leaders, such as the prince of Orange who had recently arrived there and to whom the king gave great authority in affairs of war, and all the other war leaders were looking for an honorable issue by means of an agreement because winter was approaching, there was no money, the number of Frenchmen was small, many of them were ill, and they were leaving every day without permission while others were going with the king's leave. But all these signs could not prevent those of whom I spoke from sending word to the duke of Orleans that he should not move, and they were putting him in great danger. But they were counting on the number of Germans [i.e., Swiss] about which the bailiff of Dijon was assuring us; some persons had sent word to him that he should bring whatever forces he could. And there was little unity in our company, for everyone said and wrote what he pleased.

Those who neither wanted an agreement nor a meeting to discuss one said that the king should not take the first step but that he should let his enemies talk; and they in turn said that they did not want to be the first ones to start. And time kept passing, and the people of Novara were still in distress; and their letters mentioned nothing except those who were dying of hunger every day, and that they could not hold out longer than ten days, and then eight, and at a certain point I saw them reduced to three days. But before [those three days had elapsed] the terms which they offered were accepted. Indeed not since one hundred years before we were born did people suffer such great hunger.

And while things were in this state, the marchioness of Monferrato died [August 27, 1495], and certain divisions took place in the marquisate in respect to the government, which the marquis of Saluzzo on one hand and Lord Constantine on the other were demanding. The latter was the late marchioness' uncle; he was Greek and she was the daughter of the king of Serbia; both of them had been ruined by the Turk. Lord Constantine had fortified himself in the castle of Casale and had in his hands the two sons, the elder of whom was only nine years old; they were the children of the marquis and of this wise and beautiful lady, who had died at the age of twenty-nine and who had been a great partisan of the French. Other individuals also tried to obtain the government and the question was earnestly raised before the king on behalf of those who supported them. The king ordered me to go there to settle the dispute for the safety of the children and to the satisfaction of the majority of those of the territory, fearing that because of these differences they might call the duke of Milan; and the support of that house was very pleasing to us.

I was most displeased to be leaving before I had set up means of resuming the peace negotiations; and I saw the hardships that I described to you and I saw the coming of winter. And I was afraid that these prelates might be responsible for bringing the king back to battle; and he would be poorly provided for unless reinforcement came from foreigners such as the Swiss. And even if they came in as great numbers as was reported, the king would be in danger if he put himself into their hands. For the enemy were very strong and they were quartered in a strongly situated place and were well fortified.

Having considered these things, I ventured to tell the king that it seemed to me that he wanted to put his person and his office in great hazard for a small occasion. He should remember that he had been in great danger in Fornovo; but there he had been forced to be in such a position, whereas here there was no such necessity, and he should not fail to make some honorable agreement just because of the words of those who said that he should not be the one to take the first step; and if he wished, I would see to it that they would speak in such a manner that the honor of both sides would be well preserved. He told me that I should speak to the cardinal, which I did; but he gave me strange answers. He was eager for a battle, and in his opinion we were assured of victory. It was reported that he had been promised an income of ten thousand ducats for one of his sons by the duke of Orleans, if he obtained the duchy of Milan. The next day I came to take leave of the king in order to go to Casale, which was about one-and-a-half days' journey away. I met my lord of La Trémoïlle, to whom I explained this affair since he was the king's intimate, and I asked him whether I should speak to him again about it. He encouraged me and told me that I should; for everyone wished to retire.

The king was in a garden. I took up the above-mentioned conversation again in front of the cardinal, who told me that it was up to him, as a churchman, to begin. I told him that if he did not begin, I would, for it seemed to me indeed that the king would not be offended [by my opinion], nor would his closest friends. And so I left. And at my departure I told my lord the prince of Orange, who was the principal leader of the army, that if I started anything I would submit the matter to him.

And I proceeded to Casale, where I was well received by all the members of that house [of Monferrato]; and I found most of them taking the part of Lord Constantine. And it seemed to all of them that it would be the safest solution for the children, for he could not obtain the succession, whereas the marquis of Saluzzo pretended a right to it. I organized several assemblies, which included [representatives of] nobles, clergy, and towns, and at their request or that of most of them, I declared that the king wished Lord Constantine to remain governing; for considering the king's power on that side of the mountains and the affection that the region has for the house of France, they could not oppose the king's desire.

About the third day that I was there, a major-domo of the marquis of Mantua, commander-in-chief of the Venetians, came there. The marquis was sending his condolences on the death of the marchioness in his capacity as a relative. And this man and I entered into a conversation about how these two armies might come to an agreement without fighting, for events were disposing themselves to that end. And the king was quartered in a field near Vercelli [September 12–October 11]. But to speak the truth, he had only crossed the [Sesia] river and quartered his army, which was poorly provided with tents and pavilions, for he had brought few of them and even those were lost; and the ground was damp because it was close to winter and the country was flat. [So] the king lodged there [with the army on the east side of the river] only one night, and he retired to the town the next day. But the prince of Orange remained there, and the count of Foix and the count of Vendôme, who caught a flux there from which he died, which was unfortunate, for he was a handsome, young, wise man, and he had come there posthaste because it was rumored that there would be a battle, for he had not made the trip to Italy with the king. With these persons there remained Marshal de Gié and several other commanders; but the principal force consisted of Germans who had made the journey with the king; for the French did not stay there willingly since they were so close to the town. Many were ill and many had left, some with leave and some without it.

From the camp to Novara it was ten large Italian miles, which is about the equivalent of six French leagues [about twelve and one-half English miles]; the earth was heavy and soft like [that in] Flanders, owing to the [irrigation] ditches which are along the roads, on one side and the other, very deep, much more so than those of Flanders. In winter there is much mud and in summer much dust. Between our camp and Novara was a small place called Borgo Vercelli within a league of us, which we held. And they held another place called Camara, which was within a league of their camp. And the waters [in the Sesia and Agogna Rivers] had already swelled greatly [and so it was difficult] to go from one camp to the other.

As I started to say, the marquis of Mantua's major-domo, who had come to Casale, and I continued our talks. And I told him the reasons why his master should avoid the battle; he had seen the danger in which he had been at the first one; he was fighting for people who would never increase [his reputation], regardless of any service he might perform for them; he should undertake to come to an agreement, and I would help him on our side. He replied that his master would be willing to have it; but it would be necessary, as word had been sent to me before, that we speak first, since their league, which included the pope, the kings of

the Romans and of Spain, and the duke of Milan, was a greater entity than
the king. And I told him that it was foolish to be so ceremonious, and
that the king should have precedence since he was there in person,
whereas the others had only their lieutenants there, and that he and I
as mediators could start [negotiating] if he so desired, provided that I
could be sure that his master would continue, and soon. And we concluded that I should send a trumpeter to their camp the next day, and
that I should write to the two Venetian *provveditori*, one of whom is
named Luca Pisani and the other Marco Trevisano, who are delegated
by virtue of their office to counsel their captains and to attend to the
affairs of their army.

In accordance with what we had decided, I wrote to them the substance of what I had told the major-domo; [I said that] I had found
occasion to continue my office as a good mediator, as I had agreed to do
at my departure from Venice, and that this was most agreeable to the
king and that it seemed to me to be necessary, too, for there are always
enough people around to trouble affairs, but there are few who have
both the occasion and the will to reach agreement about a great dispute
or who are willing to endure all the words that are spoken by those who
transact such affairs; for in such armies many different opinions exist.

The *provveditori* were happy about this news and they wrote to me
that they would give me an answer shortly, and that they would inform
Venice of this by their post. They soon received an answer, and there
came to the king's camp a count who was in the service of the duke of
Ferrara, who had some men there, for his eldest son [Alfonso d'Este]
was there in the pay of the duke of Milan, and this man was among
them and the duke of Ferrara had another son with the king [Ferrante,
Alfonso d'Este's younger brother]. The count was named Count Albertino [Boschetto]; and he came to see Gian Giacomo [Trivulzio],
and he addressed himself to the prince of Orange, as had been decided
upon between myself and the major-domo of whom I spoke, saying
that he had a commission from the marquis of Mantua and the *provveditori* and other captains who were in their army to ask for a safe-
conduct for the marquis and others, up to fifty horsemen, so that they
might be present to confer with such persons as it would be the king's
pleasure to designate. And they acknowledged that it was indeed reasonable that they should come to the king or his representatives first,
and also that they were willing to render him that honor. And then he
asked leave to speak to the king privately, which he did.

And in private he advised against doing all this, saying that the
[enemy] army over there was in great fear and that they would soon

decamp; and by these secret words he showed that he wanted to break this agreement and that he wanted not at all to make it or to promote it, although his public charge was such as you have heard. Gian Giacomo Trivulzio, a great enemy of the duke of Milan, was present when these secret words were spoken, and he would willingly have broken this peace. And Albertino's master, the duke of Ferrara, particularly desired the war because of the great hatred which he had for the Venetians, on account of the territories which they held from him, such as the Polesina and other places, and he came to the above-mentioned camp to see the duke of Milan, whose wife was his daughter.

As soon as the king had heard the count speak, he had me called and he brought before the council the question of whether he should deliver this safe-conduct or not. Those who wanted to break the peace, such as Gian Giacomo and others who spoke in favor of the duke of Orleans, or so it seemed to them, showed that they wanted the battle; but they were churchmen and they would not have taken part in it. They said that they were well assured that the enemy would decamp and that they would die of hunger. Others said (and I was among them) that we would be hungry sooner than they would because they were in their own country, and surely they were too powerful to flee and let themselves be destroyed, and that these words came from people who wanted us to fight for their quarrels and to have the king hazard himself and his company [for them]. Anyway, to be brief, the safe-conduct was granted and sent, and it was decided that the next day at two o'clock in the afternoon, the prince [of Orange], Marshal de Gié, the lord of Piennes, and myself in their company, would go [to a place] between Borgo Vercelli and Camara near a tower where they kept guard, and that we would have a conference together there.

And we were there, well attended by men-at-arms; the marquis and a Venetian who was in charge of their stradiots came there, and with courteous words they said that for their part they desired peace. And it was concluded that in order to speak more conveniently, the next day some of their men would come to our camp, and then the king would send some of his to their camp and would assign others; and so it was done.

And the next day Francesco Bernardino Visconti came to us on behalf of the duke of Milan, as well as a secretary of the marquis of Mantua, and we, the persons whom I have named and the cardinal of Saint-Malo, met with them. We entered into negotiations for peace [September 16–19, 1495]. And we asked for Novara, in which city the duke of Orleans was being besieged; and we also asked for Genoa, saying that it was the king's fief and that the duke of Milan had confiscated it. They begged to differ, saying that they had not undertaken anything against the king except to defend themselves, that the duke of Orleans had taken the city of Novara from them and had started the war with the king's soldiers, and that they thought their master would not do any of the things which we were asking for, but that anything else he would be willing to do in order to please the king. They remained there for two days, after which they returned to their camp, and we went there, too, Marshal de Gié, de Piennes, and myself, always in order to again request the two cities [i.e., the cities of Novara and Genoa].

We would have been well pleased if Novara had put itself in the hands of the men of the king of the Romans, who were in their army and whose leaders were Georg von Ebenstein and Friedrich von Kappeller and one Hans [Hederlein]. For we could give it help only by a battle, and that we did not want; and we said the above because the duchy of Milan is held as a fief from the emperor, and because [in this way] we could get out of the affair honorably.

Several trips back and forth were made by us to their camp and by them to ours without any conclusion being reached; but I always remained lodged in their camp, for such was the king's will, since he did not want to break up anything. Finally we returned there [September 24] and in addition the president [of the Parlement of Paris] de Ganay came there in order to put the words into Latin, and with him was a person named my lord of Morvilliers, bailiff of Amiens; for up to then I had spoken in bad Italian, but [now] we were ready to couch our articles in writing.

And it was our manner of procedure that as soon as we arrived at the duke [of Milan]'s lodgings he would come to meet us with the duchess as far as the end of a gallery; and we all placed ourselves before him as we entered his room, where we found two long rows of chairs placed one in front of the other and very close to each other. They sat on one side and we on the other. The first to be seated on his side was a representative of the king of the Romans, [then] the Spanish ambassador, the marquis of Mantua, the two Venetian *provveditori*, a Venetian ambassador, and then the duke of Milan, his wife, and lastly the ambassador of Ferrara. And on their side no one spoke except the duke, and on ours only one person; but it is not according to our temperament to discuss as calmly as they do, and sometimes two or three of us spoke at once, and the duke said: "Ho [there], one at a time."

When it came to couching the articles in writing, everything that was agreed upon was immediately written down by one of our secretaries and also by one from their side, and at our departure the two secretaries read the text, one in Italian and the other in French; and it was done once more when we assembled again, in order to see whether anything had been changed there, and also to save time. And it is a good procedure to expedite an important affair. This conference lasted for about fifteen days and more [September 24–October 9]; but on the first day that we began negotiating, it was agreed that my lord of Orleans could leave from there. And we made a truce that day, which continued from day to day until peace had been achieved. And for the safety of the duke, the marquis of Mantua gave himself up as a hostage into the hands of the count of Foix, and he did so most willingly, and more to please [us] than out of fear. And first they made us swear that we were proceeding in good faith with regards to the peace treaty and that we were not doing it only to free the duke of Orleans.

17

Marshal de Gié proceeded to the above-mentioned place [Novara] with others in the service of the duke of Milan, and he had the duke leave with only a small retinue and he left it with great joy [September 23]. And those who were in the place were so pressed with hunger and illness that the marshal had to leave his nephew, named my lord of Ramefort, as a hostage, promising those inside that they would all leave within three days.

You have already heard how the bailiff of Dijon had previously been sent to the Swiss, throughout all their cantons, in order to raise up to five thousand Germans who had not yet arrived when the duke of Orleans left the town of Novara; for in my opinion, if they had come we would most certainly have fought. And although we were quite sure that they were coming in greater numbers than we had requested, it was not possible to wait because of the extreme famine which there was in the place, where at least two thousand men died of hunger as well as illness and the rest were so emaciated that they looked more dead than alive; and I do not believe that people ever endured greater hunger, unless one wishes to bring to mind the siege of Jerusalem. And if God had made them wise enough to have stored the wheat which was in the vicinity of the town when they first took it, they would never have come to this misfortune, and their enemies would have raised the siege to their great shame.

Three or four days after the departure of the duke of Orleans from Novara, it was agreed on both sides that all the soldiers could march out; and the marquis of Mantua and Galeazzo di Sanseverino, leaders of the troops of the Venetians and of the duke of Milan, were ordered to conduct them to safety; which they did. And the place remained in the hands of the townspeople, who swore that they would put neither Frenchmen nor Italians in it until the treaty might be concluded. And thirty men remained in the castle; the duke of Milan let them have food for their money, but only as much as they needed for each day.

And no one who did not see the poverty of the persons who came out of the place could ever believe it. Very few horses came out, for all had been eaten, and there were not six hundred men who would have been able to defend themselves, although some fifty-five hundred came out. A large number of them remained on the roads, and their very enemies helped them. I know that I saved at least fifty of them with an *écu* near the little castle called Camara which the enemy held, where they were lying in a garden, and [for my *écu*] they were given soup, and only one died; on the road about four died, for it was ten miles from Novara to Vercelli, where they were going. The king showed some charity toward those who were coming to Vercelli and ordered eight hundred francs to be distributed in alms and also in payment of their wages; and the dead as well as the living were paid; and also the Swiss, of whom about four hundred had died. But in spite of any kind act that we were able to do for them, about three hundred men died in Vercelli, some from eating too much and others of illness, and many people [lay] upon the manure heaps of the town.

And about this time when everyone was out except thirty men who had been left in the castle (and every day one or the other of them was missing), the Swiss arrived to the number of eight or ten thousand men in our camp, in which there were already some two thousand who had served in the expedition to Naples. The others stayed about ten miles from Vercelli; and the king was advised not to let these two groups join, for there would have been about twenty-two thousand of them; and I believe that never had so many men from their country found themselves together. And according to the opinion of people who knew them, there were few fighting men left in their country. Most of them came even though we had [enough] of them, and it became necessary to prohibit entrance into the area [called] Piedmont in order to prevent more of them from coming, or else the women and children would have come.

One might ask whether this coming proceeded from great love, considering that the late King Louis had been very good to them and had helped enhance their glory and reputation in the world. It is true that some of the old people loved King Louis, and there were many captains who were more than seventy-two years old, and they had served as captains against Duke Charles of Burgundy. But the principal cause was avarice and their great poverty; for two of the cantons had declared themselves against us, that is, Berne and Schwyz, and nevertheless all the fighting men possessed by those [two cantons] came there [to the king's camp].[268] And I have never seen so many handsome men; and it seemed to me that it would have been impossible to put them to rout, unless they were overcome by hunger, cold, or some other necessity.

Now we must come to the principal thing about this treaty. The duke of Orleans had already lived at his ease for eight or ten days and had been attended by all sorts of people. And it seemed to him that some people were making remarks about the fact that so many men as he had with him in Novara had let themselves be reduced to this necessity. [So] he talked much about a battle, and so did one or two others who were with him, such as my lord of Ligny and the archbishop of Rouen, who were involved in his affairs, and two or three minor persons; and they worked on a few Swiss who came to offer themselves for fighting. They did not give any [good] reasons [for a battle], for the duke of Orleans had no one in the place any more except twenty or thirty men in the castle. There was no longer any occasion to fight, for the king was not pursuing any quarrel, and he had wanted to fight only to save the person of the duke and his other servants and subjects. The enemy were very strong and it was impossible to capture them inside their camp because they were so well enclosed with ditches full of water and their location was favorable and they did not have to protect themselves against anyone except us, for they no longer had any fear of the people of the town. They included about twenty-eight hundred men-at-arms in armor, five thousand light-horsemen, fifteen hundred Germans led by good commanders, such as Georg von Ebenstein, Friedrich von Kappeller, Hans [Hederlein], and others, and a great number of infantrymen; and it seemed indeed frivolous to say that one should take them there [in their camp] or that they would flee.[269]

Another matter of even greater concern was that if all the Swiss assembled together they might take the king and all the rich men in his company, which was very weak in comparison to them, and that they might take them to their country; and some signs of this were seen, as you will see by [my account of] the conclusion of the peace.

268. *Sic.* According to Mandrot and Calmette, *op. cit.*, Zurich, not Schwyz, was the second canton which declared itself against the French.

269. Calmette, III, 240, n. 4, citing another source, asserts that Commynes exaggerates the numbers of the enemy which were no more than 9,000 in all. Perhaps, Calmette continues, Commynes exaggerates in order to justify his role in pursuing negotiations for peace.

18

While all these questions were being discussed among us (and the duke of Orleans had such a heated argument about this with the prince of Orange that he gave him the lie), we returned to the enemy's camp—the marshal, the lord of Piennes, President de Ganay, the lord of Morvilliers, the bishop's lieutenant in Chartres, and myself—and we concluded peace.[270] And we believed, judging from the signs that we saw, that it would not last; but it was necessary for us to do this for many reasons which you have heard, and because the season was forcing us to do so, and for lack of money, and in order to depart honorably with an honorable peace in writing which could be sent everywhere, as it was. And the king had so decided in a grand council meeting in the presence of the duke of Orleans.

The substance was that the duke of Milan would place Genoa at the service of the king against anyone in the world and [would equip] two ships at his [the duke's] expense to go at that very moment to give help to the castle of Naples, which was still holding out, and the next year three ships. And with his person he would serve the king once again in his enterprise against the kingdom, in case the king were to return there, and he would give passage to the king's men. And in case the Venetians should not accept peace within two months and they wished to support the house of Aragon, he would serve the king against them, provided that everything which the king might take from their territories would be given to him; and he would employ his person and his subjects [to that end]. And he would discharge the king of eighty thousand ducats of the 180,000 which he had lent him during the expedition which the king had made; and he would give two hostages from Genoa as security [for carrying out the treaty]. And the castle [the fortress or *rocca* of Genoa] was put in the hands of the duke of Ferrara, as a neutral, for two years; and the duke would pay for one half of the guard that was in the said castle and the king for the other; and in case the duke of Milan did anything against the king at Genoa, the duke of Ferrara could give the said castle to the king. And he was to give up two other hostages from Milan, which he did; and those [hostages] from Genoa would have done the same [i.e., given themselves to the king] if the king had not been so quick to leave; but as soon as the duke saw that he was gone, he found an excuse.

270. The Peace of Vercelli was signed on October 9 by the negotiators of the treaty and on October 10 it was ratified and sworn to by Charles VIII. As Commynes indicates in the remainder of this chapter, this was a peace between the duke of Milan and the king only.

As soon as we had returned from having the duke of Milan swear this peace, and the Venetians had taken a term of two months to either accept it or not (for they did not want to commit themselves any further on this matter), the king also swore the peace [October 10], and the next day he decided to leave, like one who was very desirous of returning to France, as was all his company. But that night the Swiss who were in our camp began to hold various meetings, each with the men from his own canton, and they beat their drums, and they held their *Ring*, which is their form of council. And what I am saying was told to me by Lornay, who was and has always been one of their leaders, and who understands their language well; and he was sleeping in the camp, and he came to advise the king of this during the night. Some said that they should take the king and all his company, that is, the rich people; others willingly approved of this, but they said that only three months' pay should be demanded of him, on the ground that the king his father had promised them that every time they left their country with their banners, they would receive such a payment. Others wanted only the principal persons to be taken, without touching the king, and they were undertaking to put this plan into execution; and they already had many soldiers inside the town. But before they had concluded anything, the king left and proceeded to Trino [October 11], a town which belonged to the marquis of Monferrato. They were wrong, however; for they had been promised only one month's pay, and furthermore they had served only five days.[271] Finally an agreement was made with them; but before that they took the bailiff of Dijon and the above-mentioned Lornay, who had always been their leaders (these were the ones who had been to Naples with us), in order to obtain fifteen days' pay and then leave; but the others were paid for three months, and the whole thing amounted to at least 500,000 francs. They accepted pledges and hostages. And this was brought about by the French themselves, who proposed this to them, for one of their captains came to advise the prince of Orange of this and he told the king; and it was because they were against this peace.

When the king had arrived at Trino, he sent Marshal de Gié, the president de Ganay, and myself once more to the duke of Milan to ask him to come to the king and speak with him. We gave him several reasons to persuade him to come, and we told him that it would be the true con-

---

271. The terms of the treaty signed between the Swiss and Louis XI on January 2, 1475, indicate that Commynes is correct, strictly speaking, but that there were grounds in that treaty's wording for the Swiss contention also. The treaty signed between the Swiss and Charles VIII on November 1, 1495, clarified the wording in favor of the Swiss contention. See Mandrot, II, 330, n. 1, for the relevant texts and the pay accorded the Swiss mercenaries.

firmation of the peace. He gave us many reasons to the contrary and excused himself on account of certain words which my lord of Ligny had said, to the effect that he should have been seized when he was with the king at Pavia, and other words which had been spoken by the cardinal, who had all the king's credit. It is perfectly true that many foolish words had been said (by whom I do not know); but at the time the king was desirous of being his friend. He [the duke of Milan] was in a place called Robbio; he was willing to have a conference if there was a barrier or a river between them. When the king heard this answer he went to Chieri, where he stayed for only a night or two [October 18–20], and he continued on his way to pass the mountains. He sent me back to Venice and others to Genoa to arm these two vessels which the duke of Milan was supposed to give; but he did nothing of the sort and let them go to great expense and make great preparations and then refused to let them go; instead of keeping his promise, he sent two ships against us.

19

It was my mission in Venice to find out whether they were willing to accept this peace and to have three articles ratified. The first was to give back Monopoli, which they had taken from us; the second was to retire the marquis of Mantua and others whom they had in the kingdom of Naples in the service of King Ferrandino; the third was to have them declare that King Ferrandino was not included in the league which they had recently made, and in which only the pope, the king of the Romans, the king of Spain, and the duke of Milan were named.[272] And when I arrived in Venice [November 4, 1495] they received me honorably, but not so honorably as they had the first time; but now we were in open enmity, whereas the first time we were at peace.

I told them my business. The prince [i.e., the doge] told me that I was most welcome, that he would give me an answer shortly, and that he would consult with his senate. For three days they made general processions, distributed generous alms, and made public sermons, as they prayed to Our Lord that he might grant them the grace of obtain-

272. Calmette, III, 247, nn. 1 and 2, points out that Commynes couches the second and third demands of the French in misleading terms. The object of the second demand was to prevent the marquis of Mantua from going to the aid of King Ferrandino, not to reverse an action already taken. The marquis' expedition to Naples took place in the spring of 1496. Commynes, with his habitual chronological carelessness, speaks as if it had already taken place. Similarly, the object of the third demand was to prevent King Ferrandino from being made officially and openly a member of the Holy League.

ing good counsel; and I was told that they often do this under similar circumstances. And truly, it seems to me that it is the most reverent city which I have ever seen in ecclesiastical matters; and they have the most adorned and well-equipped churches. And in this respect I consider them rather equal to the Romans, and I believe that the greatness of their Signoria[273] stems from this; and it is worthy of being augmented rather than lessened.

To conclude [the description of] my business, I waited for fifteen days before receiving an answer, which was a refusal of all my requests [November 18]. They said that they had no war with the king, and that what they had done was to help their ally the duke of Milan, whom the king wanted to destroy. And they had the doge speak with me privately; he offered me an advantageous agreement, which was that King Ferrandino would render homage to the king for the kingdom, with the pope's consent, and that he would pay fifty thousand ducats a year as [feudal] dues as well as a certain amount of ready cash which they would lend. And by means of this loan they intended to have in their hands the places which they have in Apulia, such as Brindisi, Otranto, Trani, and others. In addition, Don Ferrandino would give the king or let him have a place in the region of Apulia for security; and they meant Taranto which the king still held, and he [Ferrandino] would have given one or two more. And they intended to hand over these places on that side [the eastern side of the kingdom of Naples] because it was the farthest from us and in a location which might serve against the Turk, of whom the king had talked much when he came to Italy, saying that he was making this enterprise for that purpose and in order to be closer to him [the Turk]. But this was a very bad thing [to say] because it was a lie, and thoughts cannot be concealed from God. In addition, the doge of Venice told me that if the king wanted to undertake anything against the Turk, he would have enough places in the region I mentioned, and that all Italy would contribute to it, and that the king of the Romans would wage war on his side too, and that the king and they would hold all of Italy, and that no one would oppose

273. *Sic.* Although Signoria ("Seigneurie") is capitalized in the Polignac manuscript and early editions, I believe that Commynes (who dictated his manuscript and probably did not trouble to indicate capitalization) refers here to lordship ("seigneurie") in the sense of political power rather than to lordship as a particular political institution in Venice (see n. 152 above for description of the Venetian Signoria). Conversely the word "senate" at the end of the first sentence in this paragraph, although it is not capitalized in the manuscript or editions, should be capitalized. The Venetian Senate had a membership of 120 Venetian nobles, selected by their Great Council, to which many other officers of the state, such as the members of the Signoria, were added as *ex officio* members. Thus in the fifteenth century the Senate often numbered as many as 300 members.

what they would organize; and that for their part, they would serve the king with one hundred galleys at their expense and with five thousand horsemen on land.[274]

I took my leave of the doge and the Signoria, and said that I would make a report of this. I returned to Milan and found the duke of Milan at Vigevano, where one of the king's major-domos named Rigault was ambassador. The duke came to meet me, pretending to go hunting, for they treat ambassadors with such honor.[275] He had me lodge in his castle and treated me most honorably. I begged to be allowed to speak to him privately; he said that he would grant this request, but he showed that he did not desire to do so. I wanted to press him about those ships which he had promised us by the treaty of Vercelli. They were ready to depart (and the castle of Naples was still holding out), and he was pretending that he would send them.

Perron di Baschi, the king's major-domo, and Etienne de Nèves were in Genoa on behalf of the king. They immediately wrote to me as soon as they knew that I had arrived there, and they complained about the deceit of the duke of Milan, who was pretending to send them the ships, although he had on the contrary sent two against us. One day the governor of Genoa replied that he would not suffer these ships to be manned by Frenchmen, and [another day he said] that only twenty-five men would be allowed on board each one, and he gave many other such excuses, dissimulating and waiting for the news that the castle of Naples had surrendered; for the duke well knew that there was food for only a month or so. And the army which was being assembled in Provence was not sufficient to give help without these two ships, for the enemy had a large fleet in front of the castle, [supplied] by them as well as by the Venetians and by the king of Spain.

I was with the duke for three days. One day he held a council meeting and became angry because I was not pleased with his answer concerning these ships; and [he said] that by the treaty of Vercelli he had indeed promised to help with two ships, but that he had not promised to allow

274. No other trace of the doge's offers to the French exists, according to Mandrot and Calmette. Mandrot asserts, II, 334, n. 1, that the offers must have been feints since the doge wrote at the same time to the Venetian ambassador at Rome that the Senate had already ordered stradiots and money sent to Ferrandino. (See Mandrot, II, 332, n. 3, for quotation of this epistle.)

275. This strange sentence perhaps means this: It is the custom in the duchy of Milan to treat ambassadors with such honor that the duke comes to meet them personally. This the duke did to me, and he made it seem even more of an honor for me by pretending that he was thereby interrupting a hunting expedition. Or perhaps it means this: This the duke did to me, but he pretended that he was going hunting and that he had just happened to see me on the way, so that he would not appear to demean himself too much.

any Frenchmen on board. To which I replied that this excuse seemed to me a rather lame one, and that if for example he lent me a good mule to pass the mountains, what good would he be doing me if he had it led up to me and then only let me look at it without allowing me to get on? After a long exchange he took me aside in a gallery. There I demonstrated to him the pains which I and others had taken to bring about the treaty of Vercelli and the danger in which he was putting us by proceeding in such a contrary manner and by thus causing the king to lose his castles, which meant the total loss of the kingdom, which would cause perpetual hate between the king and him. And on the contrary, I offered him the principality of Taranto and the duchy of Bari, which he already held. I told him the danger in which he was putting himself and all of Italy by being willing to consent to the Venetians having those places in Apulia. On every point he confessed that I was speaking the truth, and especially in respect to the Venetians; but as a sole conclusion, he told me that he could find neither security nor trust with the king.

After these conferences I took leave of the duke, who conducted me for half a league; and at my departure he made up a most beautiful lie (if one may speak that way of princes; and it seemed to him indeed that I was leaving with great melancholy). He told me suddenly, like a man who was changing his mind, that he wanted to do me a friendly turn, so that the king would have the occasion to give me a warm welcome; and that the next day he would have Galeazzo (one could ask for nothing more if he was named)[276] leave to have these ships sent away and join our fleet; and that he wanted to be of further service to the king by saving his castle of Naples for him; and that by so doing he would save the kingdom for him (and he spoke the truth, if he had done it); and that when they had sailed he would write me so in his own hand, so that the king would receive the first news of it from me and realize that I had done this service for him; and the courier would overtake me before I got to Lyon.

I took my leave full of good hope and proceeded to cross the mountains, and I never heard the post coming behind me without thinking that it was the one who was going to bring me the above-mentioned letter, although I had some doubts about it, knowing the man. I got as far as Chambéry and found my lord of Savoy, who gave me a warm welcome and had me stay for a day; and then I arrived at Lyon, and [still] my courier did not come. And I made a report of everything to

276. Galeazzo di Sanseverino was Lodovico's "lieutenant and principal servant," as Commynes says on p. 452 above. Entrusting him with a commission, Commynes implies, was tantamout to its execution.

the king, who was there at the time [November 7, 1495–February 9, 1496] and was busy feasting and jousting; nothing else interested him.

Those who had been angry about the peace of Vercelli were very happy about the deception which the duke of Milan had practiced against us, and their authority increased thereby. They gave me a good dressing down, as is customary in the courts of princes in similar cases. Indeed I was rather angry about it. I told the king about the offer which the Venetians were making him, which you have heard before, and I showed it to him in writing. He attached no importance to it and the cardinal of Saint-Malo, who was the one who conducted everything, even less. I spoke of it another time, however, and it seemed to me that it would have been better to accept this offer than to lose everything; and furthermore, I did not see any persons [who were fit] to manage such an enterprise, and they never called in anyone who could have helped them, or [at least] as seldom as possible. The king would have been willing to do it, but he was afraid of displeasing those to whom he gave credit, and especially those who managed his finances, such as the cardinal, his brothers, and his relatives.

This is a fine example for princes, for they must take the trouble to conduct their own affairs, and they should commission at least six persons to take care of them and sometimes call in more, depending on the matter, and they should hold them almost as equal. For if one of them is so great that the others fear him (as King Charles VIII did and has done up to now, for he has always had one such person) that person is king and lord in effect; and the master is badly served, as he [the king] was by his governors, who have managed their own affairs very well but his affairs badly; and he has been all the less esteemed for it.

20

I returned to Lyon in the year 1495 on the twelfth of December, and I had been gone on this journey for twenty-two months.[277] And they still held the castles of Naples, as I said a little earlier; and still in the kingdom of Naples were my lord of Montpensier, the king's lieutenant [who had betaken himself] to Salerno [where he was staying] with the prince of that locality, and my lord of Aubigny, who was in Calabria where he had been almost continually ill but had served extremely well there. And Gracien de Guerre was in the Abruzzi, Domjulien at Monte Sant'Angelo, and Georges de Sully at Taranto; but all of them were so poor that no one could imagine it, and so abandoned that they could

277. If Commynes' calculation is correct, he must have left home in mid-February, 1494, to join the king as he was about to proceed to Lyon (see p. 452 above).

receive no news except with great difficulty; and whatever news they did receive was nothing but lies and promises without effect. For as was said, the king did nothing on his own. And if only they had been provided with sums of money in time—and we spent six times over double the amount [needed]—they would never have lost the kingdom: I am referring to forty thousand ducats only which was sent to them when all was lost, as part of their pay for a year and more. And if that money had arrived one month earlier, the hardships and disgraces which befell them, as you shall hear, would not have come upon them, nor would the divisions; and all this came about through the fault of the master, who managed nothing on his own and did not listen to the people who came from there. His servants who were involved with this had little experience and they were lazy; and I believe that one of them was secretly in touch with the pope. And it seemed that God had entirely withdrawn from the king the grace that He had granted him on the journey [to Italy].

After he had stayed in Lyon for two months or so, he received news that my lord the dauphin, his only son, was in danger of death. Three days later he received news that he had died [December 6, 1495]. The king grieved, as one might reasonably expect, [but] not very long; but the mother, named Anne, queen of France and duchess of Brittany, conceived the greatest sorrow from this that any woman might experience, and it lasted with her for a long time. And I believe that in addition to the natural sorrow which mothers usually experience upon the death of their children, she judged within her heart that some other great misfortune would happen. The king her husband did not grieve for long, as was said, and he wanted to comfort her by having a dance performed before her; and several young lords and gentlemen came there in their doublets to dance at the king's invitation. And among them was the duke of Orleans, who was about thirty-four years old, and at this the lady was extremely sad, for indeed it seemed to her that he was happy about this death, since he was the closest in line to the crown after the king. And for this reason they did not speak to each other for a long time afterwards.[278]

The dauphin was about three years old [when he died]; he was a beautiful child and bold in his speech, and he was not afraid of things that other children usually fear; and I assure you that for these reasons the father easily recovered from his sorrow, because he was already afraid that his child would soon be grown up and that if he continued to possess these characteristics he might lessen his authority and power.

278. Louis, duke of Orleans, born June 27, 1462, became King Louis XII in 1498 after Charles VIII's death on April 7. In January, 1499, Louis married Charles VIII's widowed and childless queen, Anne.

For there was never a man of smaller bodily stature than the king, and he did not have much judgment, but he was so good that it was not possible to see a better person.

Now you may realize how great are the miseries of great kings and princes who are afraid of their own children! King Louis, who was so wise and virtuous,[279] was afraid of them (that is, of that very King Charles who reigns today); but he provided very wisely for him and he left him the crown at the age of fourteen. King Louis had frightened his father King Charles VII, and found himself in arms and in league against him with some lords and knights of the kingdom because of quarrels pertaining to the court and the government; and he told me that many times. And this happened when he was about thirteen [*sic*: sixteen] years old, and it did not last. But after he became an adult he had great divisions with King Charles VII his father, and he withdrew to Dauphiné and from there to Flanders, leaving the territory of Dauphiné to the king his father, for they did not wage war against each other. And this matter was mentioned at the beginning of these memoirs.[280]

No creature is exempt from suffering, and everyone eats his bread in sorrow and toil, as Our Lord promised them from the moment He created man, and He kept His word loyally to everyone; but sorrows and toil are varied, and those of the body are the least, whereas those of the mind are the greatest. Those of the wise are of one sort and those of the fools of another, but the fool endures much more sorrow and suffering than the wise, although it seems otherwise to many, and he has less consolation. The poor people, who work and toil in order to feed themselves and their children and who pay taxes and other subsidies to their lords, would live in great discomfort if great princes and lords had nothing but all the pleasure in this world and they had all the worry and misery; but it happens quite differently, for if I wanted to begin to write about the suffering that I have seen high-ranking persons endure, men as well as women, during the past thirty years alone, I could make a book out of it. I do not refer to those who are of the same condition as those who are mentioned in Boccaccio's book,[281] but I am thinking of the men and women whom one sees in perfect wealth, health, and prosperity; and those who did not frequent them as closely as I did considered them to be very happy. And I have often seen their disappoint-

279. See n. 135, p. 374.
280. See p. 131.
281. Commynes is presumably referring to Boccaccio's *De Casibus illustrorum virorum*, which was translated into French between 1400 and 1409 by Laurent de Premierfait and again translated, or rather drawn upon, by Georges Chastellain for his *Le Temple de Bocace* in the 1470's.

ments and sorrows founded on such insignificant reason that people who did not live close to them would hardly have wanted to believe it. Most of them are founded on suspicions and the reports [of others], which constitute a secret illness reigning in the houses of great princes, from whence comes many evils which befall their persons as well as their servants and subjects. And this shortens life so much that there is hardly a king in France since the time of Charlemagne who lived past his sixtieth year.

Because of such suspicion, when King Louis came close to this age and was suffering from another illness, he judged himself already dead. His father Charles VII, who had done so many fine things in France, took it into his head when he became ill that people wanted to poison him [and so] he wanted to eat no more. King Charles VI, who went mad, had different suspicions, and all because of reports. And this should be considered a great fault in princes that they do not verify them when they are things which concern them, even if they may be of no great importance, for by this means they would not have them so often. And it should be told to the people in each other's presence—I refer to the accuser and the accused—and by this means no report would be made unless it were true. But some people are so stupid that they promise and swear not to say anything about it, and by this means they sometimes bear these anguishes of which I am speaking, and most of the time they hate the best and most loyal servants and persecute them at the instigation and on the reports of the meanest people, and they cause great wrongs and great sorrows to their subjects.

21

The death of my lord the dauphin, King Charles VIII's only son, occurred toward the beginning of the year 1496, and it was the greatest loss that had ever happened or that could happen to him, for he never again had any child who lived. This misfortune did not come alone, for at this very time he received news that the castle of Naples had been surrendered by those whom my lord of Montpensier had left there, owing to famine, and also in order to recover the hostages whom the lord of Montpensier had given up, and who were my lord of Alègre, one of the sons of the La Marcks from Ardenne, a person named de la Chapelle from Loudun, and a person named Joan de Rocaberti, a Catalan. And those who were in the castle returned by sea.

Another shame and misfortune befell him, which was that a person named Entragues, who held the citadel of Pisa, which was the fort, and who held this city in subjection, gave up the citadel to the Pisans

[January 1, 1496], which was contrary to the king's oath, for he had twice sworn to the Florentines to give them back the city and other places, such as Sarzana, Sarzanella, Pietrasanta, Librefatto, and Motrone, which the Florentines at his arrival in Italy had lent the king in his great plight and necessity, and they had given him 120,000 ducats, of which only thirty thousand remained to be paid. It has been mentioned somewhere else. But all these places were sold; the Genoese bought Sarzana and Sarzanella, and they were sold to them by a bastard of Saint-Pol. Entragues also sold Pietrasanta to the people of Lucca, and Librefatto to the Venetians; all this was to the great shame and detriment of the king and his subjects and was the consummation of the loss of Naples.

As was said elsewhere, the first oath which the king took to restore these places was in Florence at the high altar of Saint John in the church [Santa Maria del Fiore]. The second was in Asti on his return, when the Florentines lent thirty thousand ducats in cash to the king, who was in very great need of them, on condition that if Pisa were surrendered [to the Florentines], the king would not pay anything of that sum and the pawns and jewels which they were given would be returned. And they were to lend the king another seventy thousand ducats to be paid in cash in the kingdom of Naples to those who were still there by the king's appointment, and to maintain permanently at their expense three hundred men-at-arms in the king's service until the end of the enterprise. And because of the above-mentioned malicious act, nothing of the sort was done. And it was necessary to return the thirty thousand ducats which the Florentines had lent; and all this misfortune [came about] because of lack of obedience and because of reports [whispered] in people's ears, for some of the king's intimates had encouraged Entragues to act as he did.

At the same time [or] within two months more or less, at the beginning of the year 1496, when my lord of Montpensier, Lord Virginio Orsini, Camillo Vitelli, and other French commanders saw that all was lost, they took the field and captured several small places. And there King Ferrandino, son of King Alfonso who had taken religious vows, as you have seen before, came to meet them [April, 1496]. With King Ferrandino was the marquis of Mantua, brother of the lord of Montpensier's wife and commander-in-chief of the Venetians, who found Montpensier lodged in a town called Atella [June 23, 1496], a most disadvantageous place for them to obtain food.

And Ferrandino and the marquis of Mantua took up quarters on a hill and fortified their quarters like people who fear a battle, for King Ferrandino and his men had always been beaten everywhere and the marquis came from Fornovo where he had fought against us.

569

And the Venetians held in pledge six places of great importance in Apulia, such as Brindisi, Otranto, Gallipoli, Trani, and other places. They also hold Monopoli, which they had taken from us, but it was worth little. And they lent a certain sum of money to King Ferrandino, and they estimated at 250,000 ducats the service of the men-at-arms whom they had [maintained] in the kingdom, and [whom they will continue to maintain] for as long as they hold these places. They want to count the expense of guarding them; and I believe that their intention is not to return them, for such is not their custom when they are advantageous, as these places are, and they lie on their side of the gulf. And by this means they are the real lords of the gulf, which is something that they greatly desire. And it seems to me that from Otranto, which is at the extreme end of the gulf, to Venice is nine hundred miles. The pope owns Ancona there, and other places between the two; but everyone who wants to sail through the gulf must pay duty to Venice. And it is more important to them to have acquired these places than many people realize, for they receive from them large quantities of wheat and oil, which are two things very useful to them.[282]

In this place of which I am speaking [Atella] disagreement came up among our men on account of food supplies which were beginning to diminish as well as for lack of money; for the pay of the men-at-arms was a year and half overdue, and more; and they had endured great poverty. Much was also due the Germans, but not so much; for all the money which my lord of Montpensier was able to raise in the kingdom was for them. Yet they had the pay for one year and more due to them. But they had pillaged several small towns, from which they had become very rich. However, if the forty thousand ducats which we had so often promised to send them had been there, or if it had been known that they [the forty thousand ducats] were in Florence, the dissension which arose there would not have taken place. But everyone was hopeless. However, as many of the leaders have told me, if our men had been in agreement about fighting, it seemed to them that they would have won the battle, and even if they had lost it, they would not have lost half of the people whom they lost by making such a disgraceful agreement as they did. My lord of Montpensier and Lord Virginio Orsini, who were the two commanders, wanted the battle; and they died in prison. And the agreement was not observed in regard to them. These two persons about whom I am talking accused my lord of Précy, a young knight from Auvergne, of having been the cause of their not

282. See nn. 199 and 226, pp. 452 and 492, on the Venetians' holding of these towns and others along the Adriatic Sea.

fighting; however, he was a very valiant knight, [although] not very obedient to his superior.

There were two kinds of Germans in this army. They included about fifteen hundred Swiss, who had been present as soon as the king went there. Those men served him loyally until death, and so well that more could not be said. There were others whom we commonly call lansquenets, that is to say, "companions of the country," and they naturally hate the Swiss, and the Swiss reciprocate. They come from all countries, such as those up the Rhine and from the land of Swabia. There were some from the territory of Vaud in Savoy and some from the territory of Gelderland. All this amounted to seven or eight hundred men whom we had sent there recently with two months' pay, which was eaten up by the time they arrived and there they found no other payment. Since these men saw themselves in this danger and in this need, they did not have the same affection for us as do the Swiss, and they made transactions, and they turned over to the side of Don Ferrandino. And for this reason and because of the division of the leaders, our men made a detestable and infamous agreement with Don Ferrandino, who indeed swore to observe it, for the marquis of Mantua wanted after all to secure the person of his brother-in-law, my lord of Montpensier.

By this agreement [July 21, 1496] they all placed themselves in the hands of their enemies and gave them all the king's artillery and promised him to have all the places which the king held in the kingdom surrendered, both those in Calabria where my lord of Aubigny was and also Gaeta and Taranto,[283] and places in the Abruzzi, where Gracien de Guerre was; and in return for this King Ferrandino was to send them to Provence by sea, with their baggage intact (which was worth very little). But King Ferrandino had them all taken to Naples; they numbered five or six thousand persons or more.

Such a dishonorable agreement had never been made in our time, nor had such a one been made before; and I have not read of any like it except the one with the Samnites which was made by two Roman consuls, as Titus Livius relates, who[se descendants] are supposed to be the present-day Beneventans, in a place which was then called the Caudine Forks, which is a certain mountain pass. This agreement the Romans refused to observe, and they sent the two consuls back to the enemy as prisoners.[284]

283. According to Mandrot, II, 349, n. 1, Gaeta, Taranto, and Venosa were expressly excluded from the agreement to have the other French-held towns surrender.

284. See Livy's Book 9, chapters 1–7.

If our men had fought and lost the battle, they would not have lost so many dead. For two-thirds of our men died of famine or of the plague, since so many were kept inside their ships off the island of Procida, where they were sent afterwards by King Ferrandino; and even my lord of Montpensier died there [November 9, 1496], some say of poison and others of fever, which I rather believe. And I do not believe that of all this number fifteen hundred persons ever returned, for of the Swiss, who were at least thirteen hundred [in number], not more than three hundred and fifty returned, and they were all ill. These people should be praised for their loyalty, for they never wanted to take the part of King Ferrandino, and they chose rather to die, as many did in Procida, of heat and illness as well as of hunger, for they were kept in their ships for a long time, and in such great necessity of food that it is unbelievable. I saw the return of those who came back, and especially the Swiss who brought back all their standards; and their faces showed that they had suffered greatly, and all of them were ill; and when they left the ships to take a bit of air, they had to be supported.

Lord Virginio was freed to return to his territories by this agreement, and [so was] his son; and so were all the Italians who served the king. But they detained him and his legitimate son, for he had only one; (it is true that he had an illegitimate son, a man of quality named Lord Carlo). Several Italians from their company robbed him as he was leaving. If such misfortune had befallen only those who had made this agreement, they should not be pitied.

Soon after King Ferrandino had received this honor [that is, the kingship] about which I have already spoken, and after his recent marriage to the daughter of his grandfather King Ferrante (whom he had by the sister of the presently ruling king of Castile, and who was the sister of King Alfonso, his own father), who was thirteen or fourteen years old, he was taken with an unceasing fever of which he died in a few days, and the possession of the kingdom went to King Frederick, Ferrandino's uncle, who has it at present. It seems to me horrible to speak of such a marriage; and several similar ones had already been made by that house in recent times, about thirty years ago from now.[285]

And this death occurred shortly after the agreement mentioned before, which was made at Atella in the year 1496. And the king Don Ferrandino, and also the king Don Frederick after he became king,

285. See the table in Appendix C, p. 604, for the closeness of parentage between Ferrandino's new wife, Joanna of Aragon, and Ferrandino. Married in March, 1496, to Joanna who was seventeen at the time, Ferrandino died of dysentery on October 7, 1496. Perhaps Commynes is thinking of the close parentage between Ferrante I and Joanna, the father and mother of Joanna of Aragon, when he speaks of "several similar" marriages in the house of Aragon.

offered as excuse [for the fact that they did not observe the agreement] that my lord of Montpensier was not having the places surrender, which he had promised [to do] when the agreement was made. And Gaeta and other places were not in his hands; and although he was the king's lieutenant, those who held these places for the king were not bound to give them up at his command, although the king would not have lost much thereby, for they have cost a great deal since then to guard and provide with food; and nevertheless they were lost. And I do not think I am speaking falsely, for I was present to observe being dispatched three or four times those who went to supply the castles of Naples with provisions and to help them one time, and afterwards up to three times in order to supply Gaeta; but these four trips cost more than 300,000 francs, and they served no purpose.[286]

22

After the king's return from the above-mentioned expedition, he stayed in Lyon for a long time, as I said, spending his time in tournaments and jousts, and he was desirous of not losing the places of which I spoke. He did not care how much it cost him, but he did not want to make any effort to take care of the matter [personally]. Plenty of propositions were offered him [by people] from Italy, and they were big enough and sure enough for a king of France. For France has many people, and there is plenty of wheat in Languedoc and Provence and other regions which one could send there; and there is money. But if any prince other than the king of France should desire to become involved in the service of the Italians, in their enterprises, and in aiding [them], he will always end up in the poorhouse; for he will always put up whatever he has and [still] will not achieve anything. For they do not serve except for money; and moreover, they could not do so, unless it were a duke of Milan or one of the Signorias. But a poor captain, even if he would like to serve a member of the house of France pretending a right to the kingdom [of Naples], or another pretending a right to the duchy of Milan, regardless of how much loyalty he has in him or even if he were your partisan (for one cannot ask for greater assurance in Italy than partisanship), would not be able to serve you long after the pay fails, for his men would leave him and [thus] the captain would have lost his assets. For most of them have nothing except the credit accorded them

286. Commynes' arithmetic is once again rather strange. Does he mean that he watched—presumably at Marseille—one fleet depart for Naples (after being summoned to depart three or four times) and three fleets depart for Gaeta? Mandrot, II, 352, n. 2, points out that aid was sent to Gaeta three times, in January, July, and August of 1496.

because of their men-at-arms, who are paid by their captain, and he in turn has himself paid by the one whom he serves.

But what were these propositions that I mentioned? They were so important that before Gaeta was lost [November 10, 1496] and even since, two years after the king had returned and the duke of Milan had not kept any of his promises (and he was not doing everything out of deceit or malevolence, but partly out of fear that if the king became so powerful he might overthrow him later on; and he considered the king a person of small constancy and trustworthiness), it was decided that the duke of Orleans would go to Asti with a good, large number of men. And I saw him ready to leave, and I saw all his [baggage-]train leave. We were certain [of the support] of the duke of Ferrara, with five hundred men-at-arms and two thousand infantrymen, even though he was the duke of Milan's father-in-law. [For] in order to remove himself from the peril in which he saw himself between the Venetians and the duke (already a long time before, as was seen earlier, the Venetians had taken the Polesina from him, and they asked for nothing but his destruction), he would have chosen his safety and that of his children in preference to the friendship which he had for his son-in-law. And perhaps it seemed to him that the duke would make an agreement with the king when he found himself in fear of this [alliance between Ferrara and France], and by his [the duke of Ferrara's] hand. The marquis of Mantua, who was formerly commander-in-chief of the Venetians and still was, but who was held in suspicion by them and was dissatisfied with them, joined forces with his father-in-law the duke of Ferrara, with three hundred men-at-arms. For he had as a wife and still has [Isabella d'Este] the sister of the duchess of Milan and the daughter of the duke of Ferrara. Giovanni di Bentivoglio, who governs Bologna and is, so to speak, its lord, would have supplied one hundred and fifty men-at-arms and two of his sons, who had men-at-arms and good infantrymen; and he is located in a place where he could serve well against the duke of Milan. The Florentines—who saw themselves destroyed if, owing to some great misfortune, they did not rally themselves (because they were dispossessed of Pisa and other places which have been mentioned)—would have supplied eight hundred men-at-arms and five thousand infantrymen, and this at their expense. And they had put aside [the money] for their payment for six months. The Orsini and the Vitelli and the prefect [of Rome, Giovanni della Rovere], the brother of the cardinal of Saint Peter in Chains, who were mentioned several times because they were in the king's pay, would have brought at least one thousand men-at-arms; but you must understand that the attendants of their men-at-arms are not the same as those of our men-at-arms, who have archers. But the pay is about the same, for a well-paid man-at-arms costs one hundred ducats a year, and a thousand men-at-arms 100,000 ducats a year, and we need double that amount for the archers.[287]

It was indeed necessary to pay these mercenaries; but nothing had to be paid the Florentines. Only part of their expenses had to be paid to the duke of Ferrara, the marquis of Mantua, and Bentivoglio, for they expected to gain lands at the expense of the duke of Milan or the Venetians. Now observe that if the duke of Milan had suddenly been assailed by the forces which the duke of Orleans and all those whom I have named had brought, he would not have been able to defend himself without being destroyed or being forced to turn over to the side of the king against the Venetians. And less than eighty thousand ducats would have kept all these Italians in the field for a long time; and once the duke of Milan was defeated, the kingdom of Naples would have been recovered of its own accord.

The reason why this fine enterprise was not attempted was that the duke of Orleans (although he was expected to leave any day, since he had sent before him all sorts of things which were useful to his person and no one remained to leave except him and his army, which was ready and had been paid; for he had eight hundred French men-at-arms in Asti and about six thousand infantrymen, of whom four thousand were Swiss) changed his mind and requested the king twice that he should bring this matter up before the council; which was done twice, and I was present there both times. And it was concluded without a dissenting voice (and there were always at least ten or twelve persons present) that he should proceed there, since they had so assured all the above-named friends in Italy, who had already spent money and held themselves in readiness. Then the duke of Orleans (who had been advised by someone, or else avoided leaving because he saw the king in rather poor health, and he was to be his heir if he should die) declared that he would not go there on account of his quarrel [with the duke of Milan], but that he would willingly go as the king's lieutenant and by his command. And so the council was ended.

The next day and for several days afterwards [in May, 1496] the Florentine ambassadors and others pressed the king strongly to send the duke on his way; but the king said that he never sent anyone to war by force; and so the journey was broken up. And it displeased the king, who had gone to great expense on account of it and who had great hopes of taking revenge on the duke of Milan, considering the news which he received every hour from the informers which Gian Giacomo

287. See nn. 23 and 249 on pp. 112 and 522 above on Italian and French lance-teams. Commynes' cost accounting seems to be correct.

Trivulzio had; he was lieutenant for the king and for the duke of Orleans in Asti and was a native of Milan, and he was well liked and had good relations in the duchy of Milan, where he had many persons who were in compact with him among his relatives as well as others.

When this enterprise failed, another came up immediately afterwards —or rather two and three at one time—from Genoa, whose people are inclined toward any sort of change. One involved Battista di Campofregoso, who was a great leader among the parties of Genoa. But he was banished from there and his party could do nothing there; and neither could the Doria, who are nobles whereas the Fregosi are not. And the Doria are partisans of the Fregosi and they cannot be doges because they are nobles, for no noble can become one. And Battista had been one not long before, but he had been betrayed by his uncle the cardinal of Genoa, who had put the government of Genoa into the hands of the duke of Milan not too long ago. And Genoa was governed by the Adorno family, who also are not nobles but have often been doges of Genoa with the help of the Spinola, who are nobles. Thus the nobles indeed make a doge in Genoa, but they cannot become one themselves. Battista was hoping to have his party take arms in the city as well as in the fields, and that the governmental power would pass to the king and that he and his partisans would rule and would drive the others out.

Many people from Savona had addressed themselves to the cardinal of Saint Peter in Chains, assuring him that they could give up the town of Savona to him, in the hope that they could become free; for it is under [the jurisdiction of] Genoa, and they pay the *gabelles*.[288] If anyone had been able to obtain that place, Genoa would have been reduced to great straits, considering that the king holds Provence and that Savoy is under his orders.

And because of all this news the king sent word to Gian Giacomo Trivulzio that he should support Battista di Campofregoso and should provide men to accompany him up to the gates of Genoa to see if his partisans could revolt. From another side he was so pressed by the cardinal of Saint Peter in Chains that the king immediately wrote to Gian Giacomo that he should send men with the cardinal to escort him as far as Savona; and he was told this orally by the lord of Serenon from

288. There are two problems in this phrase. "Gabelles," like "bledz" (see n. 235 on p. 506), may be specific or general in meaning: "salt taxes" or merely "taxes." We have handled this problem analogously to the way in which we handled the word "bledz": by preserving the words "gabelle" or "gabelles" in the text, the reader may interpret the context for himself (see, e.g., p. 590 below where the context easily determines the proper meaning of "gabelle"). The second problem in this phrase is the uncertain reference of the last pronoun, "they." Calmette, III, 278, n. 7, suggests that "they" refers to the Genoese. This seems absurd. It is the Savonans who want to stop paying taxes to the Genoese.

Provence, a friend of the cardinal and a very bold talker. The king sent word to Gian Giacomo that he should put himself in a position to support [both of] the two parties and that he should not undertake anything against the duke of Milan or against the peace which had been made with the duke the preceding season, as has been explained elsewhere.

Now these were rather different orders. Thus the affairs of great princes are dispatched when they are not present and when they are hasty in having letters and people sent without carefully hearing the execution of such important business discussed before them. Now you must understand that what Battista di Campofregoso was asking and what the cardinal was trying to obtain could not possibly be supplied to both at once. For to go up to the walls of Genoa without a great number of men was not feasible, for there are many people inside and they are brave and well armed. And if men were to be given to the cardinal, the army would have had to have been divided into three sections, for part of it had to remain with Gian Giacomo. And in Genoa and Savona there were a great number of people whom the duke of Milan and the Venetians had sent there, for both of them were very much afraid that Genoa might turn [against them], and so were Don Frederick and the pope.

Now Gian Giacomo had a third enterprise in his heart; he would have liked to proceed directly against the duke of Milan and to leave the other two enterprises aside; and if he had been allowed to do as he pleased he would have accomplished great things. And he began [to do so]; for under color of writing to the king that he could not protect from adversity those who would go to Genoa or Savona, he went to place himself on the high road by which it was possible to come from Alessandria to Genoa, for by no other way could the duke of Milan send men to charge upon us. And Gian Giacomo took two or three little towns, which opened [their gates] to him; and he said that he was not at war with the duke on that account, considering that it was necessary that he should put himself there. And moreover, the king had no intention of waging war against the duke in order to take Genoa or Savona, if he had been able [to take them], because he said that they are held from him [the king] and that he [the duke] had forfeited them.[289]

In order to satisfy the cardinal, Gian Giacomo gave him part of the army to go to Savona. He found the place garrisoned and his enter-

---

289. Commynes seems to be saying that Charles VIII wanted no destruction of Genoa or Savona through war, for this would be destroying what he considered already his feudal forfeit.

prise broken; and they turned back. And he gave other [troops] to Battista in order to go to Genoa, and Battista assured him strongly that he would not fail. [But] after he had marched three or four leagues those who were in his company, both German and French, began to have suspicions about him, although this was a mistake. But their company, which was not large, would have exposed themselves to danger by going there if his party had not risen.

And thus all these enterprises failed; and the duke of Milan had already made himself strong, although he would have been in great peril if Gian Giacomo had been allowed to have his way. And many Venetian soldiers had come to him. Our army retired and our infantrymen were given leave. The small towns which we had taken were abandoned and the war ended with little profit for the king, for very great sums of money had been spent for it.

23

From the beginning of the year 1496, when the king had already been three or four months on this side of the mountains, until the year 1498, the king did not do anything else in Italy. I was with him all the time and I was present at the transaction of most of his affairs. And the king went from Lyon to Moulins, and from Moulins to Tours [June–July, 1496], and everywhere he spent his time in tournaments and jousts and thought of nothing else. Those around him who had most credit were so divided that they could not have been more so. Some wanted the enterprise in Italy to continue; they were the cardinal and the seneschal, and they saw that it was to their profit and advantage to continue it; and everything was referred to them. On the other side was the admiral [Graville], who had had complete authority with the young king before the journey; he wanted these enterprises to be entirely abandoned. And he saw his profit in this, and visualized himself returning to his former position of authority and the others losing it. And thus things stood for a year and a half or so.

And ambassadors were sent to the king and queen of Castile, for the king strongly desired to appease that side, since they were at war. And they were strong at sea and on land. Although they had achieved little on land, they had given considerable help to Kings Ferrandino and Frederick at sea, for Sicily is a league and a half from the kingdom of Naples at Reggio Calabria; and some people maintain that it was formerly all land, but that the sea has formed this opening that we now call the Straits of Messina. And from Sicily, over which the king and queen of Castile were great lords, much help arrived at Naples, both men and caravels which they had sent there from Spain. In Sicily itself a number of men-at-arms were raised who passed over into Calabria along with a number of jennetaries and made war against those who were [fighting] there for the king [Charles VIII]. Their ships accompanied those of the league unceasingly, and so when they were all together, the king was much too weak at sea.

Otherwise the king of Castile did the king little harm. Great numbers of horsemen entered Languedoc and did some pillaging there and stayed camped in that region. A number of them stayed in the region for two, three, and four days, but they accomplished nothing else. My lord of Saint-André from the Bourbonnais was in this area as deputy for my lord the duke of Bourbon, governor of Languedoc. He undertook to take Salces, a small town which was in Roussillon, for they were waging war against the king from there; and this was two years after he had given back to them the area of Roussillon in which the region called Perpignan is located, and this little town is in this region.[290] The enterprise was important, for there were many soldiers there, considering the place, and there were also gentlemen from the house of the king of Castile; and their army, which was larger than ours, lodged in the field within a league [of us]. However, the lord of Saint-André conducted his enterprise so wisely and so secretly that in ten hours he took the place, as I have seen by his letters. It was taken by assault, and thirty or forty Spanish gentlemen of good reputation died there, and among others the son of the archbishop of Santiago, in addition to three or four hundred other men who had not expected to be beaten so soon; for they did not understand the power of our artillery, which in truth exceeds all the other artillery in the world.

And there you have all the fighting which was done by these two kings; but it was to the shame and discredit of the king of Castile, considering that his army was so large. But when Our Lord wishes to start to punish people, such minor hardships often befall them at the beginning; for indeed greater ones came upon the king and queen soon afterwards; and it was the same with us.

The king and queen were very much to blame for having perjured themselves toward the king, after the great kindness which he had manifested to them in returning to them the territory of Roussillon,

290. See n. 172, p. 415, for the treaty of Barcelona of 1493, by the terms of which the county of Roussillon was returned to Spain. Ferdinand of Aragon sent troops to Salces in July, 1495. Between November, 1495, and January, 1496, Spanish forces made the raids into Languedoc of which Commynes speaks at the beginning of this paragraph, and Saint-André invaded Roussillon in reply. Attacks continued in both areas through the spring and summer of 1496, and culminated in the surrender of Salces on October 8, 1496.

which had cost his father so much to repair and maintain and which had been held by him [Charles VIII] in return for 300,000 *écus*, which he had paid them. And all this was so that they would not hinder him in the conquest which he hoped to make of the kingdom of Naples. And they renewed the old alliances of Castile, which run from king to king, from kingdom to kingdom, and from man to man among their subjects,[291] in the name of which they promised not to hinder him in this conquest and not to marry any of their daughters in the houses of Naples, England, or Flanders. And this strict clause concerning marriage came from their side; and overtures were made about this by a Franciscan named Brother Juan de Mauleón at the request of the queen of Castile. And as soon as they saw that war had started and that the king was in Rome, they sent their ambassadors everywhere to make an alliance against the king, and even to Venice where I was; and there the league of which I have spoken so much was concluded between the pope, the king of the Romans, themselves, the Signoria of Venice, and the duke of Milan. And they immediately began a war against the king, saying that they were not obligated to observe the promise of not marrying their daughters to those kings of whom I spoke (and they had four daughters and one son). Yet this overture had been initiated by themselves, as you have seen.

Now to return to my subject. All these wars of Italy had miscarried, and the king held nothing except Gaeta in the kingdom (for he still held it when the peace negotiations began between the kings and the queen [Charles, Ferdinand, and Isabella], but afterwards all was lost, and moreover no more war was made in Roussillon, but each one kept what belonged to him). [Then] they sent a gentleman and one of the monks of Montserrat [September, 1496] for they have had all their affairs managed by such people, either out of hypocrisy or in order to spend less. For Brother Juan de Mauleón, the Franciscan who was [just] mentioned, negotiated the treaty [of Barcelona in 1493] concerning the return of Roussillon. These ambassadors whom I have mentioned begged the king at the outset that he should be pleased never to

291. So far as I have been able to discover, these juridical phrases, which Commynes has also used on p. 173 to emphasize the close ties between France and Castile, appear for the first time in approximately the form in which Commynes gives them in the second treaty of alliance between Alfonso XI of Castile and Philip VI of France, made in July, 1345. See Georges Daumet, *Etude sur l'alliance de la France et de la Castille au XIVe et au XVe siècles* (Paris, 1898), p. 141, for these phrases in the treaty of 1345. Daumet reprints the texts of subsequent treaties and related documents down to the treaty of 1475 between Louis XI and John II, in most of which these phrases reappear (see e.g., pp. 156, 192, 254, etc.). Perhaps Commynes derived his knowledge of Franco-Castilian diplomatic instruments from his trip to Castile in 1471 (see p. 7 ff. of the Introduction).

call to mind the wrong that the king and queen had done him. (The queen is always named, because Castile came from her side; and also she had the principal authority. Theirs was a most honorable and harmonious marriage.) Afterwards they requested a truce in which all their league was to be included and the king was to remain in possession of Gaeta and other places which he had in the kingdom [of Naples] and he was to be able to supply them with food at his pleasure during the truce and a day was to be appointed so that ambassadors from all the league could be present in order to negotiate peace, if possible. And afterwards [if peace were signed] the kings[292] wanted to continue with their conquest of or their enterprise against the Moors, and to pass the sea which is between Granada and Africa, in which the territory of the king of Fez was the closest to theirs. However, some people have maintained that such was not their will, and that they were satisfied with what they had accomplished, which is the conquest of the kingdom of Granada [1492], which was indeed a fine and great conquest and the finest that has taken place in our time and [something] which their predecessors were never able to do. And I wish out of affection for them that they had not had designs on anything else and had kept their promises to our king.

The king sent back the lord of Clérieu from Dauphiné with these two ambassadors, and the king tried to make peace or a truce with them without including the league [October–November, 1496]. If he had accepted their offer, however, he would have saved Gaeta, which was sufficient to recover the kingdom of Naples, considering the friends whom the king had in it.

When Clérieu returned [from a second embassy to Spain in January, 1497,] he brought new propositions [from the Spanish], and Gaeta was already lost before he got to Castile.[293] This new overture was that the

292. Commynes is referring to Ferdinand and Isabella as "the kings," for he is translating the Castilian term for the king and queen, "los reyes," directly into French, "les roys," as he indicates in a parenthesis on p. 584.

293. Clérieu's first offer, mentioned in the preceding paragraph, was rejected by the Spanish. Gaeta fell on November 19, 1496, and Clérieu was sent back to Spain for the second time in January, 1497; it is the result of this second negotiation that Commynes discusses in this paragraph. But Commynes himself evidently thinks that he is discussing in this paragraph the results of Clérieu's first trip to Spain in October–November, 1496, and not those of his second trip in January, 1497. This memory slip is extraordinary since Commynes dictated this passage before the end of 1498, which was less than two years after these events took place. Moreover, he knew many of the ambassadors involved personally and may even have had a hand in the negotiations himself (see Joseph Calmette, "Contribution à la critique des *Mémoires* de Commynes," *Moyen Age*, VIII [1904], 202 and 206, for these points). Commynes begins the paragraph following this one with, "Since then ... Clérieu and ... Gramont returned there...." Thus, in Commynes' mind his discussion of

king and they should return to their original and former friendship, and that they should undertake the conquest of all Italy as loot for them both and at their common expense and that the two kings should be there together. But first they wanted a general truce in which the league would be included, and they wanted a meeting to be organized in Piedmont where everyone could send ambassadors, because they wanted to leave the league honorably. In my opinion, judging from what we saw later, this whole overture was just a deception, made to gain time and to let King Ferrandino, who was still living [*sic*: died October 6, 1496], and Don Frederick, who had recently entered the kingdom, have a rest; however, they would have been glad if that kingdom had been theirs, for they had better rights to it than those who possessed it and possess it [now]. But the house of Anjou, from which the king has his title, is supposed to have priority. But considering the nature of the kingdom and of the people who live in it, I should think that it belongs to whoever is able to possess it; for they want nothing but changes [in government].

Since then [*sic*] the lord of Clérieu and a person named Michel de Gramont [*sic*: Richard Lemoyne] returned there with some propositions. Clérieu had some affection for the house of Aragon and hoped to obtain the marquisate of Cotrone, which is in Calabria and which the king of Spain holds as a result of that recent conquest which his men made in the territory of Calabria, and Clérieu claims that it is his. He is a good man who believes things easily, especially [when they come] from such persons [as kings]. The second time he returned [to France, in February, 1497,] he brought an ambassador from the kings [Ferdinand and Isabella]. Clérieu reported that they would be satisfied to have what is the closest to Sicily—that is, Calabria—in return for the rights which they pretend to have to the kingdom [of Naples], and the king could take the rest. And [he reported] that the king of Castile[294] would come in person to take part in this conquest and would pay as much as the king toward the expenses of the army. And he already held and still holds four or five fortified places in Calabria, of which Cotrone, an

---

Clérieu's second mission to Spain begins with the following paragraph and not with this paragraph (note how Commynes begins the fourth sentence of the following paragraph with the words "The second time..."). In fact, the present paragraph and the following one discuss the same embassy, that of January, 1497. Commynes also erroneously states in the following paragraph that Clérieu was accompanied on his second mission by Michel de Gramont, when in fact it was one Richard Lemoyne, not Gramont, who accompanied Clérieu.

294. *Sic.* Although Ferdinand controlled Castile's foreign policy for his wife Isabella, he was never styled "king of Castile." He was king of Aragon and husband of the queen of Castile only.

important and strong city, is one. I was present when the [ambassador's] report was made; and it seemed to many people that it was nothing but trickery and that someone who understood things well should be sent there to pursue this proposition more closely. Therefore the lord of Bouchage joined the first group. He was a very wise man who had had great authority with King Louis and still has it at present with King Charles, son of the late King Louis.

The ambassador whom Clérieu had brought never agreed to confirm what Clérieu said; but he said that he believed Clérieu would not have said it if his masters had not told him so, which confirmed the [fact that there was] trickery; nor would anyone believe that the king of Castile would come in person or that he wanted to or could spend as much as the king.

As soon as the lord of Bouchage, Clérieu, Michel de Gramont and others had arrived before the king and queen of Castile [May, 1497], they had them lodge in a place where no one communicated with them, and they had people who kept watch over them; and the king and queen spoke with them three times.[295] But when du Bouchage told them what Clérieu and Michel de Gramont [*sic*: Lemoyne] had reported, they replied that they had indeed spoken about it in a manner of conversation, but not at all otherwise. But [they said] that they would willingly concern themselves with peace and make it for the king's honor and his profit. Clérieu was very much displeased with this answer, and not without cause, and he insisted in front of them and in the presence of the lord of Bouchage that they had so told him. Then a truce which could be denounced on two months' notice was concluded by the lord of Bouchage and his companions, without including the league.[296] But they certainly included those who had married their daughters and the fathers of their sons-in-law, that is, the kings of the Romans and of England, for the prince of Wales and the archduke of Austria had married them and are still married to them; but the prince of Wales is quite young and they have another daughter to be married, for they have four daughters. And the eldest one was a widow and had married the late king of Portugal's son, who broke his neck before her [eyes] as he

295. In this and the following paragraph Commynes speaks of Clérieu's third embassy to Spain in May–June, 1497, in which he was accompanied not by Lemoyne, but by Gramont, du Bouchage, Jean Guérin and Etienne Petit (see Calmette, *ibid*., pp. 205–206).

296. In fact, as Calmette, *ibid*., p. 205, points out, a truce of two months' duration was signed at Lyon on February 15, 1497; it was a result of Clérieu's second embassy in January, 1497, and not of his third one in May, 1497. The truce described here as negotiated by du Bouchage is essentially an extension of this earlier truce and was not agreed upon until November 24, 1497, as indicated in n. 298.

went along a path on a jennet, [only] three months after he had married her.[297]

After du Bouchage had arrived and had made his report the king realized that he had done well to send him there, and at least he was assured of what he had been in doubt about. And it seemed to him indeed that Clérieu had believed things too easily. Furthermore, du Bouchage told him that he had not been able to accomplish anything except this truce, and it was up to the king to either accept or refuse it. The king accepted it; and it was a good truce, considering that it meant the breaking up of this league which had so disturbed him in his affairs. And he had found no way of breaking it up, although he had tried to by all possible means. Du Bouchage also told him that ambassadors were following him en route to the king [of France], and that the king and queen had told him at his departure that they would have the power to conclude a very good peace. And du Bouchage said in addition that when they had left, the prince of Castile, their only son, was ill.

24

Ten or twelve days after the arrival of du Bouchage and his companions, letters came which were addressed to du Bouchage by one of the king's heralds whom he had left there to conduct the ambassadors who were to come. And the letters said that he should not be surprised if the ambassadors were a few days late; it was on account of the death of the prince of Castile.[298] The kings (for so they were called) mani-

297. The four daughters of Ferdinand and Isabella were Isabella, whose husband, the Infante Alfonso of Portugal, died on July 12, 1491 (some seven months, not three, after their marriage on November 27, 1490); Joanna, wife of Philip the Handsome, son of the king of the Romans; Maria, unmarried; and Catherine, fiancée of Arthur, son of Henry VII of England and prince of Wales. Catherine of Aragon later became the wife of Henry VIII after the unexpected death of Arthur.

298. Don Juan of Castile died on October 4, 1497, not ten or twelve days after du Bouchage returned from Spain but rather some four months after he left Medina del Campo on June 7. The pompous lamentations which followed Don Juan's death, Commynes reports, delayed further negotiations between France and Spain. Discussion of these lamentations and their moral implications causes Commynes to deviate from his subject, so that he never tells his readers of the end of the Franco-Spanish negotiations discussed in chapter 23. Charles VIII, in order to achieve a more definite settlement with Spain, sent the five ambassadors mentioned in n. 295 above back to Spain in late October, 1497. On November 24, 1497, the French ambassadors signed the treaty of Alcalá de Henares which had essentially been worked out by Clérieu and du Bouchage during their earlier embassies. Its main provision was a truce between the two powers which could be interrupted on two months' notice (see the announcement of the truce reproduced in Antonio de la Torre's *Documentos sobre relaciones internacionales de los reyes católicos*, V [Barcelona, 1965], 553–54). The chronological confusions and incompleteness of

fested such extreme grief over this that no one could believe it, and this was especially true of the queen, who was expected to die rather than to live. And to speak the truth, I have never heard of greater mourning than was observed in all their kingdoms, for all the craftsmen stopped working for forty days (as their ambassadors have told me since) and everyone dressed in black clothes of coarse sackcloth; and noblemen and persons of quality rode on mules which were covered with such cloth down to their knees and only their eyes could be seen; and black banners were hung on the gates of the cities everywhere. When my lady Margaret, daughter of the king of the Romans, sister of my lord the archduke of Austria and wife of the prince, heard this sad news—and she was six months pregnant—she was delivered of a stillborn daughter.

What pitiful news [this was] in this house which had received so much glory and honor, and which possessed more lands through inheritance than any prince in Christendom had ever possessed! And in addition they had made this fine conquest of Granada and had forced the king out of Italy and had made him fail in his enterprise, which they considered to be a grand thing, and they were so honored throughout the world! The pope had wanted to bestow upon them the title of

---

which Commynes is guilty in discussing the Franco-Spanish negotiations of 1496–1497 cannot be explained away as merely the result of Commynes' "unsystematic" but "not in any way inexact" exposition, as Calmette attempts to do in the article which we have cited (see *ibid.*, p. 207) and in the notes to his edition (see Calmette, III, 289 ff.). In fact, Calmette's attempt to exonerate Commynes from almost all inexactitude causes him to annotate several passages in chapter 23 misleadingly if not incorrectly (cf. Calmette, III, 290, n. 4, with n. 294 above, and III, 292, n. 4, with this note).

These chronological distortions seem to have been caused, here as elsewhere in the *Memoirs*, by Commynes' excessive confidence in one of his sources—in this case, du Bouchage, an intimate of Commynes' since the 1470's. For the result of Commynes' presentation of these Franco-Spanish negotiations, as he takes pains to emphasize in the paragraph preceding this one, is to indicate du Bouchage's competence and Clérieu's incompetence in negotiating. Such emphasis served Commynes' turn since he, like du Bouchage, had been thrown in the shade by Charles VIII's new diplomats (the *Memoirs*, as I have tried to show on p. 20 of the Introduction among other places, served personal apologetic purposes as well as more generally didactic and commemorative ones). Commynes reproaches Clérieu for taking seriously Ferdinand's offer to Charles to "undertake the conquest of Italy as loot for them both." Yet that is exactly what Ferdinand and Charles did agree to do in a secret accompaniment to the treaty of Alcalá: forming an offensive alliance against Naples, they agreed that Ferdinand should have Calabria and Charles the rest (the treaty of Granada in November, 1500, between Ferdinand and Louis XII merely repeated this arrangement, while enlarging Ferdinand's share to include Apulia as well as Calabria). See H. F. Delaborde, *L'Expédition de Charles VIII en Italie* (Paris, 1888), pp. 683–84, and H. Mariéjol, *The Spain of Ferdinand and Isabella* (New Brunswick, New Jersey, 1962), pp. 70–71, for these aspects of the treaties of Alcalá and Granada.

"most Christian" and to take it away from the king, and several times he had so addressed them at the head of the briefs which he sent them. And because some cardinals objected to this title he gave them another one and called them "most Catholic," which title he still uses when he writes to them, and one may assume that this title will remain theirs in Rome. They had achieved great obedience and justice in their kingdom, and it seemed that God and the world wanted to honor them more than any princes in the world, and they lived personally in much prosperity.

But [their sorrows] did not cease [with the death of their son], for their eldest daughter, whom they loved more than anything else in the world after the prince their son whom they had lost, had been married a few days before [*sic*: in October, 1497] to the king of Portugal named Manuel, a young prince who had recently become king [October, 1495]. And the crown had come to him by the death of the late king [John II] who had reigned cruelly; for he had his father-in-law's head cut off, and afterwards killed his wife's brother, who was the son of the above-named person and the eldest brother of the man who is now king of Portugal; and he had him live in great fear and terror; and he killed the brother with his own hands as he was having dinner with him in the presence of his wife; and he wanted to make king one of his illegitimate children.[299] After these two cruel acts he lived in great fear and suspicion, and soon after these two exploits he lost his only son, who broke his neck as he rode on a mule and was going along a path, as I said; and it was he who was the first husband of the lady of whom I am speaking, and who has now married the king of Portugal who now reigns (and so she was in Portugal twice). She is said to be among the most wise and honorable ladies of the wise ladies of the world.

To continue with these miserable adventures which happened in such a short time to the king and queen of Castile, both of whom had lived so gloriously and happily until they had reached their present age of about fifty (although the queen was two years older):[300] they had given their daughter to the king of Portugal so that they would have no enemy in Spain, for they hold all of it except Navarre, with which they do as they please, holding four of the principal places there. And they also

299. Calmette, III, 296, n. 7, asserts that while Commynes is correct about how John II of Portugal (1481–1495) murdered his wife's brother with his own hands, he is wrong in asserting that John had his wife's father executed. Rather, it was another duke named Ferdinand who suffered John's wrath. George of Portugal was the illegitimate son whom John wanted to succeed him. Instead, the crown passed to Manuel the Fortunate in 1495, who became the husband of Isabella of Aragon in October, 1497, only to lose Isabella less than a year later (August 24, 1498), as Commynes tells us some paragraphs after this.

300. *Sic*. Ferdinand and Isabella were somewhat closer in age than Commynes believed: Ferdinand was born on March 10, 1452, and Isabella on April 23, 1451.

did it in order to settle the matter of the lady's dowry and the money
that had been given [at the time of her first Portuguese marriage], and
because some lords of Portugal had been banished from the country
when the dead king had killed the two lords of whom I spoke and had
confiscated their estates (and by this means the confiscation holds
today, although the offense of which they were accused was that they
wanted to make the one who reigns at present king of Portugal). These
knights were recompensed in Castile, and their lands were left in the
hands of the queen of Portugal of whom I am speaking.

Now it should be understood that there are no people whom the
Spaniards hate so much as the Portuguese; and they despise them and
mock them. Therefore it was most distressing to the above-mentioned
kings to have given their daughter to a man who would not be pleasing
to the kingdom of Castile and their other territories. And if they had
been able to marry her [according to their inclination], they never
would have done it; and it was another source of great affliction, and
all the greater because she had to leave them. However, after their sorrow was over, they led them through all the principal cities in their
kingdoms, and they had their daughter received as their princess and the
king of Portugal as their prince, to be king after their death. And some
small comfort came to them, which was that this lady, who was princess
of Castile and queen of Portugal, was pregnant, and the child was moving. But here the height of their sorrows was reached, and I believe that
they would have wanted God to take them away from the world; for
this lady, whom they loved and treasured so much, died as she gave
birth to her child, and I believe that it was not a month ago, and we are
now in October of the year 1498. But the child for whom she died in
labor has remained alive, and he was named Manuel after his father.[301]

All these great [turns of] fortune happened to them in the space of
three months.[302] But before the death of the lady of whom I spoke,
another great sorrow and calamity occurred in this kingdom, for King
Charles VIII of whom I have spoken so much died, as I shall explain
afterwards. And it seems that Our Lord looked upon these two houses

301. Isabella died during the birth of her child Miguel (not Manuel) on August
24, 1498. Miguel lived only twenty-three months, dying in July, 1500. Thus, Commynes must not have revised the *Memoirs* after 1500.

302. *Sic.* As in the case of the death of Juan of Castile, of Campobasso's desertion,
of Louis XI's virtual imprisonment at Péronne, and of many other unexpected
turns of events recounted in the *Memoirs*, Commynes distorts chronology to make
his moral lesson more impressive. Between the death of Juan of Castile on October
4, 1497, and the death of Isabella of Portugal on August 24, 1498, almost eleven
months elapsed. However, as Calmette maintains in III, 299, n. 1, Commynes may be
thinking here only of the time between Isabella's trip through Portugal (together
with husband and parents) and her death.

with His stern countenance and that He does not want one kingdom to mock another at all. For no change can take place in a kingdom without causing great hardships to most people; and although some people may gain something thereby, it happens one hundred times more often that people are the losers on account of it. And it is necessary to change many a custom and manner of living when such changes take place, for what pleases one king displeases the other. And as I said elsewhere, if anyone were to consider this, he would find that the cruel and sudden punishments which Our Lord has laid upon great men in the last thirty years outnumber those occurring for two hundred years beforehand, and this includes France, Castile, Portugal, England, the kingdom of Naples, Flanders, and Brittany. And if anyone were to write about particular cases, all of which I have seen (and almost all the people, both men and women), he could make it into a large and most admirable book, even if it included only what has occurred in the past ten years, whereby the power of God should be well known and understood. The blows which He gives to the great are much more cruel and much more weighty and of much longer duration than are those which He gives to the small. Finally it seems to me that, considering everything, they [the great] have scarcely any advantage in this world over others. If they are willing to see and apply to themselves what they observe happening to their neighbors, and if they fear that the same thing might happen to them, they will recognize it. For they punish the men who live under them at their pleasure, and Our Lord disposes of them as He wishes, for they have no superior except Him. And a country or kingdom is indeed fortunate when it has a wise king or lord who fears God and keeps His commandments.

We have been able to see in few words the sorrows which these two great and powerful kingdoms sustained in three months' time. Shortly before this they were so inflamed against each other and so busy tormenting each other and so intent on increasing their power; and they were in no way satisfied with what they had. I truly confess, as I said, that when such changes occur, there are always some who are happy and who derive benefit as a result; but even for them such sudden death is terrifying at the outset.

25

I wish to put a complete stop to my discussion of the affairs of Italy and Castile and to return to our particular sorrows and losses in France, and also to the joy which those who gained something from them may have had. [So] I shall speak of the sudden death of our King Charles, eighth of that name. He was in his castle of Amboise, where he had started the greatest building project that any king had undertaken during the past one hundred years, both in the castle and in the town. This can be seen from the towers [in the castle], up which one can ascend on horseback, and from what he had undertaken in the town, for which the plans [alone] represented a marvelous undertaking and expense, and [their execution] would have taken a long time to finish. And he had brought from Naples several masters who excelled in many fields, such as sculptors and painters. And it seemed indeed that what he was undertaking was the project of a young king who did not think of death, but who hoped for a long life; for he collected all the beautiful objects that were recommended to him, in whatever country they may have been seen, whether France, Italy, or Flanders. And he always had his heart set on the return to Italy; he confessed freely that he had made many mistakes there, and he enumerated them. And it seemed to him that if he could return there once more and recover what he had lost, he could provide for the retention of the area better than he had done [the first time].

He was involved in intrigues on all sides, including a recent one, to send once more to the kingdom of Naples fifteen hundred Italian men-at-arms to be led by the marquis of Mantua, the Orsini, the Vitelli, and the prefect [of Rome], brother of the cardinal of Saint Peter in Chains; and my lord of Aubigny, who had served him so well in Calabria, was going to Florence, and they [the Florentines] assumed half of these expenses for six months. We were supposed to first take Pisa, or at least the small places around it, and then, joining all forces, we were going to invade the kingdom [of Naples], from which messengers came at every moment.

Pope Alexander, who reigns at present, entered into great intrigues everywhere in order to be on the king's side; he was displeased with the Venetians and sent a secret messenger whom I conducted to the king's chamber shortly before his death. The Venetians were ready to act against Milan. The Spanish maneuvers were such as you have seen. The king of the Romans desired nothing in the world so much as his friendship and that the two of them might arrange their affairs together in Italy. The king of the Romans, whose name is Maximilian, is a great enemy of the Venetians; for they hold many things [i.e., fiefs] from the house of Austria of which he is a member, and also from the empire.

Furthermore, the king had recently made up his mind to live properly and according to God's commandments, to put justice and the church in good order, and also to regulate his finances in such a way that he would raise only 1,200,000 francs upon his people by way of taxes over [and above the money from] his domain, which was the sum that the three estates had granted him at Tours when he became king. And he wanted this sum [to be granted him] in authorization for the defense of the kingdom. And he wanted to live from his domain, as kings formerly did; and he certainly was in a position to do so, for the domain is quite considerable, if it were well managed, for it includes the *gabelle*, the salt-tax, and certain *aides*, and amounts to more than one million francs. Indeed it would have been a great comfort to the people, who are paying today more than two and one half million francs in taxes.

He took great pains to reform the abuses [in which the monks] of Saint Benedict and [those of] other religious orders [indulged]. He gathered good monks about him and heard them speak. He wished indeed, if he had been able [to do it], that no bishop should hold anything except his bishopric unless he were a cardinal; the latter might have two, but both [cardinals and bishops] would have to go and reside in their benefices. But he would have had to do much to bring order to the clergy.

He gave large alms to the mendicants. A few days before his death, as was related to me by his confessor the bishop of Angers, who is a notable prelate, he set up a public audience at which he listened to everyone and especially to the poor; and matters were well expedited there. I saw him eight days before his death for two full hours, and then never saw him again. And even if no great decisions were made at these audiences, at least they held people in fear, and especially his officers, some of whom he had suspended for pillaging.

Enjoying this great glory in [the affairs of] this world, and being [possessed by] good intentions in [affairs pertaining to] God, on the seventh day of April in the year 1498 on the eve of Palm Sunday, he left the room of Queen Anne of Brittany, his wife, and took her with him to watch those who were playing tennis in the [empty] moat of [Amboise] castle; he had never taken her there before. And they walked together into a gallery which was in broken-down condition because of the construction job, and which was called the Hacquelebac gallery because that person had then and [also] earlier had had it in his care. It was the filthiest place in the castle, for everyone pissed there and it was all broken down. And at the entrance he hit his forehead against the door, although he was quite short; and he looked at the players for a while and talked with everyone. I was not present, for I had left eight days before and had gone to my house, but his confessor the bishop of Angers and his closest chamberlains told me so. But the last word which he ever said, in conversing while he was still healthy, was that he hoped never to commit a mortal sin nor a venial one if he could help it.

As he said these words he fell backwards and lost his speech. It was about two o'clock in the afternoon; and he remained in the said place until eleven o'clock at night. He recovered his speech three times, but he did not keep it for long, as the confessor told me; he had confessed him twice that week, and once it was on account of those who came to him to be cured of scrofula. Anyone who pleased could enter the gallery; and the king was lying on a miserable straw mattress, which he never left until he gave up the ghost; he was there nine hours. The confessor, who was continually present, told me that each time he recovered his speech, which happened three times, he said: "My Lord and the glorious Virgin Mary, my lord Saint Claude and my lord Saint Blaise, help me!" And so this great and powerful king died, and in such a miserable place, when he possessed so many magnificent houses and was building such a fine one, and he could not choose anything but a poor chamber to die in at the end.

How plainly, by the two examples here described, can we realize that the power of God is great and that our miserable life is a very little thing, although we trouble ourselves so much for worldly things; and kings cannot resist it any more than a laborer [can].[303]

26

I said somewhere in my account of the affairs of Italy that there was a preaching friar or Jacobin [i.e., Dominican monk] who had lived in Florence for a period of fifteen years and who was renowned for the very holy life which he led (and I saw him and spoke to him in the year 1495). He was named Brother Girolamo [Savonarola], and he predicted many things before they happened, as I said in the place where I spoke of him; and he always insisted that the king would pass the mountains, and he preached it publicly, saying that he knew this as well as other things of which he spoke by revelation from God. And he said that the king had been chosen by God to reform the church by force and to chastise the tyrants. Because he said that he knew these things by revelation, many people murmured against him, and he incurred the hate of the pope and of many persons from the city of Florence. His

303. Calmette asserts in III, 307, n. 2, that Commynes means by "the two examples here described" the death of Louis XI, described in Book 6, and the death of Charles VIII. But it seems more likely that Commynes is referring to the deaths of the children of Ferdinand and Isabella, described in chapter 24, as the first example and to the death of Charles VIII as the second. The words with which he begins the last paragraph of chapter 24 on p. 588 are quite parallel to the words with which he ends chapter 25 here. Many modern scholars believe that Charles VIII died of syphilis (note, e.g., Commynes' description of the attack of "small-pox" which the king suffered en route to Naples on p. 460) rather than of apoplexy (see p. 593) or the blow on the head described here.

life was the most beautiful in the world, as far as could be observed, and his sermons the best; he preached against vices, and he led many people in that city to live properly, as I said.

In this year 1498 during which King Charles died, Brother Girolamo also ended his life within four or five days of the other; and I shall tell you why I have made this calculation.[304] He had always preached publicly that the king would return once more to Italy to accomplish this commission which God had given him, which was to reform the church by the sword and to chase the tyrants out of Italy; and that in case he should not do it, God would punish him cruelly. He had all his early sermons and these new ones printed and they are being sold. He wrote about this threat to the king many times shortly before his death, saying that God would punish him cruelly if he did not return. And he said it to me personally when I spoke with him on my return from Italy, and he said that sentence had been pronounced against him in heaven if he did not accomplish what God had ordained for him [to do] and if he did not keep his soldiers from pillaging.

Now about the time of the king's death the Florentines had great divisions in the city. Some still expected the king's coming and wanted it because of the hope that Brother Girolamo was giving them, and they ruined themselves and became incredibly poor because of the expenses which they sustained, since they thought that they might recover Pisa and the other places which they had given the king; and the Venetians held Pisa. Many in the city were in favor of taking the part of the league and of abandoning the king entirely, and they said that it was nothing but deception and folly to expect him and that Brother Girolamo was nothing but a heretic and a scoundrel and that he should be put into a sack and thrown into the river. But he was so well supported in the town that no one dared do it.

The pope and the duke of Milan often wrote against the friar, assuring the Florentines that they would have Pisa and other places returned to them if they gave up the king's friendship and that they should take Brother Girolamo and punish him. And by chance it happened that a [new] Signoria was selected in Florence, and it included several of his enemies, for the Signoria changes [its members] every two months. And there was a Franciscan who, either through prompting or on his own, proceeded to provoke an argument with Brother Girolamo, calling him a heretic and deceiver of the people because he said that he had revelations and similar things. And he offered to prove this by the ordeal of fire; and these words were said in front of the Signoria. Brother

304. *Sic.* Savonarola was executed on May 23, 1498, a month and a half after Charles died.

Girolamo did not want to expose himself to the fire, but one of his companions said that he would put himself in it for him against the
Franciscan; and then a companion of the Franciscan presented himself
on the other side. And a day was appointed on which they were to
enter the fire, and both of them presented themselves on the established
day accompanied by their [fellow] monks; but the Jacobin brought
the Host in his hand and the Franciscans and the Signoria wanted him
to take it out of his hand, which he refused to do; and so they returned
to their convents. And the people, who were stirred up by the friar's
enemies and by the permission of this Signoria, went to fetch him in
the convent along with two others and from the beginning they tor-
tured him incredibly. The people killed the most prominent man in the
city, a friend of the friar named Francesco Valori. The pope sent them
authorization and a Papal agent to hold a trial, and in the end they
burned all three of them. The charges were only that he created discord in the city and that what he predicted as prophecy he knew by
means of his friends who were in the council.

I do not want to either excuse or accuse him, and I do not know
whether they did well or not to have him die; but he has said many
things that were true, which those of the town of Florence would not
have been able to tell him. But concerning the king and the misfortunes
which he said were to happen to him, they did take place, as you can
see; first it was the death of his only son, and then his own. I have seen
some letters which he wrote to the king.

27

His illness was a catarrh or apoplexy; and his physicians hoped that it
would descend into one of his arms and that he might be crippled as a
result, but that he would not die from it. However, it turned out differently. He had four good physicians, but he had faith only in the most
foolish of them. And he gave so much authority to that one that the
others did not dare speak; and they would willingly have given him a
cathartic four days before because they saw the signs of death there.
And it was [indeed there]. Everyone ran to the duke of Orleans,
who was next in line for the crown.

King Charles's chamberlains had him given very sumptuous funeral
ceremonies; a service was immediately begun for him, which never
ceased by day or night. For when the canons finished the Franciscans
began, and when they were through the Bons-Hommes [hermits of
Saint Francis], whose order he had founded, took over. He remained
in Amboise for eight days, partly in a room which was beautifully hung

and decorated, and partly in the church, and everything was richer than for any other king. And all his chamberlains and those closest to him and all his officers never moved from the side of the corpse. And this service lasted and this company remained until he was buried, which was for a period of about one month [April 7–May 2, 1498]; and it cost forty-five thousand francs, as I was told by the people in charge of the finances [*sic*: 200,000 francs].

I arrived at Amboise two days after his death and went to say my prayers where the corpse was; and I was there for five or six hours. And to speak the truth, I have never seen such a mourning, nor one that lasted so long. Moreover, his intimates, such as his chamberlains and ten or twelve young gentlemen who were attached to his chamber, were better treated and had larger estates and gifts than any king had ever given, and it was too much. And in addition he had the most humane and sweet speech that any man ever had, for I do not believe that he ever said a word to anyone that would displease him. And he could not have died at a better time to remain in great reputation in histories and to be greatly regretted by those who had served him. And I believe that I was the man in the world to whom he was most unkind, but since I realized that it happened during his youth and that it did not come from him, I never held it against him.

After I had slept one night in Amboise I went to this new king [Louis XII], with whom I had been as intimate as anyone else [in the world]; and because of him I had incurred all my troubles and losses.[305] However, for the moment he did not remember that very well. But he began his reign wisely, for he did not change anything in the pensions for that year, which was to last for another six months, he abolished few offices, and said that he wanted to keep everyone in his estate and position (and all this was very proper for him [to do]), and as soon as possible he wanted to have his coronation, which I attended. As for the peers of France, the following persons were present: the first was the duke of Alençon, who served for [i.e., performed the feudal functions of] the duke of Burgundy; the second, my lord of Bourbon, who served for the duke of Normandy; the third was the duke of Lorraine, who served for the duke of Guyenne; the first count, Lord Philip of Ravenstein, who served for the count of Flanders; the second, Lord Engilbert of Cleves, who served for the count of Champagne; the third, my lord of Foix, who served for the count of Toulouse.[306] And the coronation

305. The personal calamities and personal friendship with Louis XII to which Commynes refers here are described briefly on p. 13 and in n. 188 on p. 440.
306. Since the fiefs of Burgundy, Normandy, Guyenne, Flanders, Champagne, and Toulouse had all been absorbed into the royal domain, other feudal titularies

of King Louis XII, who reigns at present, took place in Reims on May 27 in the year 1498.

He was the fourth king who came [to the crown] from a collateral line [rather than inheriting it through direct descent]. The first two were Charles Martel or his son Pepin and Hugh Capet; both of them were masters of the palace or governors of the kings, and they usurped the kingdom from their kings and took it for themselves. The third was King Philip of Valois, and the fourth the present king. But these [last] two obtained the kingdom justly and loyally.[307] And this is so if we count the first generation of the kings of France from Merovech. There had been two kings in France before Merovech, that is, Pharamond, who was the first to be elected king of France, for the others had been called dukes or kings of Gaul; and Pharamond had a son named Claudion. Pharamond was elected king in the year 420 and reigned for ten years; his son Claudion reigned for eighteen years. Thus these two kings lasted for twenty-eight years. And Merovech, who came afterwards, was not Claudion's son but his relative; so that it would seem that there have been five changes in these royal lines. However, as I said, we consider the first generation to start with Merovech, who was made king in the year 448. And it has been one thousand and forty-eight years up to the coronation of King Louis XII, who reigns at present, since the genealogy of the kings of France began. And those who wish to start it with Pharamond must count thirty-eight [*sic*: twenty-eight] more years, which would make it one thousand and eighty-six [*sic*: seventy-six] years since a king was first called king of France. From Merovech to Pepin, the Merovingian line lasted for three hundred and three years. From Pepin to Hugh Capet the true line of Pepin and Charlemagne his son lasted for two hundred and thirty-seven years. Hugh Capet's line lasted as a true line for three hundred and thirty-nine years and ended with King Philip of Valois. King Philip of Valois's line lasted as a true line until the death of King Charles VIII, which was in the year 1498; and he was the last of that line, which lasted for one hundred and sixty-nine years and during which seven kings have reigned, who were King Philip of Valois, King John, King Charles V, King Charles VI, King Charles VII, King Louis XI, and King Charles VIII.

---

substituted for them in the traditional ceremonies involving the holders of these fiefs at the coronation.

307. *Sic*. Pepin the Short and Hugh Capet did not belong to collateral lines of the Merovingian and Carolingian dynasties, in contrast to Philip VI and Louis XII who did belong to collateral lines of the Capetian dynasty. The continuities in the royal line which Commynes asserts here and in the following sentences, where he treats the legendary kings Pharamond, Claudion, and Merovech as historical figures, are chiefly interesting as evidence of the way in which his royalism was founded in part on what he felt was the durability of the French crown.

Appendixes

APPENDIX A

When Volume One of this translation was published, page numbers referring to Books 6, 7, and 8 of Commynes' *Memoirs* could not be given in the footnotes to the Introduction, since Volume Two had not yet been completed. Consequently, references to Books 6, 7, and 8 were given to Calmette's French text of the *Memoirs*. For the convenience of the reader, we provide here a list of the page numbers in Volume Two which correspond to these references to Books 6, 7, and 8 in the Introduction to the *Memoirs* in Volume One. The list is given in this form: the reference to page 281 of Calmette's Volume II which is given on page 3, footnote 1, of our translation, corresponds to p. 399 in this volume and is therefore given in this Appendix as 3, 1. C, II, 281: 399.

3, 1. C, II, 281: 399.
12, 20. C, II, 337–40: 431–32.
12, 21. C, III, 17–18: 444–45.
17, 32. C, II, 299: 410.
18, 36. C, II, 247: 378.
44, 99. C, III, 300: 588.
44, 100. C, III, 3 and 256: 438 and 566.
45, 101. C, III, 266: 570.
45, 103. C, III, 307 and 313: 291 and 593–94.
45, 105. C. II, 278: [*sic*: 289]: 405.
49, 115. C, III, 238: 557.
50, 121. C, III, 300: 588.
53, 130. C, II, 282–99, 308–24: 400–410 and 415–24.
53, 132. C, II, 340: 432.
54, 133. C, II, 322–23: 423.
54, 134. C, II, 323: 423.
55, 136. C, II, 321–22: 422.
55, 137. C, II, 324: 424.
70, 180. C, II, 320: 422.
79, 203. C, II, 341: 433.
80, 205. C, II, 340–41: 432.

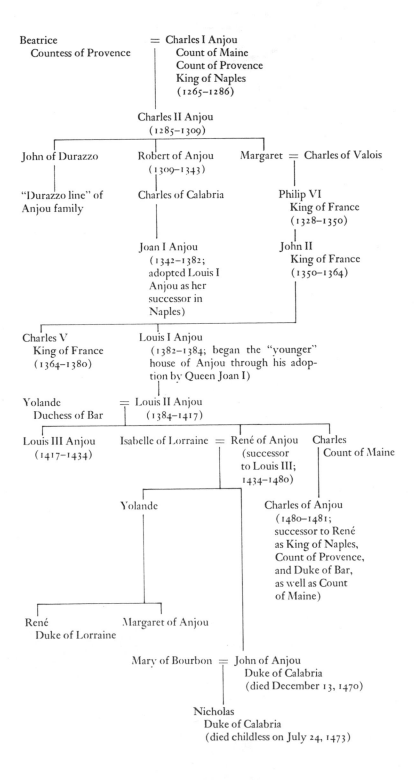

Beatrice   = Charles I Anjou
  Countess of Provence   Count of Maine
                              Count of Provence
                              King of Naples
                              (1265–1286)

                    Charles II Anjou
                      (1285–1309)

John of Durazzo   Robert of Anjou   Margaret = Charles of Valois
                      (1309–1343)

"Durazzo line" of   Charles of Calabria   Philip VI
Anjou family   King of France
                                                (1328–1350)

                    Joan I Anjou   John II
                      (1342–1382;   King of France
                      adopted Louis I   (1350–1364)
                      Anjou as her
                      successor in
                      Naples)

Charles V   Louis I Anjou
  King of France   (1382–1384; began the "younger"
  (1364–1380)   house of Anjou through his adop-
                      tion by Queen Joan I)

Yolande   = Louis II Anjou
  Duchess of Bar   (1384–1417)

Louis III Anjou   Isabelle of Lorraine = René of Anjou   Charles
  (1417–1434)   (successor   Count of Maine
                                           to Louis III;
                                           1434–1480)

                    Yolande   Charles of Anjou
                                                (1480–1481;
                                                successor to René
                                                as King of Naples,
                                                Count of Provence,
                                                and Duke of Bar,
                                                as well as Count
                                                of Maine)

René   Margaret of Anjou
  Duke of Lorraine

        Mary of Bourbon = John of Anjou
                            Duke of Calabria
                            (died December 13, 1470)

                    Nicholas
                    Duke of Calabria
                    (died childless on July 24, 1473)

APPENDIX B

The complicated rights of inheritance of the house of Anjou to the duchy of Bar, the county of Provence, and the southern Italian kingdoms of Naples and Sicily are more easily represented in a genealogical chart than they are explained verbally. This chart does not include the so-called Durazzo line of the Anjou family in whose hands Naples remained during most of the period between 1382 and 1435, in spite of the claims of Louis I, Louis II, and Louis III of the younger house of Anjou. It was through the "Durazzo line" that the royal house of Aragon derived some of its "rights" to these kingdoms (see Appendix C). Charles I of Anjou, founder of the dynasty, was the brother of King Louis IX of France and was enfiefed with the kingdom of "the two Sicilies" (that is, the mainland kingdom whose capital was Naples and the island of Sicily; the whole was sometimes called simply the "kingdom of Sicily," as Commynes does on page 439) by the pope and with the county of Maine by his brother. He possessed Provence through his wife. Yolande, King René's sole surviving heir when her father died, signed over to King Louis XI of France her rights to the duchy of Bar, and to King Charles, son of Charles, Count of Maine, her rights to the two Sicilies and Provence. King Charles, who died childless on December 11, 1481, willed all his possessions to Louis XI. King Charles's will had been almost dictated to him by his uncle, King René. That is why Duke René of Lorraine, as Commynes reports on page 439, not only protested King Charles of Anjou's will but also accused King René of wrong-doing. Charles of Anjou should never have received King René's inheritance, the duke of Lorraine maintained, because Charles was merely René's nephew while he himself was the direct descendant of King René through his mother Yolande. King Charles VIII's reply, Commynes says, was that Provence could not be inherited by women (nor, the king asserted, could the kingdom of the two Sicilies, as Commynes brings out later in the first chapter of Book 7), and therefore it passed necessarily to King René's brother, Count Charles of Maine, rather than to Yolande. On the other hand, the duchy of Bar was handed over to René of Lorraine in exchange for money, and the duke was given further compensation by being appointed on August 7, 1486, to the "important position" of grand chamberlain, as Commynes mentions on page 439.

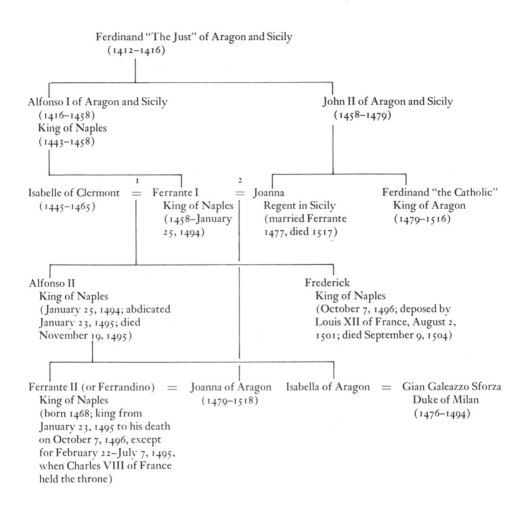

Ferdinand "The Just" of Aragon and Sicily
(1412–1416)

Alfonso I of Aragon and Sicily
(1416–1458)
King of Naples
(1443–1458)

John II of Aragon and Sicily
(1458–1479)

Isabelle of Clermont   =   Ferrante I   =   Joanna
(1445–1465)   King of Naples   Regent in Sicily
                    (1458–January   (married Ferrante
                    25, 1494)   1477, died 1517)

Ferdinand "the Catholic"
King of Aragon
(1479–1516)

Alfonso II
King of Naples
(January 25, 1494; abdicated
January 23, 1495; died
November 19, 1495)

Frederick
King of Naples
(October 7, 1496; deposed by
Louis XII of France, August 2,
1501; died September 9, 1504)

Ferrante II (or Ferrandino)   =   Joanna of Aragon   Isabella of Aragon   =   Gian Galeazzo Sforza
King of Naples   (1479–1518)   Duke of Milan
(born 1468; king from   (1476–1494)
January 23, 1495 to his death
on October 7, 1496, except
for February 22–July 7, 1495,
when Charles VIII of France
held the throne)

The story of the Aragonese occupants of the throne of the kingdom of the two Sicilies is no less complicated than that of the Angevin claimants (see Appendix B). Since Commynes refers in confusing fashion to a number of these occupants, a brief summary of the Aragonese succession should be given here.

In 1282 nobles on the island of Sicily revolted from King Charles I of Anjou in the famous rebellion called the Sicilian Vespers, transferring their allegiance to King Peter III of Aragon, who had a claim to inheritance of the kingdom through his wife. From this date onward Angevins and Aragonese vied for the kingdom of the two Sicilies. Agreements were frequently made to divide the kingdom, leaving the Aragonese in control of the island of Sicily and the Angevins in control of the mainland. King Alfonso I of Aragon, whom Commynes mentions, held the island from 1416 onwards, and he worked to reunite island with mainland. Queen Joan II of the Durazzo line of the Anjou family held the mainland kingdom. Childless, she was persuaded to adopt Alfonso as her successor to the throne of Naples in 1433. However, Joan adopted René of Anjou as her successor instead of Alfonso in 1434, and when she died in 1435, René was able to make good his claim to Naples. In 1443, however, Alfonso conquered Naples from René and retained it together with Sicily until his death in 1458. His will divided the two Sicilies once more. Aragon, Sardinia, and the island of Sicily passed to his brother John II, while the mainland kingdom was given to his illegitimate son Ferrante I. Through his marriage in 1476 to John II's daughter Joanna, however, Ferrante reestablished control over both Sicilies. This was the situation when the French invasion began to take shape. Then in less than three years' time (not two years, as Commynes maintains at the end of chapter 14 of Book 7) five kings—Ferrante I, Alfonso II, Ferrante II (or Ferrandino), Charles VIII of France, and Duke Frederick of Calabria—succeeded each other on the Neapolitan throne, as indicated on the genealogical chart.

By the time of Frederick's death in 1504 Ferdinand of Aragon had been able to conquer the whole kingdom, mainland and island, from the armies of Louis XII of France. Henceforth the area was governed by Spanish viceroys until the time of Napoleon.

List of Errata

Following the example set by Calmette's edition of the Memoirs, *we have adopted the expedient of including a list of errata. The items in this list have come to our attention over the years of translating, editing, and reevaluation as we have attempted to resurrect that which cannot be resurrected in all its fullness—an exact picture of feelings, thoughts, and words five hundred years old.*

p. 13, paragraph 2, l.2: the thirteen-year-old King Charles VIII

p. 14, paragraph 2, l.3: The story that Commynes gave the chains

p. 19, paragraph 1, ll.7–8: He dictated . . . the *Memoirs* in 1496–97, revising and completing them in 1498.

p. 49, n. 115, l.4: on the road about four died. . . ." (i.e., delete "though" and "back")

p. 54, ll.5–6 of first quotation from Commynes: he placed ten crossbowmen in the moat at each one of the iron cabins, so that they could shoot at anyone

p. 54, ll.9–10 of first quotation: the captains of the guards posted their ordinary gate keepers and ordered their archers

p. 54, ll.13–14 of first quotation: major-domos and persons of that sort did not present themselves before him.

p. 54, l.3 of second quotation: had [only] a small courtyard

p. 54, l.5 of second quotation: had himself guarded (i.e. delete the second "himself" in this line)

p. 57, l.11: the young son of Charles VIII

p. 78, paragraph 1, ll.4–6: Commynes' didactic commentaries give a sometimes wry and sometimes anguished twist. Whatever shape the twisting gives to the event, such commentaries are best seen as part of Commynes' feelings about his time, rather than as separable, and separably formed political, historical, or moral judgments.

p. 79, paragraph 2, l.3: the great and the small are

p. 79, paragraph 2, l.6: moment, in accordance with the works

p. 83, ll.11–12 *accorder ses vielles* (to harmonize).[2]

p. 90, paragraph 3, l.2: in the volumes,

p. 91, l.1: My lord Archbishop of Vienne

p. 91, ll.3–4: (may God pardon him)

List of Errata

p. 98, n. 7, l.2: *Mémoires*, ed. Calmette (Paris, 1924–1925), I, 9, n. 1, henceforth cited as Calmette, I, 9, n. 1.

p. 124, paragraph 2, l.7: pensioners from his household

p. 132, paragraph 2, l.7: he found the fortifications of the Saint-Antoine Gate [of Paris]

p. 141, paragraph 3, l.5: Compiègne

p. 146, l.7: disenchanted, heavy-lidded store

p. 169, paragraph 4, l.1: Besides, we are diminished [in stature] by age, and we do not live as long

p. 211, n. 78, l.1: The father, Earl Rivers,

p. 216, paragraph 1, l.5: the marquis

p. 216, paragraph 3, l.9: the marquis

p. 268, paragraph 1, ll.3–4: a company whose members] receive twenty *écus* [a month].

p. 341, paragraph 2, ll.4, 6, 7, 13: city, not citadel (Note 127 on p. 341 is superseded by n. 156 on p. 397)

p. 398, l.3 of note: rubber-rimmed goggles.

p. 407, last line: San Bernardino in Aquila

p. 450, paragraph 1, l.6: Our [queen, Anne]

p. 456, paragraph 1, l.5: [Castello d']

p. 457, l.7: Alberto [Lomelino].

p. 481, paragraph 1, l.8: Savelli

p. 485, l.2: brothers, the duke of Melfi, the duke of Amalfi

p. 513, paragraph 2, l.3: [Castello d'] Annone

p. 514, l.6: [Castello d'] Annone

p. 535, paragraph 1, l.15: Città

p. 580, n. 291, l.8: between Louis XI and Alfonso V of Portugal, pretender to Castile,

p. 584, n. 297, l.2: husband, Alfonso of Portugal

Index

Previous indexes of the Memoirs *have been limited to entries identifying some persons and places. We have listed all persons and places without exception, together with indications of geographical location, of feudal titles and offices, and even of familial relationships, wherever possible. In making this index, we have used the relatively complete indexes of persons and places in the editions of Mandrot and Calmette. But unlike these editors, we have introduced entries of a conceptual kind ("economic conditions"; "fortune"; "society, classes in"; "Commynes, didacticism of") and we have also ordered the subdivisions of major entries topically rather than chronologically. Mandrot's and Calmette's entries for "Commynes" consist of seven page-long columns which offer chronological summaries of the author's life, page by page and book by book. Our entry "Commynes" consists only of topically arranged references by Commynes to himself and of topically arranged references to the author's life, character, and thought made by the editor. Thus, references to aspects of the author's thought not commented upon specifically by the editor are classified as main entries rather than as subdivisions of the category "Commynes."*

Several other categories besides "Commynes" might at first glance seem to require listing every page of the Memoirs. *We have restricted the category "Memoirs" to topics of primarily historiographical concern ("chronological procedure in," "composition of," "causation in"). (Topics which pertain more generally to Commynes' writing are listed under "Commynes," such as "realism of," "dualistic thought of.") We have restricted the category "God" to Commynes' references to this entity; references to other and more general aspects of Commynes' religious sense are listed under "Commynes, religious beliefs of." Under "Political affairs" we have listed only the editor's explanations or assertions in the Introduction. Other aspects of Commynes' concern with politics are listed under such topics as "Commynes," "Princes," "Military affairs," "Negotiations," "Political thought of Commynes," "Tyranny, tyrants," and "Fiefs and feudalism."*

The following conventions have been used: whenever an item in the Index refers to editorial opinion in the captions accompanying illustra-

tions in the volumes, and "e" ("editor") follows the page number reference; whenever an item refers to material in the notes, an "n" follows the page number reference; whenever Commynes is referred to, his name is abbreviated as "C," except in the case of the index category called "Commynes;" whenever the Holy Roman Empire is referred to it is abbreviated as HRE. Because both volumes of the translation are prefaced by pages numbered with identical Roman numerals, we have inserted an arabic numeral referring to the volume number in parentheses following references to these pages, e.g., xii (1) for p. xii in Volume One and xii (2) for p. xii in Volume Two. We have also followed the convention of listing at the beginning of a category with subdivisions those pages with only passing references to the category in question; the more important references follow, ordered by alphabetically arranged subtopics.

Personal names of important figures are usually listed under the person's given name, not family or dynastic name ("Louis XI" is listed under "Louis," not "Valois"). Less important figures are listed under the family name ("Pierre Clairet" is listed under "Clairet," not "Pierre"). Commynes often refers only to a person's title, which may represent either a family or dynastic name or a name derived from the place-names of fiefs (ecclesiastical or secular) held by the person. Such persons are accordingly listed either under the family or under the name of the fief. Cross-references are given whenever Commynes has referred to a person in more than one way, i.e., by family name, given name, or feudal name. These cross-references include both the generally accepted titles given Commynes' characters today and the often erroneous titles which Commynes used. (The reader will have observed that, unlike outright errors of proper names, place-names, and dates, we usually have not corrected the mode in which Commynes designates persons and places in the text of the translation—e.g., "count," not earl, of Warwick; "count," not duke of Northumberland; "castle," not Tower, of London. We felt that the manner in which Commynes referred to his subjects was best preserved in as exact transliteration as possible, and this has necessitated multiplying the cross-references in the Index.)

The names of places have been identified as follows: provinces in France and Spain have been located in the north, south, east, west, or central (N., S., E., W., C.) parts of those countries; provinces in Burgundy and Italy have been located in the north, central, or south (N., C., S.) thirds of those countries; towns have been located by province only ("Bruges, town in Flanders") if the province is a main entry in the Index; towns have been located by province and country ("Blois, town in county of Blois, C. France") if the province is not a main entry in the Index.

Whenever a town is located "in Burgundy" in the Index, the reference is to the duchy of Burgundy. Whenever a county, duchy, or other region is located "in Burgundy," however, the reference is to the total holdings of the dukes of Burgundy in 1477, as shown on the map in Volume One of this translation.

Much of the credit for the completeness and novelty of this index goes to Peter Williams, who compiled it in cooperation with the editor.

A

C

D

E

F

G

H

I

J

M

645

N

O

P

Index

Pensioners; *see* Military affairs, gentlemen-pensioners

Penthièvre, count of, 76n

Pepin the Short, 595

Percy, Henry, duke of Northumberland, 280

Péronne, town in Picardy, 7, 9–10, 27, 35, 72, 77, 134, 166, 167, 172n, 200, 231, 266, 267, 292, 293, 332, 333, 336, 340, 342, 346, 349, 398; interview at, 19–21, 167–69, 351n, 410n, 587n; peace of, 30–34, 179, 191, 195, 200, 206, 235, 335n

Perpignan, town in Roussillon, 579

Perugia, town in Papal States, 508

Pesaro, prince of; *see* Sforza, Costanzo

Pescara, marquis of, Alfonso of Avalos, 482, 485

Petit Châtelet, in Paris, 414

Petit, Etienne, 583n

Pharamond, legendary king of France, 595

Philip I, king of Spain, 57

Philip VI of Valois, king of France, 580n, 595, 600

Philip the Handsome, count of Flanders, archduke of Austria, 384, xiii(2), 413, 583, 584n, 585

Philip the Bold, duke of Burgundy, xii(1), 39n, 294, 326, 330

Philip the Good, duke of Burgundy, xii(1), 6, 21, 95, 97, 98, 99, 106, 114, 117, 122, 131, 145–53, 136, 139, 142, 149, 150, 163, 164, 246–47e, 256, 294, 326, 327, 337, 338, 339, 342, 344, 350, 397, 413, 426, 428; character of, 96, 97; death of, 152

Philippe, a "certain theologian," 419n

Piacenza, town in Milan, 461, 462, 540

Piatti, 490

Piazza San Marco, in Venice, 500

Picard, Guillaume, 138

Picardy, province in N. France, 140, 141, 143, 150, 202, 240, 261, 340, 342, 352, 379, 383n, 394, 401, 411, 427

Piccinino, Iacopo, count of, 476

Piccinino, Nicola, father of Iacopo, 476

Piccolomini, Alfonso, duke of Amalfi, 485

Picquigny, town in Picardy, 45, 77–78, 206, 299; meeting of Louis XI and Edward IV at, 278–83; peace of, 377

Piedmont, terr. in Savoy, 296, 305, 309, 311, 404, 557, 582

Piennes, lord of; *see* Hallwin, Louis de

Pierrefort, town in Luxembourg, 256

Pietrasanta, town in Lucca, 463, 464, 465, 512, 514, 569

Pike-bearers; *see* Military affairs, pike-bearers

Piombino [now Porto Azzurro], town in Florence, 474, 546

Pirenne, Henri, 22n, 23n

Pisa, town in Florence, 354, 456, 459, 463, 464, 465, 496, 509, 510, 512, 514, 519, 568, 569, 574, 589, 592; people of (Pisans), 509, 512, 568; revolt against Florence, 566, 568

Q

R

S

T

U

V

W

Y

Z

Volume Two of the Memoirs *has been designed along the lines of Volume One, which was designed by Damienne Grant. The typeface used for both text and display is Janson, a typeface noted for its well-matched roman and italic. The initial letter on the title page and the ornaments used throughout the book were selected from the early typographical decorations of Erhard Ratdolt (1442–1528), German printer and type cutter, which were used widely in Commynes' day.*

Composition by Heritage Printers, Inc., Charlotte, North Carolina. Printing by offset lithography on Warren's University Text, an acid-free paper noted for its longevity and watermarked with the University of South Carolina Press colophon emblem, by Universal Lithographers, Inc., Lutherville-Timonium, Maryland. Binding by L. H. Jenkins, Inc., Richmond, Virginia.